Joseph L. Sutton, 1885–1980

Praise the Bridge That Carries You Over

Shepard Krech III

Praise the Bridge That Carries You Over:
The Life of Joseph L. Sutton

Schenkman Publishing Co.   Cambridge, Massachusetts

Copyright © 1981 by Schenkman Publishing Co.

Library of Congress Cataloging in Publication Data

Krech, Shepard, 1944-
  Praise the bridge that carries you over.

  1. Sutton, Joseph L., 1885-1980. 2. Talbot
County (Md.)—Race relations. 3. Afro-Americans—
Maryland—Talbot County—Social life and customs.
4. Afro-Americans—Maryland—Talbot County—Biography.
5. Talbot County (Md.)—Biography. I. Title.
F187.T2S894   975.2′3204′0924 [B]   81-1292
ISBN 0-8161-9038-0   AACR2
ISBN 0-87073-650-7 (Schenkman: pbk.)

This publication is printed on permanent/durable acid-free paper
MANUFACTURED IN THE UNITED STATES OF AMERICA

Contents

Foreword

Talbot County, on the Eastern Shore of Maryland, is noteworthy as the birthplace, about 1817, of the onetime slave and eloquent spokesman for human dignity, Frederick Douglass. It is in Talbot County that Douglass' grandmother Betsey, an accomplished nurse, gardener, fishnet maker, and fisherwoman, who had taken care of white folks as her own, was finally placed in a wretched hut to die. It is from here that Douglass, as a boy of about seven, was sent out on hire to Baltimore. Yet it is also here that black people retained faith, strength, and deep attachments to kin and place despite the burdens of their oppression. All this is to be found in Douglass' writings, especially the *Life and Times of Frederick Douglass: The Complete Autobiography* (1885).

Praise the Bridge That Carries You Over reaffirms Douglass' picture of Talbot County through historical records and especially the recollections of Joseph Sutton, born in 1885 in a former slave community. Sutton's account continues the story of Maryland plantation society and its decay up to the present time. Sutton shows how the savagery of racism, including such sport as the wanton killing of blacks by cars, was long rampant in Talbot County. The last documented lynching took place in the 1930s and integration began only in the 1950s.

Joseph Sutton's biography is a rich source of black ethnography. It confirms in detail the vitality and manifold functions of the extended family. It brings out the warm relations between grandparents and grandchildren. It stresses the central value attached to landholding. It refers to, although it does not detail, such institutions as preachers' central roles in dispute settlement, and family graveyards. In these ways, this study adds to such classic descriptions as Thomas J. Woofter's *Black Yeomanry* (1930) and Herbert Gutman's *The Black Family in Slavery and Freedom, 1750-1925* (1976).

Above all, Joseph Sutton's biography is a personal account of a man retaining strength, detachment, and quiet humor through lifelong poverty, repeated betrayal by employers and other wielders of power, much illness, and bereavement. Joseph Sutton was not a deeply religious man. He sought neither leadership nor wealth but rather accommodation and survival. He feared to leave his roots. Yet in his fondness for dogs and hunting, in his perceptions of night and day, of people and animals, in his lifelong home, in his occasional comments on the greater world, in his stoic philosophy, he showed multiple dimensions. Under a mantle of simplicity, this was a complex, thoughtful, sensitive man.

Sutton's biography can best be appreciated through comparison with Theodore Rosengarten's *All God's Dangers: The Life of Nate Shaw* (1974). A black tenant farmer in Alabama, Nate Shaw was a darer and a doer. He was driven to seek property, including a car. He joined a farmers' union and took part in a shoot-out with sheriffs' deputies. For this he was imprisoned in 1932 for twelve years. Sustained by religious conversion and newborn caution, he survived, although the costs to his family were great. After his release, he lived out his days. Unlike some others who carried on into the flowering of civil rights, Nate Shaw could do no more.

Sutton and Shaw, tragic and heroic figures alike, epitomize the human costs of plantation society and our nation's shameful racism.

Praise the Bridge That Carries You Over is important in its content. It is also a model of careful scholarship, meticulous in recording and transcribing, in defining and verifying. Methodologically as well as substantively, it adds impressively to the body of basic studies on black culture and the black experience.

—DEMITRI SHIMKIN

Introduction

This narrative of Joseph L. Sutton's life has been set chronologically and edited from conversations he and I have had over the past several years. The first time we talked the breadth and complexity of Joseph Sutton's comments were impressive for someone his age; he detailed the early nineteenth-century death of his great-great-grandmother a few miles away from his house in Talbot County, Maryland; the founding of Copperville (an all-black hamlet in Miles River Neck, Talbot County) in the years following the Civil War; his childhood in Copperville during the 1890s; the treatment of blacks in South Africa and Rhodesia, and the confrontation between North American Indians and the government at Wounded Knee.

These initial conversations took place during the winter of 1975-76, when Joseph Sutton was ninety years old and when a fellow anthropologist, Jerry Wright, and I were contemplating a joint fieldwork project in several black hamlets in Talbot County. We were interested in the adaptations of blacks living in this rural Eastern Shore county, in the growth of persistence in black hamlets in Miles River Neck, the role of kinship ties in daily life, and the connections between people who emigrated and their kin who remained behind.

Wright and I talked with several older men, one of whom was Joseph Sutton, and his eye for detail and knowledge of genealogies and land transactions, his great animation as a storyteller, his sense of humor, and his openness and willingness to talk with us were exciting. In short, Joseph Sutton offered a very promising starting point for some understanding of the history, society, and culture of late nineteenth- and early twentieth-century blacks in this section of Talbot County.

My collaboration with Wright never materialized, for reasons related more to the separate pulls of our other research interests and teaching duties than to anything else. But my taped conversations with Joseph Sutton continued intermittently for eighty hours during 1976, 1977, and 1978, and the transcripts were subsequently edited as this life history. The decision to edit a life history was not made easily, for I had not lived in classic anthropological participant-observer fashion in Miles River Neck prior to the elicitation of data. Furthermore, I had grown up in Miles River Neck and hence could be placed by Joseph Sutton in the race and class structure of the county. These both were sources of possible bias. In spite of these drawbacks, several factors —primarily Mr. Sutton's advanced age but also his articulateness, our developing rapport, and the methodological steps that I could take to counteract or at least minimize the biases—convinced me to edit the narrative.

My aims did not alter substantially from the interests which had led Wright and me to this area: the primary concern was Joseph Sutton's life in the context of Talbot County, the various influences on him when he was growing up in the late nineteenth century, and the subsequent development of his character. Questions were designed also to elicit information on the nineteenth-century antebellum period (for most of the founders of all-black hamlets in Miles River Neck had been slaves in an area where Frederick Douglass, the great nineteenth-century abolitionist, spent his youth); on the Civil War experiences of blacks from Miles River Neck; and on the adaptations of other blacks (and whites) in Talbot County in the late nineteenth and early twentieth centuries.

These interests were more descriptive and cultural—and ultimately humanistic—rather than intended to reveal the development of a personality (although it is hoped that this latter will also be accomplished in part).

In this introduction, brief comments on Joseph Sutton's family, his life, and on the growth of Copperville, are provided, in order to set the stage for his narrative. Details on the methods used in this study, on reliability, and on dialect and the transcription are presented in one appendix; an historical survey of blacks in Talbot County, culled mostly from documentary sources, is contained in another.

The Narrative

Joseph L. Sutton was born in 1885 in Copperville, a small, all-black hamlet in Miles River Neck, Talbot County. Miles River Neck is a 15,000-acre section of Talbot County, bounded by water on three sides (Figure 1). When Joseph Sutton was growing up there, it had a definite social and geographical identity: people living there considered themselves residents of Miles River Neck, in contrast to Oxford Neck or Deep Neck or some other section of Talbot County; within the Neck, people lived "up the Neck" (north), "down the Neck" (west), "in the other Neck" (south), or in a particular village or hamlet. In 1900, when Joseph Sutton was fifteen years old, there were three main hamlets in Miles River Neck: Tunis Mills, an all-white village whose residents worked in a lumber mill, in agriculturally-linked tasks, or who oystered and otherwise "followed the water"; and Copperville and Unionville, villages inhabited by blacks, some of whom worked by the day on farms,

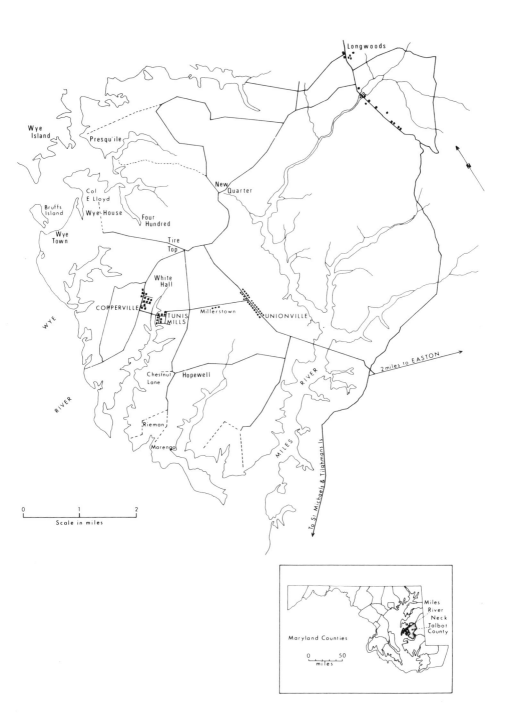

Figure 1. Miles River Neck, 1910.   Drafted by J. L. KRUPA

others in construction or mill labor, and others as oystermen in winter. There were also three small named black hamlets, each consisting of several houses in 1900: Germantown, Chestnut Lane, and Millerstown. Approximately 900 people lived in Miles River Neck at this time; 250, in Unionville; 100, in Tunis Mills; and 70, in Copperville.

Although Miles River Neck is a small section of Talbot County, the county's best-known and most influential nineteenth-century residents lived there: Frederick Douglass, who prior to his career as abolitionist and statesman had lived as a slave on the estate of Edward Lloyd; and Edward Lloyd, who owned most of the acreage in Miles River Neck and several hundred slaves and who was just one in a succession of Edward Lloyds who had been influential in colonial, state, and national affairs since the seventeenth century.

Many of the men and women who settled in Copperville and Unionville in the second half of the nineteenth century had been slaves or were the children and grandchildren of slaves, many of whom belonged to Edward Lloyd. Both of Joseph Sutton's grandmothers and his father's father had belonged to Lloyd. His mother's father was a free black. His father also was a slave and his mother was born the year of the emancipation.

Praise the Bridge That Carries You Over begins in Part I with what Joseph Sutton remembers being told of his father's and mother's families. His knowledge of his mother's side is much deeper, both because his father died when Joseph Sutton was only four years old and because he spent much time with his maternal grandmother and great-grandmother when he was a child. He remembers being told about the death of his great-great-grandmother (Figure 2). This woman's son, Solomon Deshields, and her daughter, Hester (Joseph Sutton's great-grandmother), were among the first settlers in Copperville. Hester's daughter, Charlotte, married a free black, Alexander Flamer (born

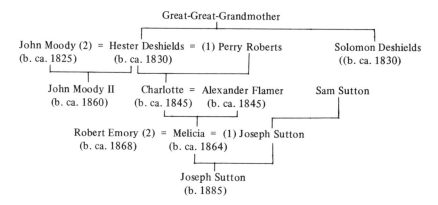

Figure 2. Joseph Sutton's Genealogy.

Table 1. Dates of Purchase by Blacks of Lots in Copperville, 1867–1920

1867	**1887–1889** *continued*
John Copper	Philip Moaney
Solomon Deshields	Henry Goldsborough
	Alexander Flamer
1876–1885	Peter Copper
Isaac Johnson	Ezekiel Emory
Samuel Hinton	
John Moody	**1893**
Perry Blake	Daniel Johnson
William H. Thomas	
John Blake	
Richard Blackwell	**1895**
Trustees of the African	Morena Mooney
Methodist Church	
Isaac Copper	
James Parker	**1910–1920**
Harrison Roberts	George Cooper
Alexander Flamer	Alexander Viney
John Blackwell	Richard Blake
William Gibson	Robert Lewis
	Charles Hinton
1887–1889	Charles Lane
Murray Roberts	Solomon Kellum
Eliza Kellum	Concert Band

in 1845), and they also lived in Copperville. Charlotte Flamer's daughter, Melicia (born in 1865), was Joseph Sutton's mother.

In Part I, Joseph Sutton also provides an oral history of slavery in Miles River Neck and of the participation of Miles River Neck blacks in the Civil War, and he details the postbellum beginnings of Copperville (the purchase of lots is presented in Table 1).

Part II begins in 1889, when Joseph Sutton was four years old, and ends in 1898, when he was thirteen; during these years, he lived for the most part in Copperville (Figure 3). Sutton provides, in addition to the substantial amount of data on his childhood, information on the economic occupations of Copperville residents, and on the social, economic, and political structure of Miles River Neck and Talbot County at that time. Talbot County was not unlike other areas of the South when Joseph Sutton was growing up: it was rural, with an economy based on agriculture (and oysters); there were few wealthy, large landowners among the many poor; and blacks were at the base

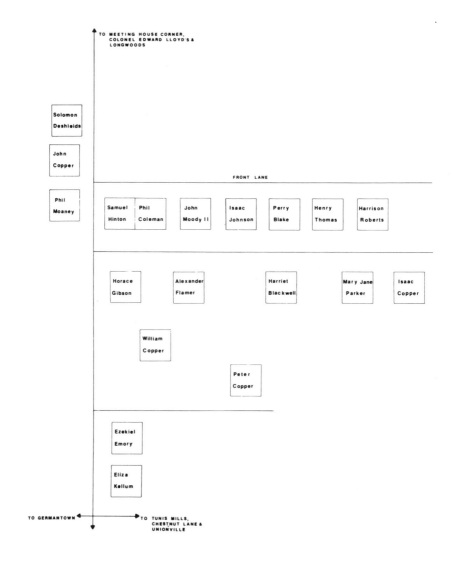

Figure 3. Copperville Lot Ownership, 1895.

of a rigid and at times brutal stratification system. The stratification order seems to have affected Joseph Sutton in a different way than it affected other blacks in Copperville. As a boy, he associated with white boys in nearby Tunis Mills, and his developing relationship with them assumed—retrospectively, at least—as great a significance as his relationship with other blacks. He grew up with a dual association, to kin and others his age both in Copperville and in other areas of Miles River Neck on the one hand, and to young whites in Tunis Mills on the other. The importance of both of these associations begins to emerge in this part of the book.

Joseph Sutton was born in 1885 into a community of people linked in complex ways by kinship. His father died in 1889, and when his mother went to Baltimore to find work, he lived with her mother, Charlotte, and Charlotte's husband, Alexander Flamer, in Germantown and Copperville. Charlotte Flamer's mother, Hester Moody, also lived in Copperville, as did Hester Moody's brother, Solomon Deshields. In 1889, Joseph Sutton's mother returned from Baltimore and married Robert Emory, and they lived in Copperville. Thus Joseph Sutton grew up in a small hamlet surrounded by kin. His half-brothers and half-sisters and mother and stepfather lived in the same household. In separate households were his mother's mother and mother's father (and their children, his aunts and uncles); his mother's maternal grandmother and her son; his mother's maternal grandmother's brother (Solomon Deshields) and some members of his family; and his stepfather's father. The meaning of these (and other) kinship connections became evident on numerous occasions when Joseph Sutton felt the pressures of others' expectations of him as a member of an extended kinship group.

Other people growing up in Copperville surely felt the same pressures, for although households tended to contain husbands, wives, and their offspring, these households were linked by primary kinship ties to other households in Copperville (Figure 4). The ties between Copperville households and households in Germantown, Unionville, Millerstown, and in tenant houses on various farms in Miles River Neck were also complex. And, whereas many blacks moved away from Miles River Neck (many via steamer from Tunis Mills and Miles River Bridge to Baltimore) to find work and a better life, some returned on a regular basis to reestablish and reaffirm their links to the Neck and to their kin residing there.

Part III begins with the move of Joseph Sutton (at age thirteen), his mother and stepfather, and his half-siblings to Chestnut Lane, a small cluster of three houses "down the Neck," and ends just before his marriage in 1908. The move to Chestnut Lane was Joseph Sutton's ninth in thirteen years. He would move approximately twenty-five times in his life (Table 2), largely because he never owned a house and as a tenant was at the mercy of the owners, or because he had to move to the place where he happened to be working. Joseph Sutton had started to work at age nine, and he had several

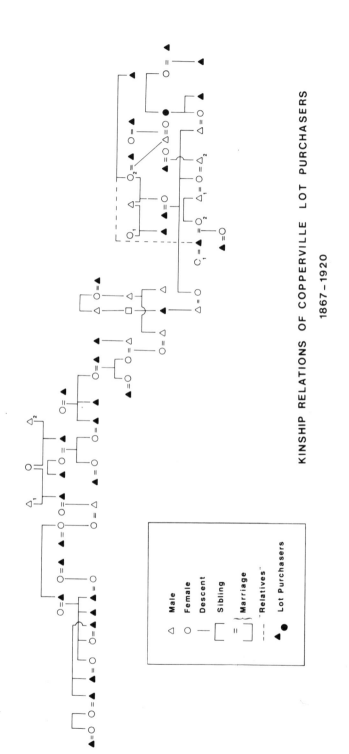

KINSHIP RELATIONS OF COPPERVILLE LOT PURCHASERS

1867–1920

Legend:

△ Male
○ Female
| Descent
⌐ Sibling
= Marriage
--- "Relatives"
▲ ● Lot Purchasers

Figure 4. Kinship Relations of Copperville Lot Purchasers, 1867–1920.

jobs during this period (1898-1908), but the ones which loomed largest were those which he performed for landowners named Rieman and Hall, and he contrasts this work with the work he had done for whites who rented farms.

Joseph Sutton married in 1908 at age twenty-three, and Part IV describes his early married life–the years 1908-1917, when he lived first with his in-laws and then in his own household in the small black hamlet of Millerstown. All four of his children were born during this period.

In approximately 1917, Joseph Sutton moved opposite Hopewell Farm, on the way "down the Neck," both close to where Chestnut Lane had been (the houses were torn down) and near the spot where his great-great-grand-mother had died years before. He lived here until 1935 in a house that he thought he was buying but which it turned out he could not buy. Part V describes these years. It was during this period that Joseph Sutton was sick: in 1916, blood poisoning in one hand slowed him down and in 1921 he was operated on for ulcers–after having been progressively affected by them over the preceding several years.

Part VI describes the years from 1935-1945. In 1935 Joseph Sutton moved out of Miles River Neck for the first time since he had worked briefly for a renter when he was thirteen years old. He had a number of jobs during this period and increasing contact with people in Easton. In 1945 his wife died, an event detailed with some bitterness by Mr. Sutton: hospital facilities at this period were still rigidly segregated and blacks remained second-class citizens in the eyes of whites.

Following the death of his wife, Joseph Sutton lived in several houses until 1953, when he moved to Unionville and stayed with his daughter. He was sixty-seven at the time, and he has remained on the same lot in Unionville since that time. Although he does not say a great deal about this most recent period in his life, his comments are drawn together in the final section (Part VII) of the narrative.

Adaptation and Stress

One theme that emerges repetitively in Joseph Sutton's comments concerns the great difficulty that blacks had in becoming economically successful in Miles River Neck. Not only did whites effectively bar blacks from many jobs, but also it was difficult to save money since sharing what one had was positively valued. Joseph Sutton once remarked, somewhat contemptuously, of a man that he was "so close he wouldn't give you a match. I guess that's the way you'd have to be to save anything." Many blacks emigrated in order to find work.

Table 2. Residence Changes and Some Events in Joseph Sutton's Life.

Date	Age	Residence	Events
1885		Copperville	Born in great-grandmother Hester and John Moody's house.
1885–89	0– 4	Copperville	Lived with mother in great-grandmother Hester Moody's house; father on farm, died 1889.
1889–90	4– 5	Germantown	Lived with grandmother Charlotte and Alexander Flamer; mother in Baltimore 1889–91.
1890–91	5– 6	Copperville	Lived with grandmother Charlotte and Alexander Flamer; alternated from grandmother to great-grandmother Hester Moody's house.
1891	6	Copperville	Mother returns from Baltimore, marries Robert Emory. Lived in Robert Emory's father's (Ezekiel Emory) house.
1892	7	Doncaster	Lived with father's brother William Sutton on farm.
1893	8	Hope House	Lived with mother and stepfather on farm.
1894–96	9–11	Copperville	Lived with mother and stepfather; rented Harrison Roberts' house; church school; work on schooner (age 9) culling oysters, carrying milk.
1897–98	12–13	Copperville	Lived with mother and stepfather; rented Harriet Blackwell's house.
1898	13	Chestnut Lane	Lived with mother and stepfather, rented house; worked on farm at Little Hopewell.
1899	14	Chapel	Lived with white farmer (renter).
1899–1902	14–17	Chestnut Lane	Lived with mother and stepfather, rented house; worked for farmer; worked for landowners Rieman, Hall.
1902	17	Copperville	Lived with great-grandmother Hester Moody; oystered.
1903–08	18–23	Chestnut Lane	Lived with mother and stepfather; stayed some time at Rieman's and Hall's.
1908	23	Hopewell	Married Mary (Mamie) Jackson 1908. Lived with her mother and father (Robert Jackson) for nine months.
1909–15	24–30	Millerstown	Rented house from Charles Dobson. Lived with wife, all four children born. Mother and stepfather also moved to Millerstown. Started raising Chesapeake Bay retrievers. Worked for bridge builders on farm, for contractors, chauffering (Arringdale), sawmill.

Table 2 continued.

Date	Age	Residence	Events
1915	30	Down the Neck	Worked and lived on a farm several months.
1915-16	30-31	Millerstown	Rented house from John Deshields. Various jobs. Blood poisoning.
1916-35	31-50	opposite Hopewell	Rented house (thought was buying) from Rittenhouse; cut corn, contractors; ulcers; duck shooting, raised Chesapeakes, run off the road, lynchings in Salisbury, Princess Anne.
1935-36	50-51	Unionville	Lived in wife's cousin's house.
1936-38	51-53	St. Michael's Road	Lived on farm, worked for Lipscomb. Pigeons. Time spent in Easton pool hall, garage.
1938-39	53-54	Unionville	Rented house from wife's sister's husband, James Blake. Butchered, worked on cars.
1939-40	54-55	Millerstown	Rented house from Richard Moaney. Wife's mother died.
1940-46	55-61	Unionville	Lived in wife's mother's house. Butchering. Wife died 1945.
1947-48	62-63	Millerstown	Rented house from Henry Green.
1949-50	64-65	Down the Neck	Lived in Rieman tenant house; worked on farm, odd jobs, cared for dogs.
1951-52	66-67	Down the Neck	Lived in Mead tenant house. Robbed.
1953-80	68-94	Unionville	Lived with daughter, Dorothy Lewis, in Unionville until his death in 1980.

The constraints against economic success were reflected in other areas of life, both in the nineteenth and twentieth centuries. Joseph Sutton revealed a deep distrust of banks and insurance companies ("all of em are slick . . ."). He once took 850 dimes to the bank, received credit for 800 only, told them to count again, and the extra fifty turned up. He hesitated in the beginning of our conversations to reveal monetary information, and was at first vague about the amount of his social security check ("Darned if I know!") and about the amount he earned working for someone ("What are you, the Revenue man or something?").

Jim Crow reigned in Talbot County until desegregation pressures started in the schools and hospital in the early 1950s and Joseph Sutton was at first reluctant to discuss the Eastern Shore lynchings of the late 1920s and early 1930s: "It don't pay to talk about it," he said. Later he was more than willing to talk about these and other events. He has also said, "There's good and bad in all. I'd pass just as quick with my children people of my own color as people of the other color. The poorer they was the worse they was against it. Color don't make a man, it's the way he conduct hisself."

Joseph Sutton equated the slave days and some more recent nineteenth- and twentieth-century events with contemporary South Africa, and he also commented that he thought "justice" would come one day, that "the bottom rail will be the top rider." He continued:

> And you take in Africa, the diamond mine, the whites went right in and took over. Blacks got to work for them in they country, and it should be their mines. And then they got very strict laws, very strict laws on em. The men can come and have to work so many months before they can go home to their family. Then, once a year, the family can come and stay with them a month and they got to go home. Well, anybody any heart or common sense, know that that's wrong. If I'm in your house, I'm goin to do as you say, I ain't goin to go in your house and rule your house. But, I think it'll all work out—course I'll be gone, and I guess all probably here be gone— but it's going to rule out after while. God say the time come when the bottom rail will be the top rider. And they are doin everything they can to keep them down. It's so bad England has . . . spoke against what the United States was doin, and England was doin the same thing. And you see how England went down. She lost every- thing that she possess, but England. And even at that, they are very poor there, in a way. Now, I think we'll go through the same thing. Someday the black man will get justice. It won't come overnight.

Joseph Sutton and other blacks in Talbot County devised several strategies to cope with the pressures and constraints on them. One black man who grew up and stayed in Miles River Neck would tip his cap every time he saw a white man, and Joseph Sutton commented: "Others thought it was his mind to do it, said he was crazy. Well, it paid off. He only had two jobs." He elaborated on this key to adaptation:

> Honesty, truthful, and mannerly: that's the three things the old people said. I used to wonder why it was when I was a boy in Copperville, I could go to Tunis Mills and the boys there wouldn't get after me, but all the others, they'd run em. Fix me bread and butter and sometime sit down at the table after, found out what manners I had. I could go to Tunis Mills and get this girl and carry her to meet her boyfriend. And her parents never said anything about it. And old people said, "Know your place." I don't think another child in the family was brought up way I was. Wasn't strict on them as was on me. And I thought it'd hurt me, but it didn't hurt me. That's what great-grandmother used to always tell me.

> What you do when you're small hurt you when you get big. Be
> truthful and honest, don't go stealin from people, don't go lyin.

Joseph Sutton insists on the truth and refers often to his great-grandmother,
who suggested guides for coping and surviving in Talbot County.

Another way to cope was to emigrate, but, although many Miles River
Neck blacks chose to head north to Baltimore and other cities, Joseph Sutton
turned down the few opportunities he had, afraid to be left without resources
in any area far from home. He once took a bus trip to Pennsylvania and said
he went "two times in one: first and last." He did not particularly like to
travel.

Still another way to cope is through humor, and Joseph Sutton rarely
failed to tell some joke during the months that I knew him. A man who
stopped by one day when we were taping asked Joseph Sutton how he was
feeling, and his response was quick: "With my fingers." Another time he
asked me if I had ever eaten groundhog. I said I had not. He then asked, "Did
you ever eat pork sausage?"

"Yes."

"Well, that's groundhog. Ain't that groundhog?"

"Yes, it is."

"Well, you've ate groundhog, then. I got the ladies up here at the Safeway
store, too, on it. One of them said to another one, 'No, I wouldn't think of
eating one of them nasty things.' I say, 'You haven't ate groundhog?' 'No,
I haven't ate groundhog. I wouldn't eat it.' I say, 'Have you ate pork sausage?
Say, 'Yea.' I say, 'Well, that's groundhog.'"

Another way to cope is to look after yourself and not to become too
deeply involved in the problems of others. Thus, it "don't pay to talk about"
lynching. The old people told Joseph Sutton, "Praise the bridge that carries
you over," no matter what happens to the next person who comes along to
cross that bridge, and in a very important way this has guided Joseph Sutton's
relationships with his kin and with blacks and whites in Talbot County. He
said one day, "A person treat you good, appreciate it and don't be against
them" no matter what they do to someone else; this is the meaning of "Praise
the bridge that carries you over," a literal and figurative bridge between black
Copperville and white Tunis Mills.

A theme repeated often in his comments was that people who cause others
to suffer will suffer themselves in the end. Joseph Sutton said once of a man
who hit a black man: "When he died he had nothing so he suffered some hisself. I don't know what extent he'll suffer at judgment, for he'll be judged."

Joseph Sutton today is not a churchgoer, but he is a religious person in
that he believes in the supernatural (but not in ghosts—"I don't believe in em.
Think when you're gone you're gone."). I once asked him which church he
belonged to. He answered:

All of em. Man told me there is a hundred and eighty some denomi-
nations and I can't understand it. And the denomination ain't got a
thing to do with it if you don't do right. You can belong to any
denomination and go to hell if you don't do right. So I don't go by
no denomination. You got to do right to make it. I don't care what
church you go to. It's only one place to go to and prepare for and
it's just like a city with different roads run through it and they all
come in on the right road, I mean, the most of em, maybe all on the
right road but their chances is just as good as other fellow comin on
another road. I don't think that's got anything to do with it. I
mean that you bein saved, that denomination. If you're right, you're
right and if you're wrong, you're wrong. It ain't the name of the
denomination and I don't think is going to help you.

One almost unavoidable result of growing up poor and black in Talbot
County was a nutritionally marginal diet and a certain amount of psycho-
social stress. Joseph Sutton may have experienced more stress than most
others, for he never wished to take the step to emigrate and his association
with Tunis Mills whites never brought tangible rewards. One sign of this
stress may have been his "ulcerated stomach," which plagued him through
the 1920s and afterwards:

Been opposite Hopewell. . . . I just had stomach trouble. Dr. Seth
was my doctor and I had him pretty near two years. I just set
around the house. I never tried to work until I could do it. I wasn't
able to work. Some come by and say, "You look bad." That'll make
you feel bad. One mornin I thought I was gone. My wife wanted to
go cross road and tell the doctor and I told her not to go, I'd be gone
before the doctor come. I suffered day and night.

It was getting worse and worse and woman told me about Dr.
Messick. He was a stomach specialist. Advised me to go to him. And
he treated me I think for two years. And wasn't getting any better,
if anything, gettin worse. And then Dr. Travers operated on me. He
had X-ray taken of it, ulcerated stomach. The operation was all right,
but he said it was the worse of that kind he had seen. And he didn't
give me the right diet. . . . And I went to the hospital again and we
had headquarters in the cellar, and I said to myself, if I'm goin to die
I'm goin to die home, I'm not goin to die here.

Went home, met Dr. Ferris, made me strip down to waist and
lay on sofa and he examine me, say, "I can't find nothin organic
wrong but you're just on the wrong diet." And I never know what
he meant by organic. After I got better I laugh about it.

Well, he knowed what was the matter with me the whole time
and he told me what to eat and he give me those things to eat, cream

of wheat, pettijohns and somethin else. I couldn't keep anythin
in my stomach. Sent one of the boys to get one of the things. And
felt better from the first meal.

This incident is reported here and in the narrative in some detail because
it looms large in Joseph Sutton's mind and because, at the time, it apparently
affected both his ability to work in demanding jobs and produced a lasting
feeling of indebtedness to Dr. Travers, who never charged him, and with
whom Joe Sutton afterwards shot ducks on many occasions.

Is Joseph Sutton a typical or "average" Miles River Neck black? This
question is difficult to answer, in part because there are few people his age
still alive and articulate who grew up in this section of Talbot County and
whose experiences can be compared to his. It would be presumptuous and
irresponsible to claim that he is representative. Clyde Kluckhohn, an anthropologist, pointed out long ago that anthropological informants are sometimes
individuals who are poorly adjusted in their own culture, which should serve
as a warning to those who would argue that any particular informant's life
is an average life. Moreover, I suspect strongly that Joseph Sutton's life is
unusual, especially so in his relationship with Tunis Mills whites and in his
attempts to associate closely with other whites. In other ways, however—
for example, in the importance of an extended kinship network and extended
kinship group to Joseph Sutton when he was growing up and in the difficulties he encountered in adjusting to the stratification system—Joseph
Sutton's experiences were surely typical.

Memory Selection and the Editor's Role

The process of memory selection or retention is one that affects the entire
oral-history endeavor; as Jan Vansina, an historian, points out, memory is
selective, it streamlines some events and symbolizes others, and what is or is
not recalled does not depend as much on memory loss as on an "active choice
of items to remember." Active choice and streamlining are characteristic of
Joseph Sutton's recall, and affect the various emphases in the document; his
selection or choice depends ultimately on his evaluations or perceptions
of what is or is not historically important, and it is this, more than falsifica-
tion, which becomes important in any exercise exploring the historical
"truth" of a document (see Appendix B).

Equally important to recognize is that *Praise the Bridge That Carries You
Over* is the product of interactions between an anthropologist and an informant, and thus some understanding of my assumptions, aims, and role is
crucial. Two aspects of my own background have affected this document.
The first involves my understanding of what is most important about people's

behavior and their culture, mainly that they are adaptive and that, to be understood, they must be placed in a broadly conceptualized environmental context. This emphasis on culture as a means of adaptation is a direct result of interests formed during postgraduate studies in anthropology; these assumptions had been major ones underlying research and a subsequent dissertation on socioeconomic changes in a Canadian Subarctic Indian community. This orientation has led me in this life history to ask certain sorts of questions and to ignore others, and to focus on the adaptations of Talbot County blacks—of a single black man—to the environmental, social, and cultural context of Talbot County.

The second aspect is that I was returning in this research to a region where I had grown up, and realizing for the first time how very incomplete and inadequate my knowledge of this area was. In the process of interviewing Joseph Sutton, reading accounts of Talbot County in nineteenth- and early twentieth- century newspapers, in archival collections, and in a variety of secondary sources, I became aware of the distortions and one-sidedness of "history" of the Eastern Shore. If anything, blacks are conspicuous in their absence from accounts of the Eastern Shore. I hope that *Praise the Bridge That Carries You Over* will begin to fill a substantial gap in historical accounts of the Eastern Shore. This is not just history of common folk; it is history of black common folk. This I consider important, even if it is a history of a single life; that I do is a reflection of a recognition that there exists a need for this type of history, of my previous experiences in the lives of Canadian Indians living in colonial conditions in Canada's Northwest Territories, and of the consistently humanistic influences of my father, a general practitioner for over two and one-half decades in Talbot County.

I brought this background to the taping sessions. My promptings influenced the material elicited, and my rearrangements—chronological and otherwise—of Joseph Sutton's raw data have left a stamp on the document; some of the methods that I used are considered in greater depth in Appendix B.

On Anonymity

Joseph Sutton's name, the names of his kin, of Copperville, Unionville, Miles River Neck, and of other people and places have not been changed to pseudonyms. It is important to note that this represents a departure from standard anthropological practice but also that it follows the express wish of Joseph Sutton. One of the major anthropological responsibilities is to protect one's informants and one way that this is done is to assign pseudonyms to people and places. Although I did explain this to Joseph Sutton, he insisted that everything he told me was the truth as he understood it, that this was his understanding of history, and that he wished neither names nor incidents altered. I have respected his wishes in spite of my discomfort and inclination to do otherwise.

There were, however, several occasions on which Joseph Sutton either didn't wish to divulge particular names or, if he did, wished the information treated confidentially. For example, he said that he loaned some decoys to a man who never returned them, and when I asked who this was, he said, "Wouldn't want you to put that down. . . . Wouldn't want anybody to read his name. Anything like that. He's one of my best friends. I went to his funeral." At other times he told me that he didn't want certain information in any book. All such occasions—which were few—have also been respected, either by not mentioning names or incidents or by eliminating the material completely so as not to compromise our confidential anthropologist-informant relationship.

Acknowledgments

I am indebted to a large number of people in the preparation of this book. My largest and most incalculable debt is, of course, to Joseph Sutton, who time and again and with great patience instructed me on his own life and on the lives of other Miles River Neck residents.

Many others in Miles River Neck—Dorothy Lewis and William Sutton especially—and in Talbot County extended their hospitality to me and provided background information; particularly helpful were John Bailey, Hazel Clark, Bertha Copper, Jack Daffin, Arlington Flamer, Ken Griffith, William Jackson, Varley Lang, Robert Lewis, Charles Lipscomb, Sidney Mielke, Mitchell Parker, Elizabeth Schiller, Howard Sherwood, Pat Shortall, Cecelia Soulsby, Emily Welsh, and McKenny Willis.

My parents assisted me in many ways throughout this research, for which I thank them both. I owe an intellectual debt to Demitri Shimkin and Jerry Wright, both of whom contributed to the formulation of questions which guided this research; they and Herbert Gutman commented on an earlier version of the narrative, and I thank them for their time and apologize for the shortcomings which remain. I am grateful for the support of this research by the Wye Institute, Inc., and the George Mason University Foundation.

Jackie Hancock provided exceptional typing of transcripts of the tapes and the complete narrative; additional typing and proofing was performed by a number of people, including David Crowlie, Joann Hickey, Jenny Kelsey, Mairi Kennedy, Mary Rousselot, and the George Mason University Typing Service.

Finally, I dedicate my own contribution to this work to my daughters, Kerry and Teal, whose incessant curiosity about Mr. Sutton and constant astonishment at his age have intensified my own interest in this project, and to my wife, Dill, whose sustenance at the end of this project is greatly appreciated. In time, I hope that they will read and appreciate Joseph Sutton's account and realize why I spent so much time away from them.

Chevy Chase, Maryland
February 1980

On March 29, 1980, Joseph L. Sutton died. Almost two years earlier, he had been talking about premonitions or presentiment when discussing the sickness of a friend, Jacob Ockimey.

"I was a young man then, I was workin to Rieman's, and I keep hearin that [Jacob Ockimey] was sick. So I said to myself, we was boys together, I believe I'll go out there Sunday to see him. Went in, Jake was sittin up in a rockin chair. And I went back again some time after that, forgot now how long it was and he was in bed. And Aunt Charlotte told me to go upstairs and what room to go in and got up there turned toward what side the room would be on and he was just as bright as he was the first time I saw him, he was settin in the rockin chair. I walked in and I say, "Well Jake, you're laying down." He say, "Yea." I say, "Well it better for you, you can rest better layin down than you can sittin up." "Yea," say, "I got to lay here until the 20th of June." And that was in, must have been first part of May. Say, "And I was told to tell two people," say, "and you are one and Uncle Bill Moaney," say, "was the other." Spoke just as bright as he would have if there wasn't anything the matter with him. So I was out in Unionville the 20th of June and there was a bunch up here. And somebody said, "Well," say, "Jake passed away this mornin." Then I got to studyin bout time. He say, "It's the 20th day of June." I thought about that a long time. It was the 20th day of June. And he certainly told me he had to lay there till the 20th of June. Cause I said to myself, brother, you won't get up from there unless somebody help you up. And I thought he was talkin out of his head. But he wasn't. And if he was, he certainly struck the day all right. And I said to myself, poor fella you haven't got enough mind to tell somebody take you up. And that's what he meant. That's when he was goin to die. I thought about that a long time. And some people know when they gonna die. I don't believe, I'm sure."

Joseph Sutton continued, turning to himself: "I don't think I'll make it. I won't see the book. My great grandmother I think she was eighty-seven when she died, and that was very old them days. I'm older than my uncles and aunts, no one in the family this old. There's only one thing I crave for— when I do leave here it's to go where there're little children. I think I'll be satisfied. I'd rather see them than see grownups. And I notice little children pay more attention to me than they do to other grownups. Just like it was with me and dogs."

The Service of Triumph, attended by family, kin, neighbors, and friends, was held at St. Stephen's AME Church in Unionville, Maryland on April 3, 1980. Joseph Sutton's family had wondered whether to bury him in Copperville or Unionville. He had said, two and a half years before, "Well I'd rather for them to decide that sometime accordin to the convenience and then that's one thing you ain't gonna worry nobody, when you're gone you're gone." Joseph Sutton, a man of dignity, warmth and humanity, and one who insisted on judging each person as an individual, was buried in Unionville, next to his wife and son.

Chevy Chase, Maryland
30 June 1980

Part I

My mother told me I was born on October fifth on a Saturday night, I think, and twelve o'clock. It could've been the fifth, or it could've been the sixth, it was so close to twelve o'clock, well, they took the fifth. This was in 1885. It was in my great-grandmother's house and the nurse may've been my great-grandmother cause she was one of them wet nurses. Copperville is my home, where I was born. I've been in Copperville for a good many years. Left there first twelve years old and I went back there again at seventeen and that was the last, but I feel that it's my home.

I was a Sutton. My father was born in slave time, but they was nothin but children. His parents was Colonel Lloyd's slaves. My father's father, Sam Sutton, wasn't at the Wye House, but I don't know what farm he was on. He worked in the field. I never heard nothin about my grandfather Sutton's parents.

My mother's mother, Charlotte, belonged to Colonel Lloyd. Charlotte was on the New Quarter, on the farm. And they never come down to Wye only some big times like thrashin wheat, sometimes gettin up hay and sometimes killin hogs. She said she was down to New Design there once. Because I heard her talkin bout the big bull frogs were there up in that ditch. The children used to catch em and take a switch and whip em. And I heard my grandmother say some of em would cry like a baby, make a noise.

My grandmother married Alec Flamer. He was my mother's father. The Flamers were free. My grandfather Flamer's mother hadn't heard nothin about when they were set free, they had the whole generation of that day come up as free people and that was unusual, and then the Flamers bought little farms and things where the slaves wasn't able to buy em, cause they had got the start on em. My grandfather Flamer had a brother. He own two farms. What they called the "Big Farm" was in Talbot. It was right on the line and that's where all the Flamers was, some over the line in Talbot and some over on the Queen Anne side. They was able to grow their own food— hogs and chickens, poultry, like that, and a big garden—and made they own clothes with a spinning wheel. And he had no kick comin, for they had some place to go, these others didn't have any place to go. They was the ones said that. But I heard one say that they were better off when they was slaves, cause they have nothin, they had no way to make a living. I heard my grandfather say that the slave ones didn't like what they called free niggers. And their children comin up together and played together, then they'd start to fuss like they used to do, "Oh, you better go home, you old free nigger."

I think my great-grandmother had Charlotte before she was married. My grandmother's father was Perry Roberts. But Perry Roberts wasn't my great-grandfather because he wasn't married to my great-grandmother. John Moody was married to my great-grandmother. He was my great-grandfather. And I called him Uncle, cause his son was my mother's uncle and naturally he was my uncle. That was a rule that the colored people had in them days, callin anybody that was older than they was, that if it was a man, they call him Uncle. That's to respect em callin em Uncle. And they called all women, Aunt. That's the way they was taught. And they did that whether they was any relation to em or not.

And Perry Roberts cut his throat out, out in Unionville one Sunday night. Somebody brought the report down to church, and I heard my mother, said she was in the bunch. Pretty near all of the church went up to see it. And when they went up there, blood was all over the floor. And the ones he was staying with said they noticed him had an old razor with no handle on it. He had been whettin that thing all day Sunday. And Sunday night after the people went to church, he cut his throat. I don't think his mind was very good.

I don't know what farm my great-grandmother Hester was born on; New Quarter was the place she spent her young days. She had one brother here that I know of and that was Solomon Deshields. I don't know whether she had any that was sold or not. And she work in the field. I heard her say she'd haul wood out of the woods in the winter times with oxens; men cut the wood and women hauled it. And then that snow would pack and it would freeze hard enough to hold the weight of the ox cart and the wood and the oxen. And they'd wrap their feet in old bags, in grass sack.

My great-grandmother was named Hester Deshields until she married John Moody. They got married right down at Miles River Bridge, at that old church. That was well back in slavery. And John Moody was a thoroughbred African. It used to be a tribe of them Africans, they had a mark on one ear, some kind of a mark in the flesh. You see that mark on one of em, they come right from Africa here. They wasn't no descendants or nothin like that. And he had that. Colonel Lloyd, I guess, bought him when they used to bring em from Africa here. I saw some others with that mark. I heard the old people say they was Guineas. I don't think they'd have to be bred with that mark; they must've been marked when they was babies.

They lived in Queen Annes on Wye Island. Some called it Peekers, later days they called it Packers Island. They lived there for years. He belonged to whosomever owned the Island and he come over to this side and courted my great-grandmother. He courted her and married her and then it was up to Colonel Lloyd to let her go over there to live and it was up to his master, and let him come over here, but Colonel Lloyd give in to him and let him take her over there on in Queen Annes. Course, they was Colonel Lloyd's slaves and he had to give her permission to leave Wye, to go to Queen Annes to live, cause was his property. Say he'd give in and he would let a woman change her home quicker than he would with a man, naturally, cause the man did more work.

My mother was born in '65, same year the fightin ended. And great-grandmother raised my mother. They lived on this point on Wye Island right across from Bruff's Island. Lived down near the water. And they call that point two names, Felix Point and Hessie Point. And whenever they did go shoppin, used to go in a ox cart. And Uncle John Moody had been carryin some corn in his boat. He called it a boat; well, it was just a dug-out log. Say you couldn't cut tobacco in your mouth in it; say if you did, it'd turn over. And anyhow, he had some big fryin chickens and he had a rooster he was goin to turn out and the boat tied on the shore. The rooster got in there and was eatin a shot of corn and he heard the rooster holler and looked, there was a mink that had this rooster. He went to the wood pile and cut a stick about a couple of feet long and he went down to the shore and throwed the stick in the boat to kill the mink, and killed his rooster, and the mink jumped overboard and went on bout his business. Used to hear my moher tellin it, cause her and her grandmother saw it. Saw him hurryin from the boat to the wood pile. And saw him cut this stick about two or three feet long. And was rushin down to the shore, they watched him, saw him when he throwed it. And when he throwed it, the mink jumped out of the boat. Course, they dive like a muskrat. And they saw him go to the boat, pick the rooster up. It killed the rooster dead, never hurt the mink.

My great-grandmother's mother and father come from down in Princess Anne. Colonel Lloyd's sister married a man from Princess Anne and that man's father, he had a bunch of slaves like Colonel Lloyd did. And when they got married, he give his son my great-grandmother's mother and father. And they lived on Hopewell.

My great-grandmother's mother died over here in Hopewell field cuttin wheat. The men cut wheat with a cradle and the women used to bind it. Every man with a cradle had a woman to bind after him. And she died under a big tree; the body was eight or ten feet across and the limbs was big and long, and why it growed like that, somebody cut the top out of the top of it when it was a sapling comin up. And she had a baby just a little over a month old. She would nurse it fore she would go to work in the mornin and then they'd bring the baby out in the field to her nine o'clock. They always had an old woman was too old to go in the field to work or a young girl wasn't old enough, to take care of the children. And this was either the mornin session or evenin session cause they used to bring em out again at three o'clock in the evenin. And it was awful hot and she went under that tree to nurse the baby and that sudden change—cool. She died right under that tree.

Most of em around here belonged to the Lloyds. It wasn't many of em worked in the house, I mean men. Course, they were cooks and what they called chambermaids and they were all women. If you got in the house, that was a big promotion. But they have a boy in the house, that was old man John Copper. They called em houseboys. John Copper was off-relation, he was uncle by marriage: he married my father's sister. They tried to get the most intelligent ones in the house; old man John Copper, he was very intelligent. He was the one that learned how to read and never went to school. And Colonel Lloyd's brother started him off. He used to go down in the garden and hide, and set and carry the books down there. Then when he started readin, after he got to something he couldn't spell, couldn't pronounce, why, he'd call it somethin quite loud so they could hear him. He wouldn't ask them, he'd call it somethin else and then listen. And then they'd say, "John, that ain't right. I told you such and such." And then he'd go on. Say he could depend on em to do that. Better than it would be to ask them what it was. It would have been just too bad on the boys and Copper, too, if the boys' father had knowed he was teachin him. That's the way he learned. Fred Douglass said, in Baltimore, he learnt similar to that. The people that owned him, I don't know what kind of work this man's doin, he was goin on Monday, I think they said, and wouldn't come back till the end of the week. And the boys started him off readin. Then after he got started, he just kept on. But at the same time, they tell me if they caught a slave with a piece of paper, say they'd whip him worse about that than they would if he had stole somethin. Didn't want to see you lookin at a piece of paper.

The house people thought they was better than the farm people. You take somebody that was workin in the house, well, he just felt he was way above the other fellow. And sometimes he was a whole lot stupider than the other fellow. I know it was better in the house, cause you got better food and more of it. And you had to go dress better. It was a whole lot better being in the house. Them people that wasn't in the house and had to work, why, they had a job to get enough to eat. That's why they used to steal chickens and pigs. You what they called "allowanced out." When you ate that, you had to try to get somethin to eat some other way. In the summer season, the men used to fish. They couldn't do nothin with crabbin, because they couldn't see the crabs, to dip em at night, but they used to fish. They used to hunt.

They found a lot of scary people them days. They used to scare each other. Colonel Lloyd had a man, name was Max Carter, he used to go from Wye Town, way up around New Quarter, White House Neck, places like that after he stopped work, go up there night-time to scare people. Then he'd go right back the second night and they wouldn't know nothin bout it, just as scared of him they was the first night. I heard Uncle John Copper said he worked in the house there to Wye and another old lady and her daughter, was her daughter who he finally married for his first wife. Her mother was a cook to Wye and the daughter worked in the house. But they worked in the house and they'd all get off the same time and he would walk with them down to the quarter where they used to stay. And one night, old man Max Carter had been down that way, where Wye Town and Bruff's Island was. And Uncle John say when they left the kitchen they was talkin about it. Say, "John," say, "if you see anythin," say, "you wouldn't run and left us, would you?" "Mam?" Say, "John," say, "if you see anything," say, "you wouldn't run and left us, would you?" Said, "God Almighty no! No! I wouldn't run." They got to the rail fence and it was a ditch on the field side of this rail fence. They got there and started to get over say he saw this big white thing layin in the ditch right down where the little boards they had to go across the ditch. Say he hollered, "Lord, God Almighty," say, "look a-here! Look a-here!" That thing started raisin up and he was carryin home a bucket of clabber for em. This thing started raisin up in the ditch, say he didn't drop the bucket of clabber, say he throwed it away! And left them women, and just told em that he wouldn't leave em. Say he left them! And they come along later, and then they had to come right back up to the big house again. They got up there, say he was sittin down. Old man Carter got a kick out of it. Walkin best part of the night, had to work the next day.

And great-grandmother's husband, John Moody, he belonged to what they called then the Peekers on Wye Island, but he used to come over nights to see her. He come to see her one night and old man Max Carter was there. Well, he wasn't married to her and he couldn't say nothin to old man Max, so he got hisself a brick and went to the door and called old man Max. Said, "Brother Max. Come here, Brother Max." Said he hit old man Max Carter in the stomach with that brick. And he runned, he was afraid old man Max'd follow him. He said he walked and runned all that night. He went up Wye Mills and turned in there, and then he sit down and rest, went to sleep and woke up again, and the next time he was home on Wye Island. And that started up here, New Quarter. "Yes," say, "I hit Brother Max," say, "right in his belly with that brick."

The men them days didn't have any beds to sleep in; they used to lay on a board. Cold weather they'd put the foot of the board in the fireplace and had somethin they'd put under the other end of the board to get it higher than your feet and that's the way they slept. And old man Bill Moaney, he was a slave on Wye Town, and he had been worryin the overseer about a new ax. All of his talk was a new ax. Keep tellin the overseer if he had a new ax that he could cut more wood than any man on the place and wouldn't be afraid of the Devil. And he got his ax, and old man Carter thought he'd have some fun off him, and old man Carter was goin to spend the night there with em. I guess they had an extra board.

They was on their boards, been talkin and old man Bill used to sleep with the ax right by him cause they played tricks on him, they'd hide his ax if he'd go to sleep. And somethin woke him up. Somethin come in there had a bell on it. Them days, a man with a flock of sheep, he'd have one or two with bells on em. That made it easier to find em when they was feedin. And they heard this bell and there was great big buck sheep they say walked in. Course, they had no lights on, and he commenced to blatin, "Baaaah," say. And Bill say he peeped and looked and one of these old men was lookin. The other one was still asleep. Say, this sheep was just inchin up on em. And bout that time, that other old man, he woke up and he looked. He hollered, "Get that sheep out of here before he butt me in my belly." He had a big stomach. "Get him out of here before he butt me in my belly." Old man Bill say he jumped up and one of em said, "Bill, get your ax. Get your ax!" Old man Bill say he said, "Goddamn the ax, let me get out of here!" Say he left his new ax layin on the floor. He went out that door a flyin. And he went down to the quarters, I think they say where the women used to sleep, slept that night out. And he come to find it wasn't a soul, only old man Max Carter.

And one time, he come down to Wye. That was in the slave quarters, after a while, they tore it down. And they had like stalls in the place. An aisle run down and them stalls was on each side. And this old lady, that was Aunt Rosie, she was a young woman then, she was workin up to the house and she has a son, good-size boy, and he used to tend to the baby. That was John Blackwell. Old man John Blackwell had his sister on his knee rockin her and singin about somethin. And had one little slidin window in that hut where they was, and it blew open a little. And Max Carter hollered in there, say, "Is that all you say, John?" Say, "Can't you spare me a little more?" And he jumped up and throwed the child clear back of the back log. Throwed back of the fireplace! Fire in the fireplace. Just was lucky she went back of the back log where it wasn't any blaze. Old man come to the window and scared him that night.

And they couldn't have any enjoyment at night. They couldn't have a gatherin. If they had em, they had men round here called theirself white caps or night riders, they'd come break it up. Them that belonged to that ring horse ridin, they had a white cap. And then when they did, they did what the colored people masters want to do. They afraid they'd get together and make up plots. But there was one man that owned some slaves, lived on Marengo, and he didn't believe in that, and he wouldn't whip em, and he wouldn't let anybody else whip em. That used to be the overseer's job, but he wouldn't let the overseer whip em. He was nice to his slaves. One time he went away, they thought they'd give a dance. They called it a dance and had a crowd. And they was in this house dancin, a rap come on the door, and somebody hollered, "White caps! White caps!" They blowed the lights out. And they had their chunks ready sittin handy. And open that door wide. And they could discern the man outside better than the man outside could discern anybody inside. And one of the night riders called in there for one of the slaves. And he come to the door and was talkin. The man said, "Light that light." "No, come in, gen'men, come in." "No. I said light that light." "We run out of oil," they said. "Come in, gen'men, come in." That man backed up. He didn't come in there. He said what he was goin to do. He was goin to kill him right there, and his master wouldn't let the law do anythin with em. He was sure of that. And this other fellow that was workin for the master that owned these slaves, he said somethin, and they caught his voice, and when the master come home and they told the master about it, the master went right down and fired him right then and told him to get off'n that place just as soon as he could get off.

And I heard that the man that owned Hope wouldn't even hit em. Old man Jim Viney, when he was a boy, his father lived there. And their master, if they did anything wrong he just call em to him and ring their ear. And his orders was for his head man on the place not to touch one of em. Say, "Anything they do wrong," say, "you let me know," say, "I'll correct em." And he wouldn't hit a slave and wouldn't let nobody else.

That was the kind of master he was, but they all wasn't like that. A lot of em want to be rough on em. Other people, well, they had a man just to whip em; they wouldn't whip them theirself. Down to Lloyd's, they used to take em in a barn. They had a place there they would chain their arms up. And you give em so many lashes. Make them take their shirts off. Right on their bare back. And then rub salt in the sores on their back. I don't know whether Colonel Lloyd ever whip em, but that was his head man orders.

Dr. Decoursey, he lived in Queen Annes and he was related to the Lloyds. He killed a slave right in the field, he was plowin, and Dr. Decoursey come out and said somethin to him about the plowin or the horses or whatever he was usin. And then he unhooked the single-tree and took it and bust his head. And I heard the old people talkin about it when I was little, that was the old men that was big enough at that time to remember when it happened. But he lived a miserable life before he died, though. He lost his wife and it was hard for him to get anybody to work for him.

Old man Copper said one time down here to Wye, slavemen stole wheat and sold it. Boats used to come up to get Colonel Lloyd's father's grain, and if they didn't get all, that night, the slavemen would carry God knows how many bushels down to the boat on their backs. And Captain Horney lived outside of Tunis Mills, up the head of the creek. His boats used to lay up there. He used to run grain for the farmers. That was his job way back in slave times. Slaves used to steal wheat and corn and carry it to him at night. Walk from Wye some of them other farms. It'd always be three or four of em or more, together. They would take bout two bushels of grain and walk miles with it, bring it down to him. They couldn't use the ox team, no horses, nothin, because the overseer could hear em. Course, he didn't give em good as nothin for it, but anyhow, it helped their livin. That money was the whole lot to them, cause if they didn't get money that way, they didn't get any money to Lloyd's. Then the boat went on to Baltimore, and the overseer went in the barn and missed the wheat they had saved for seed wheat. And the overseer told the men, say, "I know some of you men got it," say, "but I got to tell the truth about it. I got to tell Mr. Lloyd." So he told Mr. Lloyd about it, and he come where was workin and told em what he was goin to do. Said he was goin to send everyone of em down to Georgia.

And they was afraid to go to Georgia, and they didn't know what to do. It used to be a woman up here a little distance from Matthewstown, they called her Kitty Hubbard. So they got together, say, "Well," say, "we'll go up there tomorrow evenin." And they left after dinner and they walked from Wye to the corner where she used to live. And they walked and was speakin about goin to her. And one old man said, "Yeah," say, "we walk all this distance," say, "goin to her. Ol hussey." Say, "Can't tell us nothin." When they stepped in the door and closed the door, she said, "Well," said, "here's the old hussey." And the men got scared, cause that's just what they said, and then she told em what they had done, had stole this wheat. And the one that doubt her tellin em anythin, well, his eyes come open then. Cause she was tellin them true things just like it was. And she told em they left there late that evenin, said, "You're goin to see a big black snake," say, "and if that snake don't run," say, "you all better get out tonight, better leave tonight." Say, "And if he runs," say, "you'll be all right." Say, "He ain't goin to sell you down to Georgia." Say and they heard this leaves rustlin in the side the woods, said, and they looked, there was the biggest black snake they ever saw in their life. And that snake run. And she told em, said, "Tomorrow mornin," say, "you all be in the barn, doin somethin in the barn." And say, "Now when he step in the door," say, "all of you say, 'good mornin, master,'" say, "and keep your head down. Don't look at him anymore." And they did that and said that was all of it.

And they had another man there, he died out here to Unionville. I believe his name was Isaac Sampson. And he was down there to Wye, sayin he used to sneak around night time to see what the men was doin, whether they was stealin pigs, or stealin sheep or somethin like that. Course, they had to take somethin to live, from what they got to live on. And Colonel had a gill net and made an agreement with three or four of em, they was goin to set that net. Take the net and set it, and put it back where they got it from. And one of em said, "This is all right, if that man don't see it." Said, "If he see it, we gonna get a whippin." And another one said, "Well," say, "if he come down here," say, "let's drowned him." Hadn't no more got it out and looked, here he was comin around the shore. And they said, "Here he come now." Say, "Don't say a word to him." Say, "When he get up here, grab him. And we can take him out chere and drowned him," say, "and they'll never find him." So one of the men, when he got close there, went to meet him and grabbed hold of him, said, "Come on, boys." Say, "Here he is." Say, "He won't get our backs cut tomorrow." Say, "Let's drowned him." And this old man cried some and prayed and begged. Told em if they didn't drown him, he'd never do anything like that again. And that broke em up. Said he didn't tell no overseer. But say he was bad about that. He just sauntered around night time to see what they was doin. Sometime he'd tell the overseer that the man had been on somebody else's place and stole somethin. You'd have to go a long distance to get off from Colonel Lloyd's place.

Well, they had a hard time. Just to think a man walkin several miles with two bushels of corn or wheat on his back. And didn't get much for it. And in that time, they used to sell whiskey out at a place they call Todd's Corner. Used to be a store there, way back in slave time. And they'd take that money, them that drinked it, they'd get theirself somethin to drink. One old man, he carried a pail to get his in, and they were doin something around the barn, and he had his pail there in the barn takin a nip every once in awhile and other tellin him, say, "You better watch for Marsa Eddie." Say, "Don't let him walk up on you. If you do, you're gonna get a whippin." And he'd go to the door and look and carry the bucket. One time, he went to the door, he looked all around, he didn't see Marsa Eddie and he stood right in the door, he was drinkin. Marsa Eddie come around the corner of the barn and hit the bucket on the bottom, and then hollered at him, "What you doin?" When he hit the bottom, he spilled all the whiskey on this man. Throwed it all up in his face and his neck, but he didn't get no whippin for it. And that was bad days, them days.

And them was sold, pretty near all of em went down south. Well, I know my great-grandmother said she remembered when, I believe it was, a brother and sister was sold, and that's what they found out, they carried em down south and never did hear talk of em no more. And that was somethin.

Some people that owned slaves, they set em free, turned em free. I heard some of the old slave people talkin bout was a man they said come from down on Bay Side, bought four head and was carryin em home, and they sang and prayed so until he stopped and told em they was free; they could go back home. And I don't know whether them was Colonel Lloyd's slaves or the slaves they bought in Easton to what they used to call the Market House— that's where they used to auctioneer slaves off. And I heard an old man say they had certain days to sell slaves like they sellin calves and sheep and stuff like that. I don't know what they got for em. They didn't get as much as a good horse'd cost, I'm pretty sure. This day, they was sellin, this man say he was with his mother, and when she was sold and the people bout ready to take her away, he grabbed her dress and commenced to cryin; he was a little fellow. And the auctioneer come along and didn't pull his hand loose and struck him on the arm and broke his grip on his mother's dress. And she was sold and he never knowed where she went and never heard from her no more. That was terrible, though.

I heard em speakin of John Blackwell's mother, puttin the hay in the barn. And they had heard talk of this getting free. And the Colonel rode up, and they asked him, say, "Master Eddie," say, "I heard we was going to be freed." Say, "We goin to be freed?" "No!" Say, "You'll never be free as long as I've got a nail on this thumb. And put that hay in the loft." I think the war had started, but the North couldn't whip the South. The Colonel made a bad guess, though.

The North couldn't whip the South, that's the way the slaves got free. And then, after that, they got the slaves in there, that made thousands and thousands of more help for the North, and then the North could whip the South. And the Quakers, I believe, was the cause of the black man gettin free, cause they had suggested gettin the slaves on their side and some of the others said, "No, we don't want them. The first time you hear a gun fire," say, "they'll run." And the Quakers told em, "You'll never know that unless you try it." And that's the time they commenced recruitin the black man.

And they found out he had more nerve than the other man did, cause he was used to bein told what to do and he had to do it. He tell em to take a place, well, they would go until the last man was shot down. They carried a bunch of em down to Sumter, South Carolina, and the fort was facin the water, and they carried em ashore, facin this fort. And sent em ahead with no white man leadin em. And they cut em down, just a cuttin em down. Come back, regroup again, send another group, and they'd do the same thing. Just go as long as they was told to go. Have to call em back. And after the second wave, well, the officer decided they was all right, say, "They'll stand." And he just did that just to try the nerve of em. And then they was a big help to em. Hadn't been for that, the South would've whipped the North.

The man that was recruitin soldiers went to all of em that owned farms here and picked up the men, cause there was no law to stop em. That was Ben Blackwell, he was relations to John Blackwell. Well, he went around to all Colonel farms. There was one old man was very bow-legged, I heard this man tell it hisself, said, when he come recruitin them, say he was in the field plowin and Ben Blackwell come lookin at him and told em, said, "They wouldn't want you." Say, "You'll do more good here growin food." Say, "There ain't no use a carryin you, you won't make a soldier." He was so bow-legged you could roll a barrel between his legs. And that come from somethin the children should'a had when they was babies and children comin up. That was Davis Farm, and Uncle Perry Blake say he was in the field plowin.

Ben Blackwell was one time, maybe the onliest he was over here, recruitin down at Colonel Lloyd's farms. He had pretty near a dozen farms besides Wye, and old man Harrison Roberts was born and raised up to that time on Four Hundred. That's where his mother and him lived. Well, he didn't want to go, and Ben Blackwell told him he had to go. "If you don't," say, "you're gonna put in jail." And when called on Uncle Harrison, they noticed he was slow movin. Old man Ben Blackwell says, "Harrison," says, "hurry up." Say, "I got a lot of places to go yet today." And they was walkin. So he kep his gait and then say, "Come on." So he went with em and he got out to the meetin house, he stopped and told Ben Blackwell he had to go in the woods to do a job. And old man Ben stopped the men and they waited for Harrison to come back. They wait, wait, and wait. And old man Ben say he thought there was somethin wrong. He commenced callin Harrison. No Harrison answered. So old man Ben told the men, "Well, come on, we'll go," say, "and I'll report it and they'll get him." In the meantime, before he stopped the men for goin in the woods, one of em said, "Harrison," say, "you gonna leave them two big fat hogs you got there at Four Hundred?" That's the time he say he had to go in the woods. And then went on and old man Harrison from that day, went back down to Wye to be close to Colonel Lloyd for protection and he stayed there until he was disable to work.

And they never saw old man Harrison until the war was over. And they come back here again. Old man Harrison had pulled that woods over em. That was the first day he went down to Wye. Course, the Colonel kept him, and was glad to get him because all his able men was gone. Colonel Lloyd was against the recruitin. He didn't do nothin to help the side he was on. No indeed, there'd never had been no war if people like that had their way. He had too much to lose. That was his wealth they was takin away from him.

Old man Matthew Roberts, he belonged to Colonel Lloyd, and the overseer wanted to whip him and he runned off. And he ran from Wye over to New Design, and they got after him on horseback. Well, he could distance em, cause he could run in the woods or he could run from field to field, and if there wasn't a gate there, they'd have to go a long distance sometimes to get into the next field. He got down here to the head that creek when they got about halfway to the field. And he runned down and throwed his hat overboard. Sailed it out as far as he could like he had gone across to the other side. And then he turned shore and wheeled around and gone around to the edge of the shore where was lots of these wild grapes vines, and they was up high and you couldn't see a man down in the bank if you was up in the field. And he hid hisself in these vines. When they got down to the shore, he was close enough to hear one of em say, "There he is." Say,

"He's gone overboard." And the overseer of the place where he ran from say, "Yeah," say, "let him go." Say, "There's his hat." Say, "He drowned hisself and ain't no use lookin for him." Say, "I'm glad he did." And old man Matt was layin in them vines. They didn't see him. Then when they left, he got out and went down here to Miles River Bridge. They used to have a day boat, steamer run up to Miles River Bridge. And he got on that steamer and went to Baltimore. When they was recruitin soldiers in Baltimore, course, they got him. And then they had that big battle in Virginia and he got crippled in the leg. After the battle, the enemy side was goin over the field killin all that was wounded. They didn't pick em up to help em. They killed em. And Mr. Louis Trail, he lived in Easton, him and another man was together and they come to Matthew Roberts. Matthew was talkin and tryin to get them not to kill him and this man, he had drawed the butt of his old gun back to hit him in the head, and Mr. Trail looked and he hollered this man, said, "Don't hit that man! Don't hit that man!" Say, "I know him." He must've knowed him through bein down to Wye. Say, "I know him. He come from home," say, "and I want him to carry a message to my father." When he come up there, he spoke to old man Matt. Old man Matt recognized him. He told him whatever it was he told him to tell his father. Say, "They gonna send you home. You're wounded." Hadn't been for that, he'd a got killed.

Trail fought for the South. A lot of em North fought for the South. They used to go down to the closest place where it was a Southern soldier and I think that was Virginia, and God knows how many of em waited until night and they'd get in a sailboat and go down where it was. Lot of em from here.

Old man Matthew was shot somewhere in the leg and that's what killed him. He come home there and lived several years, but he used to always have trouble with his leg. And towards the last, it would swell up twice its size and smell, and they want to cut it off. He wouldn't let em cut it off, and after awhile it killed him.

My grandfather Flamer said they tried you out to see how you could shoot. Said, to make a sharp-shooter out of you. And he say he was in the bunch they was trying out and he was hittin the bull's eye every time. The other men shootin off from it, missin. Wasn't nobody in the nother bunch, unless it was once or twice, that hit the bull's eye. So after it was over, the men got together, no officer around, they got to talkin. They said, "They gonna make a sharp-shooter out of you." He say, "I'm already a sharp-shooter." They say, "Well, that's what they was tryin you out for. There you see, we didn't hit that target." And my grandfather said it scared him then. They carried him out again and he said he didn't hit nothin. He was bad as they was, cause a sharp-shooter's life is a whole lot shorter than the other man.

My grandfather, I overheard him speakin about was a man in their company. They didn't have any tents down South, the bunch my grandfather was in, and nights they'd stay in the woods. And they had a man there that carried a pocketful of knives, and he was always off to hisself. He'd be in hearing distance and he'd stick them knives around in a circle and that's where he'd stay. And some of em tried to creep up on him just to see what he was doin, but he never turned his back. He said, "Far and no farther," say, "cross that line," say, "you'll die." And they'd fly back to their company again.

And John Copper fought in the war. Well, he didn't fight, either. Old man Copper heard if you lose your forefinger on the hand that you pulled the trigger with, why, you wasn't no good as a soldier. And he shot his forefinger off and that settled him. I think they sent him home. But say he did that on purpose. Put his finger right over the muzzle of the gun and tripped the trigger and that blowed his finger off. He was just a little smarter than the majority of the soldiers. He'd rather lose that finger than lose his life, and he should've done it, because it was a benefit to him and the others.

I forgot where that long battle was fought. I believe that was in Virginia that big Battle of Bull Run. And I heard old man John Blackwell say he was in it and Ike Johnson, that was one of the Colonel's slaves. And this man was carryin the flag, well, he got shot. Ike Johnson saw the flag fallin and he run and grab it sayin, "I ain't gonna let it hit the dirt." And he carried it the rest of the war. Didn't get killed. Now they was brave, and they knowed if they won the war they'd get free; they had somethin to fight for.

They had several men that was small that wouldn't make a soldier—not that they were scared, but they was small. And they'd tend to the horses and mules; they didn't go into battle. It's a place in Virginia, Geesbury, somethin like that, that was a great place for the government horses. And that's where they stayed. And they were just to handle the horses—fed em and clean em, hook em up when they need em. They didn't even carry a gun.

And then when war was over, they didn't get no pension. They never got a cent. They wasn't in no battle, but they was in a position that they could've got killed, cause the enemies could've made a raid on the place where they was takin care of the stock. And they was workin for the government just like the others was. Course, they wasn't takin as big a risk.

Old man Alfred Hayward, he lived on one of Colonel Lloyd's farms, he was little and Uncle Zeke Emory, my stepfather's father, he was very little. Them was the two I used to hear speak of Geesbury. They say they was too small to make a soldier. And John Moody, he may've been a horse tender. Them ones was teamsters, never got no pensions. They were there, they was puttin up their life there, they never got a cent.

After the Civil War and they come home, they had no place to go, and some of em claimed that they was in worse fix than they was when they was owned by a Master, because some of em, they didn't get work enough to feed theirself decent. Some of em said they fared better in slave-time. In slave-time they could bet on somethin to eat and after they was freed, well, the women didn't get anything to do. Maybe some of em got a job washin for somebody, but they eventually stopped workin in the field. Then the men that worked and had families, and they had to work to feed the wife and feed the children, but before that, they got some allowance for children. And lay-in, they call it, for the wife and lay-in for the man.

When men came back from the war, the Colonel took one old man back, that was John Blackwell. His old parents belonged to Colonel Lloyd. Some of em didn't come back to work, but John Blackwell come back and worked for the Colonel until, well, figure that he was disabled.

John Blackwell was a soldier, but them days didn't give you a pension until you got disabled and when you did get it, you only got eight dollars a month. And old man Blackwell had put in for his and they had men send em around to see if the ones that put in was able to work. And they come to Colonel Lloyd's, they was threshin the wheat and he asked for John Blackwell. And somebody point him out and while he was there talkin with the colored, the Colonel got on to it. And he talked with the Colonel and he told him what his errand was; he wanted to come down to see Blackwell, see if he was able to continue work. And Colonel Lloyd told him, "Yeah," say, "he's able to work." Said, "He'll do more work than any man I've got on the farm." And old man Blackwell didn't get his pension for sometime after that. But still, your freedom meant more than all the money.

But a lot of em didn't go back down to Wye. Old man John Copper, Colonel Lloyd thought a lot of him because they was boys together. Colonel Lloyd still liked old man Copper. I know they used to oyster, used to walk down to Bruff's Island. That's where they kept their boats. And them that did it, he didn't force em to do it, but he'd ask em to give him a day's work when he was cuttin corn. And he paid em for the day, but all of em would do a day's work for goin on his place, cause he owned Bruff's Island then. There was a fellow he had found out that old man Copper wasn't goin to work, so he said, "Colonel," say, "John Copper," say, "he ain't goin." "Well," say, "hell with that." Said, "John Copper ain't able." And that surprised him. Old man Copper couldn't gone then, cut and carry that heavy corn. But the Colonel was always ready to speak up for old man Copper, cause they was boys together.

One thing about the Colonel them days, you could run any place you want if you didn't come up around the big house. Time wasn't like it is now. And wasn't like it has been for a long time. He never bothered about runnin. I remember one time they was huskin corn and it was blowin hard, they didn't go to work, and the wind fell sometime during the day. And they went rabbit huntin. It was a bunch of em. Colonel come along and stopped, "Are you men rabbit huntin?" Say, "Why don't you come down to help?" But he didn't tell em to get off'n the place. And they could rabbit hunt on any of the places. Well, I guess he should let em do it as long as they had been workin for him for nothin. But he was good about that.

I never heard of John Copper workin for him unless it was some day work. But he always kept in touch with him. And Colonel Lloyd used to give old man Copper old clothes now and then. And it was another old man, his name was Perry Blake, he used to do the same with him.

They had no place to go, and that's the time they scattered all over the place, cause there wasn't the work to do around here then, and you had to go and look for it. John Copper went up in Delaware and got a job on a small farm. And that man, he said they'd never been able to keep a colored man on the place. In fact, the colored people wouldn't work for him. And he went there and got along all right. And the people around, white and colored, they asked him how he got along with that man. He told em, said, "I have no trouble gettin along with him. I do what I'm told to do." And he got along with him good. He stayed there for a long time and then that was the time he was building his first house. And he come back, him and Sol Deshields, and built a home.

And John Copper and Solomon Deshields, and Phil Moaney was the first bought over in Copperville. And that land was bought from Captain Horney, man that owned the woods from Tunis Mills corner on up to other side of Copperville, in line with Colonel Lloyd's woodland. That's the man that used to run the grain in slave-time, he lived in Tunis Mills.

Solomon Deshields and John Copper was related, but I don't remember now in what way, how close. But they was related and that's why they built the first houses, double house. And John Copper's caught a fire and course, Solomon Deshields house had to go. They built em far enough apart the next time. And John Copper was in the most intelligent class, when a lot of the others of the same race didn't appreciate it. They would think they knowed as much as he knowed, but they didn't. He had years jump on them. He was raised in the house, what they call the houseboy. And he could learn a lot that way. And some of em used to go to him for advice on different things. Only one thing, he was just like my grandfather, he couldn't write. Could read, but he couldn't write. Solomon Deshields's as intelligent as John Copper and live a decent life. And the surroundins was just as good. That makes a big difference. Sometime your surroundins pulls you down and the ones you associate with.

And Solomon Deshields' wife had a son, Isaac Deshields. He went by Isaac Deshields, but he wasn't a Deshields. He was my wife's mother's half-brother, same father. He belonged to a man come up here durin the war from Virginia. He come here when wasn't no men here, only them that was disabled. That man wasn't here when Isaac was growin up. He went further north. Well, Solomon Deshields found out when he come back and they went livin together just like they had been before he went. And got along good together.

They didn't blame their wives. She didn't know whether he'd come back or not, not anymore than he knowed whether he'd come back or not. He raised him with his other children. Course, you could see it was a difference in him. He looked different from Deshields' children. Think or see that it was some kind of cross there, and the disposition was different from the others. Some people think that doesn't make a difference, but it will. It will make a difference in breedin dogs. Some dogs will go back to what some of their parents are. Some, if its good, and nine out of ten, if they're bad. And if they got bad habits, they'll take that after their parents.

None of that land in Copperville was leased. All Copperville was sold or was bought. My grandfather Flamer bought two lots from man named Robinson. Alec Flamer had brothers, but they was all up in Queen Annes. I remembered when their mother died, one come down here to either buy the grandfather's share out of the home place, or see if he'd give it to him for he wanted to buy it, but grandfather told him, "No, I won't charge you nothin. You go ahead and get it fixed." He said, "I'll give you my part. I got more land than I need now." He drove down here from Queen Annes and by the talk, it seemed like to me he was drivin from Philadelphia down here. Places seemed to be so much further apart them days. None of his people come down here. They stayed up there. Them that when they left up there they went to the city.

Alec Flamer come here because this was his wife's home, and I guess he figured it was a better chance here than it was up there, cause the whole bunch up there then was poor white and colored. So he come down here to get into a better work for a better class of people. And when he come down here, he worked for a man by the name of Sewell. And I don't know how many years he worked for him. And then he worked for the man next to him that was Robinson. He worked on the farm; was no house to work in when you come from up Queen Annes. Them was all poor people up there.

And my grandfather was just about like the rest of em, he wanted a home and the man he was workin for, Robinson, sold him the land. Them had a home was a whole lot better off than them that didn't have a home them days, cause they worked for nothin. Supposed to be paid and got slave treatment, all exceptin the whippin em.

He had one brother was down here to the Almshouse. It was near Trappe where they put crazy people. That's where the brother died. And he was put down there when my mother was a child and he was livin years after I was a man. He stayed in a shanty. My grandfather never went to see him that I know of. Course, you couldn't get around them days. Old man John Copper's mother was there to the Almshouse. He went down to see his mother cause he was in a little better fix than the average—he had a nice horse.

And Jim Dootz went to Almshouse from over here to Copperville. He was a Roberts, but he was a boy, they nicknamed him Jim Dootz. His mind was very bad. They sent him there he was a boy. Jim Dootz was born in slavery. They used to have what they called a quarters for the slaves and they had a big building with a passageway down the middle of that building with little rooms on each side of it. And I heard the old people say one night he got to hollerin and his mother got to hollerin and they went in there, had a fire-place, and she was on fire. And they put the fire out, but she died. And the door was bolted on the inside and Jim Dootz, who was nine years old and hadn't walked, that night he got up and opened the door. He got up the night his mother caught fire, he got up and opened the door.

And Perry Blake say when he come to Copperville, was right after slave-time; he had belonged to Lloyd, too, and that way his house was built. He worked at Colonel Lloyd's. About the only place he ever worked after he got free.

And my great-grandmother and John Moody come to Copperville from Hessie Point. And poor people, slaves, they got a house, they felt like they had a mansion. Phil Coleman and Sam Hinton, they come up here from Virginia during the Civil War. Maybe they had freedom, the part that they left. They came up here together and built together in Copperville, and lived together with no trouble, fuss, or nothin like that. And old man Phil Coleman, he was a little short man. Sam Hinton, he was a larger man. Sam Hinton, I guess they first come up here he worked for Colonel Lloyd. Lived down there. And Phil Coleman, he worked for Colonel Lloyd and then worked for Mr. Oliver, Fairview. That's the onliest two he ever worked for. They was decent people. They wasn't the low kind that kept all kind of house, I mean, people around. They had nothin, but they was decent.

Mary Jane Parker come to Copperville. Her husband died down to Wye Town. That was after what they call freedom. He was workin there and every once in a while he'd be sick and couldn't work, had to lay off two or three days and he'd go to work again, work a few days and have to do the same thing till one last time, he had to stop. Colonel Lloyd used to ride horseback then all the time. The Colonel rode up to the house and he was sittin in a rockin chair, his wife said, between the two doors to get a good breeze going through the house. And Colonel spoke to him and he spoke to Colonel. And Colonel asked him when would he be able to go to work. Say, "We need you." He told him, say, "Colonel," say, "I don't know." Say, "I don't feel any better." "Well," say, "if you can't work," say, "I want to put a man in my house that can work." Turned around and rode off. And this Parker man, he was sittin in a rockin chair and he just layed back in the chair and fore the Colonel there was out of sight of the house, he died. It worried him that much, he died. His wife said she heard a noise, when she looked, he had throwed his head back, he was dead. And what it was, it was his heart when he was havin that trouble. The Colonel wasn't out of sight of the house.

After the war, they come back, they had no place to go and they just scattered out. Charles Kellum, he went to Philadelphia. He got married, Philadelphia. Then he left that woman, come back, and picked Aunt Liza up. And then that's the time he got the children by her and he couldn't marry her because he didn't have no divorce. And when he was on what the old people call deathbed, the old women from Copperville used to go up the road goin towards Wye and Copperville. It was a clear lot and a house in there, and that man worked on New Design farm and he got sick. They had, I think, four children. She had work doin anything she could get to do takin care of the children. And he was sick in the bed. It'd be some of the old women from Copperville would go up there every day and clean and cook for him. Till one day my great-grandmother said he was an awful big liar. Say if you knowed him, you didn't believe nothin he tell you. Say that day he was talkin bout he got married, said, "I got married," say, "when I left here. I went to Philadelphia." They asked him where was his wife? "She up there, I guess." Say, "Why'd you leave her?" Say, "We got on an argument that mornin," say, "and I cut her head with a tin cup." Say, "I knowed I got locked up and I left and come back home again."

And he died and Aunt Liza tried to get pension for the children and she couldn't get a cent. Never got a cent. Some of the old soldiers tried to get pensions for their children cause she had a time to raise them children. And they tried and they wanted to know about a marriage certificate and had to write back and explain to em that she wasn't married to him. Course, they had no way to prove that them children was his, so she didn't get anything.

Old man William Copper and Pete Copper was brothers and they moved to Copperville. Peter Copper live down the same lane where old man William Copper lived. William Copper lived with his wife, Liddy, and his wife's mother. Her name was Sally; we used to call her Aunt Sally. Dan Johnson was Liddy's brother. He owned land in Copperville, but never did build a house out here. Liddy Copper and Dan Johnson were light skin and their mother was just as dark as a person could be. And she must've been part Indian, cause her hair, when she'd let it out, would come down to her waist pretty near. And the Negroes they brought from Africa, they didn't have hair like that. And so was my grandfather on my father's side. He must've been part Indian, cause he had two daughters and both of them had hair like that— long and thick and crimpy. And one of em, John Copper from Copperville, married. Course, I know her well, and her hair, she'd comb it out, it'd come down to her waist. And she was part Indian, must've been. That was on her father's side. That was on Sam Sutton's side.

I don't know whether William Copper's parents was Colonel Lloyd's or Dr. Tilghman's. I first knowed him fore they built the house, he was livin to Tilghman's. I've got an idea Tilghman owned him in slave times. Old man William had white blood in him, plenty of it, and Liddy's father was white. And I don't know whether some of the Tilghmans was his father or not.

We had respectable people out chere in Miles River Neck. I forget now how many years Unionville had started before anybody from the town went to jail. It was several years. And this fellow went to jail and the colored had a brass band in Easton and that night, they walked out and the people thought they was serenadin the town because the fellow went to jail. That was dumb to do that, and they got mad and runned every one of em. Somebody went down ahead and runned the draw off at Miles River Bridge. That draw used to slide, runned her back. And the head man, he come here run right overboard, right up on it before he saw the draw gone. And another man next to him, when he saw him stop, and he stop. Run up on this other fellow and course, he stopped right there and they jumped on him. Was goin to whip him. And he was supposed to be coward, and he turned around and tore that man up when he got close enough to him. And the man was whipped by bein surprised. He was surprised, cause they used to call him a coward. Say he tore that man up.

And Mr. Cowgill, he was the one who sold and leased em land in Union-ville, he was a Quaker. He wouldn't tell on em. I heard em say that was after slavery, the men went over in Goldsborough Neck. They went over there and they got a sheep. I think they skinned it over there, and they had it in a sack, had cut it up so one man wouldn't have to carry the whole weight. Say and when they got out of the boat gettin ready to leave, Mr. Cowgill stepped out of some bushes. They had started and he walked up on one of the men that had part of the sheep and caught a hold the sack, and he called the man name, say, "Is he fat?" And that man jumped and let go of the sack and flew. They looked, all em that had sacks, they dropped theirs and Mr. Cowgill called em, "Come back here! Come back! Come back!" Say, "I ain't gonna have nothin done with you. It ain't mine." Say, "Give me piece for my breakfast." And they let him pick the part that he want and give him. And that was all to that. And still, they was great them days about stealin pigs, shoats, and some of em were grown hogs and lambs. And if it wasn't lamb time, they'd get the whole sheep.

And one time it was two men, and sheep was in the field feedin back by what they call "the thickets" on Big Dundee. And this man left his brother to watch, to make a noise if the man on the place come out. And his brother went down and got around the sheep, goin to run em up here to the lane in a corner and both of em would catch one. So he got around, started em on up, but was a gate there then to go in. And when they started back with em runnin, he looked over in the road and he saw a man he thought was his brother. "Ike," said, "I told you I could beat you runnin." And they was keepin ahead of this man. And the one was to the gate, end the lane there, watchin, he got suspicious, cause he knowed his brother wasn't runnin no sheep out in the road. The sheep was in the field. Say he hung down the woods and this man, when he got near up to where he was goin to corner them, he got close to the fence and he looked, by God, it was a white man. And he turned around and you talk about runnin. Say he distanced that man just like it would be a horse and carriage and a automobile. He got ahead the man enough to get over that rail fence. Down the woods he went. And one of em got lost in the woods and he was there when it got light in the mornin. He didn't get out time enough to go to work on time and I heard the older men tell it, say that man didn't get them. But they had to do somethin to live them days. When they worked, they didn't get nothin for the work, not enough to feed families. What they stole, mostly from Colonel Lloyd's farms.

And Colonel Lloyd never offered one foot of land to John Copper. Didn't offer anybody. Course, it wouldn't be right to offer one land and all the others not any. He had a man there, George Cooper. Course, in them days, George Cooper a young man; he wasn't old as the slaves, but he worked for him for years. First he lived on Tire Top, for years and years. And then they put him on New Design. And old man Cooper got his leg broke workin for Colonel Lloyd and they had to take his leg off. Well, he never give him nothin. And there was half-brother, Robert Lewis, the same, both of em worked for him as long as they was able to work. He didn't get any land. George Cooper bought a piece of ground at Copperville and built a house. Rob Lewis, he bought a house as you go to Germantown, and he bought a place in Copperville. And Cooper bought the land and had a house built, but he didn't get none of Colonel Lloyd's land. And Cooper didn't do any more work after he come off from Wye. Bob Lewis, he worked on the farm till he got good age on him, then they took him up around the house where it wouldn't be so hard. And they told him they was goin to give him a horse and a cow. And he ain't got the horse or cow either, yet. He promised both of em, they say, the same thing. That wasn't the Colonel, that was Mr. Howard, the Colonel's son. And I mean them days, you worked. A man went there to work, he had to work, too. Didn't, they would fire him. But Robert Lewis was on the farm for years and years. And he got disabled and they saved money enough, God knows how, and bought that place down at German-town. And George Cooper's family is still livin in the house that he had built. And you got up them days, three and four o'clock in the mornin. You had your bell there, man was a head man, get up and ring it, and you could hear several them days ringin that time of the mornin.

Part II

My father died when I was four years old. He shot hisself in the arm, carelessness with a shotgun and he turned to lockjaw. People used to get me to tell about how he died. Some of em used to say there wasn't another boy in Copperville could tell it like I could. Before my father died, my mother lived to my great-grandmother's. My father was there off and on. He worked and most the time, he stayed where he worked. He come often to Copperville to see my mother, but he never made it his home there. My mother was raised by my great-grandmother so that was her home. My great-grandmother took her when she was four years old. My grandmother had several children and great-grandmother took her to take care of her. Times were tight.

My mother went to Baltimore when my father died. When my mother first went away, I was with my grandmother regular, but my grandmother built and moved to Copperville. My grandmother and grandfather Flamer come from Germantown while my mother was in Baltimore. Before Germantown, they lived at a farm what they called Charity. And that was joinin the farm they called Faith. Grandfather went with a man called Robinson to the next farm. And Robinson owned the house at Germantown. That was the help's house. And while they was there, they built a house to Copperville. In fact, they had part of it moved there from somewheres close by, then they built on to it. I was born in my great-grandmother's house. My grandmother Charlotte Flamer lived right opposite her property, but across the lane. And naturally both was close. After I got some size, I was backs and forths, each one. For a time, I stayed to my great-grandmother's in the day mostly and then stayed to my grandmother's at night. Grandmother's was where I was supposed to be, but I actually go to my great-grandmother's and stayed. What used to keep me goin there, back and forth, was the feedin. Was just a little lane between em, so I didn't have any distance to go. I used to have some kind of attack the doctors called it, get tired. But when I'd stay down to my grandmother's, a much cooler house, because we used to set up by a fireplace down there. When I'd go up to my great-grandmother's, it was a small room and much hotter fire, easier to heat. And it was more warmer; then that cold would break down on me. And go down to my grandmother's.

In bout a couple days, it'd be all cleared up. And I remember when I was a little fellow before I put pants on, I used to call myself racin with the moon. I used to think one time it was two moons or more. That was nighttime, I used to go back and forth. That's the way I come up from a little child.

And I remember somethin happened when I was with my grandmother. My grandfather come home one dinner time. I was sittin down in the floor; I had a cup with milk and bread, with a spoon. I was a little fellow tryin to eat the best I could, and there was a big black snake layin right across my lap. And my grandfather, he watched me, and I'd take a spoonful and then I would get another one and put it to the snake's mouth. The snake'd draw his head back far, as far as I could reach. He didn't take it, then I'd take it and eat it. There was no noise made about it because my grandfather wasn't afraid of em. He had one stay in his house several years. I don't know where it went in the winter, but it'd show up in the summer.

And my great-grandmother had told me about gettin on the road playin horse. Then, boys wore a dress until they were four or five years old. And I was somewhere round five years old and I was wearin a dress. So I went down the lane from home and fellow had reins on me. I was his horse, and another boy had reins on another child. And we come up that lane side and side. Why, if it hadn't been for them, the boy that was drivin me and the other boy's big mouth, she wouldn't've caught me. And when I looked up, she was through the gate. "Come on, son, I'm waitin on you." Took me in and tore me up. Where they had this harness that come under my arm, it always kept them stitches broke under my arm. They never go no more of that harness on me from that day.

My mother come home from Baltimore when I was near six and got married again down here. Married Robert Emory. She went in with Robert Emory's mother and father. We lived in Ezekiel Emory's house. Ezekiel lived up to Grosses for awhile on the farm. Then when we left there, we down to Hope House. And we had to move from Hope. My stepfather, he was oystering. He had his boat right down to Hope. There was water runnin right back of the house, what was called Lloyd Creek. And that's where he landed boat fore they ever moved there. He wasn't workin for the man that owned Hope. He was rentin a house and oystering and the man that owned Hope wanted a man to work on the farm, and he hired this man and he wanted his house. So we moved to Copperville.

We moved to Harrison Roberts' house when we came back to Copperville, not in Ezekiel Emory's house. They didn't have any more room. They only lived there when they didn't have any other place to go. Ezekiel Emory had one son that was home. It was the old man and his wife Millie and young Ezekiel. And mother, stepfather Robert would rather be to theirself than to be somebody else house. Ezekiel Emory had other children, but they left, went to Baltimore and some went to Philadelphia, like that. There was Prissy,

Hanna, Rosetta, and then Robert and Zeke. Prissy stayed up around Wye Neck, somewhere up in there. Lizzy and Sally and Zeke, they went back Queen Annes again. They married where they went back to. That's bout like eggs being brought from places, and when the birds grow up, the ones that hatch out of the eggs go back. So that's the way it was with the Emory children.

The old man wasn't working when I was a boy. His son, Ezekiel, was livin at home; he wasn't nothin but a boy. He was older than I was, but he wasn't grown at that time, and he stayed home till his father died, first; some years after that the mother died, and when she died, he left Copperville. And he had relation in Queen Annes and that's where he went. Didn't stay in Queen Annes till he died, but he stayed there, and he lost his wife and then he went on Kent Island. His wife come from up there to Queen Annes. And that was funny, certain. He went on the back end of Kent Island and I can't think of the name of the little town, when they was runnin a ferry from Claiborne across. Well, that's where you got off, right there at that little town where he was, right close to it. And that's where he died. He worked and all, but he didn't have a 75 percent mind and he got with a woman, her mind was the same way and they got married and her parents took her away from him after they was married for some time and sent her away. I think they sent her to Crownville. And when they did that, course, that broke em up and Zeke, he end up on the island, and way back on the end of the island.

He worked on the farm. He was workin on Mr. Stilwell's farm when I used to go up there and look after the dogs, but wasn't workin for Stilwell, he was workin for a man that rent the farm. And he certainly was glad to see me. I had a time to get away from him. I hadn't seen him for a good many years. One time, I dreamt on a Saturday night, that I saw Zeke and his wife and they was to this place, it was a public place, and one was standin on one side of the door and the other'n on the other, and they was facin out where the cars and things was. That was the main door to go in; they was standin back out of the way. And I drove by and parked, I carried two or three people there, it was the same family and after they got out of the car, I look I saw these people stand, a man was on one side of the door, the woman was on the other, and it come to me it was the same picture that I saw the night before that. I said be-dog if it ain't the same thing I dreamt bout and the same people that I saw. I got out of the car and walked up to the door, there was Zeke and his wife, and I dreamt on a Saturday night they were standin just like I saw em when my dream. One on one side of the door and one on the other'n. Both of em very near the same height.

Dreams a funny thing. I don't remember many of em coming true like that. I remember when I was a child, I had heard old people talkin bout a woman and I had never heard her name before and I had never seen her. And I kept it on my mind and I dreamt bout her. And after that, I saw her and it was the same woman that I dreamt bout. I saw the picture. And nobody understand dreams. But that was true wonders for me. And this woman even was dressed like I dreamt she was when I saw her.

We lived in Harrison Roberts' house for two years. I'm pretty sure rent wasn't over two or three dollars a month. We had bought the land and had that house built. There was a man around all this section that built some of em. Harrison Roberts was hired by the lifetime. Old man Harrison was what they called coachman. And he was on the farm until the old man got too old for to trust him with a fiery horse. And one time, two of Colonel Lloyd's sons was home and they brought two fellows with em. And Uncle Harrison was to take em to Easton. And they was sittin back in the carriage and they thought they'd have some fun on Uncle Harrison. And they said, "Harrison," ridin along, "you ever been to London?" "Yes, sir." Say, "I took your father there one time. I drove the carriage." And these other fellows, I guess they commenced laughin at old man, snickering at old man Harrison. Say, "Well, I did." Say, "We went out through Hardwood Gate. The sun was just risin just coming up over Gruffson Woods." And that's the name of that woods to your left when you leave Wye comin out. "What time did you get back, Harrison?" "We got back just when the sun was goin down over yonder." Made it between suns; the sun was just going down. Well, he didn't know no better. And I was big enough to remember the time Colonel Lloyd give him a couple of calves. He was the first one around there had the cows, white face in the head, Herefords. And there was two calves come speckle, and Colonel Lloyd didn't want them in the bunch and he give them to Harrison. And Harrison lent them to some fellow on Hopewell Farm to pasture them for him. And he left the calves there and old man Harrison tried to get em, he told em, say, "They ate they heads off." Say, "You ain't paid me nothin." He lost both of them. But the farmer didn't gain by it. Years after that and he died, he had nothin. He had worked men like dogs. We lived at Chestnut Lane and Hopewell, right across from where we lived, and I've seen lights there half past two and three o'clock around the stables. That the time he got em up in the morning. But it come home to him. Before he died, he didn't have nothin.

Then old man Harrison wanted us out; he had a lot of relations and children. And we left Harrison house, we went to Harriet Blackwell's house to Copperville. We stayed there until 1898. Harriet Blackwell had a lot, but she didn't live in Copperville. I never knowed her to live in Copperville. She lived up here to Grosses. I think she had been there ever since she was a little girl, may've been born there. That's where her people was. And then she worked in the house there at Grosses for years and years until she got disabled. She was a woman with good age on her, way older than my mother. Lot of people lived in her house at Copperville.

When we were there, she had lost her husband. His name was Richard. He was what they call a coachman there to the Grosses, carriage driver. I don't know how he held that job, cause he like his drinks, but I guess he knowed how to handle em, that was what kept him there, I guess. And I don't think he drink on his job—if he had, wouldn't't've had no job.

Stayed to Grosses until he died. He got sick. Dr. Tilghman sent him to Baltimore John Hopkins, there was no hospital here, and he didn't trust the doctors here, and that's where he died. When he come back from Baltimore, they was notified not to open the coffin. People marchin around was fixed to do it, want to see him, but it wasn't explained to the people that they couldn't open the casket, but them that made it around there told others that it was closed. Then they told them that they got a notice not to open the casket. I don't know why. I don't think it was any disease he had that was contagious. I went to his funeral. Didn't make a practice of goin to a funeral, but I went to his. I was a little fella come out to Copperville during the thing. Exceptin church, he'd be full and he'd grab me and tell the people I was tryin to throw him and he'd be holdin me.

Harriet Blackwell kept her house just like old man Harrison Roberts had his, just for to be sure if he had to leave where he would have some place to go. I judge that's what it was. And it wouldn't make sense owned it and let it sit there idle when they could make money to pay the upkeep on it by rentin it.

Copperville was called Copperville ever since I can remember, and I guess before my mother could remember. I guess it was named after John Copper; he was the first Copper that lived there. And the nickname for Copperville was Rabbittown. You call it that, a lot of the older ones would laugh at you. But that was an insultin name; they didn't want their town to be called Rabbittown. I know the time when all the town had somebody rabbit hunting. And they nicknamed Unionville, Cowgilltown, and you call it Cowgilltown, you'd have to fight. Don't mistake about it, the women get into you, children, men, you call it Cowgilltown. I remember it was a great insult. Tunis Mills, course, the people didn't get insulted about Tunis Mills. That was named after a man had a saw mill there, he owned the biggest part of this land.

There was a number of families in Copperville when I was a boy. Samuel Hinton, John Moody, Isaac Johnson, Perry Blake, Henry Thomas, and Harrison Roberts was on what they call the Front Lane. And the other side of the road goin through Copperville, it was three houses, Phil Moaney, John Copper, and Solomon Deshields. That was land was bought from another man. There was another lane: Horace Gibson, Alec Flamer, Harriet Blackwell, Mary Jane Parker, and Isaac Copper was on that lane. The church come up to Horace Gibson's property and that was the beginnin of the cemetery and the church land. On the other side of the church was William Copper, Peter Copper, Ezekiel Emory, and Eliza Kellum. Next to grandfather Flamer's house was two empty lots, two on one side. One was John Blackwell's and the other one was Richard Blake's. They was growed up in bushes. They had to be cleaned off. It was very important to own land. To have a home to go to. Some of em old fellas bought land. It was right hard on them the wages they had workin, but still, you could buy new ground then for ten dollars an acre. You had taxes to pay, but they'd say it wasn't nothin, two or three dollars, something or other like that.

My grandfather Alec Flamer was in Copperville by hisself, cause my grandmother, she went to Baltimore to work and stayed with a daughter in Baltimore. My grandmother had a daughter named Emma. She married a man from Queen Annes, George Wally. They went to Baltimore. They may've been in Baltimore when they got married. Emma's sister, Hester, also went to Baltimore. She died in Baltimore when I was bout seven years old. She had what you call appendicitis, and it burst. And had a knot to come up on her side and she had a doctor for some time then she got another one, the last doctor she got, he told her had she got him sooner, he could've brought it to a head and had it burst on the outside. They wasn't even operatin on for no appendicitis them days. Work was more plentiful there than it was here and it was more money. And at that time, three of the boys had gone there. And the youngest child that was a girl, Nanny, stayed chere with my grandfather for awhile. And then years after that, grandmother got older and wasn't able to work everyday, and she come back home. My grandfather used to go up to Baltimore about every two or three months to see her. But see, she got regular work in someone's house up there and more money and she stayed up there. It was more money than she could get chere and she could pick out a class of people there to work for. But in that day, she couldn't here. The nearest place was at Tunis Mills and all them was workin people and they wasn't able to pay much cause they didn't get much theirself. Them that had the money moved here, they had the servants, some they had there since slave times. Course, they could get jobs sometimes washin and ironin, something like that. And then some of em again that had more money they had the washin and ironin done right on the place, like down at Wye, places like that.

Many people went to Baltimore. There wasn't work enough here for em all. Some were house servants there. Dan Johnson was caterer. His nephews worked for him in Baltimore. They used to visit Copperville in the summer. They was big shots up there then. But I don't know whether they ever thought of that—they didn't make any fuss over him. And he didn't do any visitin. When he come, he stayed right there, spent so many days there, and go back to Baltimore. Course, Dan Johnson felt he was above, I guess, the others, and he didn't do any visitin anymore than his sister. Baltimore was the onliest place they did go from over here. Cause you take other places out of Miles River Neck, up around Newtown, places like that, they went to Philadelphia. Or even Easton, well, some went from Easton to Baltimore, but the big majority of em went up north. The boat used to run to Tunis Mills every day. I was pretty near grown when they stop runnin that boat to Baltimore from Tunis Mills. When I was a boy, the trip took pretty near a day.

They say when this boat was down at Miles River Bridge, the old people used to pick blackberries and huckleberries and some had chickens, they'd get on there and carry em to Baltimore and sell em. Cause they had one old woman on there, that was only a tale they told her, say they got in sight of Baltimore, just about light, say and they runned and runned and runned, they couldn't get no closer, said the captain got worried, say, "What's the matter?" Say, "We've been lookin at Baltimore for over two hours," say, "and we ain't a bit closer." He was talkin with the mate, say, "I don't know what's the matter." So he went down on the first deck and looked this old woman, when they got in sight of Baltimore, she got up and went up in the bow and was lookin at Baltimore. And the captain hollered, say, "Here's the trouble." Say, "This old woman," say, "is standin up here," say, "is so ugly." Say, "Baltimore is runnin from us." Say, "Old lady," say, "I won't charge you nothin for bringin you up here if you'll go down in the hold and stay there till we get tied up."

They used to go from out chere to Baltimore to do their dealin. Cause one old man, he went up there and bought some stuff and he had more than he should've tried to carry, he was crippled anyhow and a young fella overtakin him and people was passin him, and the young fella started pass, "Hey. Hey, you young buck." Say, "Help your uncle Dan down to the wharf." And he had the sack of flour and he give him that; it was the heaviest thing. He give him the sack of flour and something else, that fella took it, he could walk faster than this old man, he went right through the crowd. This old man never did see him no more.

And they used to go to Baltimore then when it was holidays. Was another old man out here by the name of Charles Henry Gibson. He went up there this Easter Holiday. Them days, it was a tobacco advertisement, it was an old Indian, that thing would stand up. He had a bunch of cigars in his hand, had em reached out. This old man looked, say, "No, sir." Say, "I don't chew the one." Say, "Just tell me where the boys gone." It was a tobacco sign. They used to make up all kind of tales on old people them days. My grandfather, he had a daughter living in Baltimore and he had somebody's old address they give him. And he was walkin with this piece of paper in his hand, and he stopped a cop, say, "Mister," say, "will you tell me where my Bertha Ann lives?" He handed him the paper, the man read it. Said, "No, sir. I don't know nothin about your Betsy Anna," and handed the piece of paper back to him. That was just jokes they was tellin on old people.

I never know my grandfather Flamer to do anything. When I know him, he was a man with good age on him. He had been out of the Civil War twenty years, and I don't know how old he was when he went in there. He used to work on the farm. He was an old soldier, gettin that pension, and he used to fool around at the store over there at Tunis Mills. Man had a store by the name of Hill, and he worked for him. He was handyman for him, just little jobs for years up until he died.

And John Copper was gettin some age on him when I was a boy. He was oysterin then. I don't think he did anything between oyster season. He was his own boss when it come to oysterin. That makes a whole lot of difference. If he gone and worked for somebody else, they'd want to see him move around, but he was his own boss when he was oysterin. He had his own boat. I don't know where he bought it from, but it was boat makers over at St. Michaels. He had a boy that used to cull for him, Charles Copper, but not any relation. He was landin in Wye River, and it would be an oyster bar in Wye River. He used to come clear up here back of Linton, what used to call Paul's Spring.

John Copper used to own a seine, and he used to haul the seine in warm weather, and the men he used to give them an interest in the fish he caught. He shipped what he caught, I guess, to Baltimore. He's the only colored man that ever owned a seine over here. Then lot of em didn't like that, lot of the white ones. He hauled that seine until one time he had it on the shore dryin, had it strung out and man burned it up. They knowed who did it, but if he had had him arrested, they wouldn't've done nothin with him, and I don't suppose in them days, they'd even arrest him. It was an old white man, a different nationality from the American people, and he used to live in a cave. Somebody said the cave was up here around Wye Heights and Uncle John stretched his seine out somewhere up there on the shore, stretched it out to dry. And he said he was burning the grass around the shore, that's all he'd tell em, he was burning the grass around the shore and it got away from him. Said it burnt up, that settled it. I heard the old people talkin bout it. I remember when I was little, it was fresh then to hear em talkin bout it. You know if he hadn't wanted to burn it up, he wouldn't've burnt the grass around it.

My grandfather Flamer, he was afraid of water. He worked with John Copper one day. He didn't go no more. See, you work on percentage of what you catch. They caught somethin, but was a storm come up and my grandfather keep sayin, "Put me ashore! Put me ashore! This ain't my home out chere." He wasn't used to water. Up there around Queen Annes, ain't no rivers or nothin. "This ain't my home, put me ashore." And he never did go back anymore.

Solomon Deshields done days work around, whatever he could get to do. He never oystered, he never follow the water. He worked Tunis Mills a long time. Work there when I know it was hauling out slabs and logs they was sawin. They had a place that they send them right out on the outside. And he had a horse and cart belonged to him, and that was his job, keeping that clear. Course, somebody said he could send the horse in with the cart to his place where he'd usually be to get the slabs when they come out, and the horse had got so he'd go up there and back around just as nice as a person could back him around.

I remember Perry Blake haulin wheat, thrashin wheat when I was fourteen years old. He never did work for nobody but the Lloyds. He was born a slave, and he was always a field man. He didn't know nothin bout the water, and knew nothin about oysterin. Only for a little while, he went down to saw mill and they was in the summertime. He was goin to work seven o'clock and stoppin at six and he wasn't used to it and he got to fussin. Say he wasn't used to it, being on no place, not going to work until dinner time, say, and then stoppin before sundown. Well, he hadn't been used to goin to work not any later than four o'clock in the mornin. He stopped and went down to work down to Wye again, days work, where he was makin more an hour to the saw mill and some of the others that was slaves, they'd gone there and then puttin in less hours at the saw mill and went back to the old slave time. I don't know what Colonel paid. I judge about fifty cents a day. Old man Perry was one of the old men that used to do the ditchin for Colonel, and he wouldn't let the younger men do it. They had been ditchin ever since in slavery. And them the men he got to do the ditchin, and he'd always clean out every field ditches, every three years.

I was a grown man when old man Perry died. I was seventeen years old and his wife, she wanted to still stay at the house and the children let her stay there awhile and after that, they just made her move cause she shouldn't't've been there by herself, and they wasn't able to hire anybody to stay with her. And she went to live with her oldest son.

Isaac Johnson was one the ditchers. He'd work by the day after he was there in Copperville there in his house. Isaac Johnson had a girl around my age and a boy was much older. And both of them lived down to Wye where their mother cooked. Mother's a cook there for years; Lord knows how many years. It may've been from slavery. They called her Cook Mary. Cook Mary must've stopped cookin around about 1898, when we left Copperville. She was old, she stopped cookin, and that was a pretty good job. You'd be sure to get enough to eat if you didn't get no money. I never heard any complain about the job. I've heard more complain about the ones they worked for than the job, cause I guess when they went on a job like that, they expect to work, which'n they should. And livin apart was a choice of theirs. There was no compellin em. It made it good for their two children. They didn't have to pay them board, didn't have them to feed. They was fed down to

Wye for nothin. And Cook Mary and the children would only come out to Copperville when her day was off. It may've been just Sunday.

Perry's oldest son, Richard, was livin in New Design when I was a boy. He was livin in that old slave time house. Some people hired on the farm, lived on the farm, cause they had no other place to live. And some, again, that was the onliest kind of work they was suited for. I think the wages was around about ten dollars a month, and they got up year around except in thrashin season. Wheat time half past three and four o'clock in the mornin, work until sundown, come in, and feed, it'd would take em more than an hour to do the feedin. Richard Blake got a little flour and meat and cornmeal. I believe it was about a half a bushel of meal each month, and somewheres around about thirty pounds pork. Some give a little more of eats than some others did. That was the lay-in, they called it. I remember when some of the women worked in these private homes, that's what they got.

Richard Blake used to come to Copperville church. That was their church. His children, them that went to school, walked to Unionville. Some of em walked from Presqu'ile school out to Unionville. It was some come from the other way on the other side of the bridge. As far down as Kirkham, they walk to Unionville to school. That was back before I was a boy. I heard the older ones talkin about it.

Old man Phil Moaney was doin day work on the farm when I was a boy. That was when crops was bein put in and bein harvested, like that. Course, wheat is put in in the fall, corn in the spring. Them's the two main crops. You needed labor when puttin the crops in and savin the crops. Cause, like corn, the monthly men cultivate it and put in wheat. You got up about two o'clock in the mornin. And some of em used to use a lantern to see their tracks, their wheel tracks when they was seedin it. They'd work until you couldn't see, work until dusk, and I've heard that some of em worked a little later, use a lantern in the afternoon, but mostly the lantern was for the mornin. Then they had to go in and feed the stock, that was the hogs, the cows, the sheep, stuff like that. Then the men went home to get their meals, and it was usually eight o'clock or after when they ate. And they had been up there since about two o'clock in the mornin. In fact, they'd get up and feed the team, go back and get their breakfast. By the time they got through their breakfast, the team'd be through eatin. They put in a whole lot more hours than the team did.

I don't guess any of em liked this work, but they had to do it. Wasn't nothin else for em to do, cause if they didn't do it, somebody else would and they had to live, so that's why it wasn't much kicking on that. But a lot of them'd pick for a place where you didn't have to get up that early. They used to have bells. The foreman had the bell to his house and when he got up, he'd ring that bell for every man to get ready to go to the barn, and I've been hearin distance of two and three bells and more than that. Some way off you just could distinguish that it was a bell. And then, some of em would try to beat somebody else up by ringin the bell. There was a bell at Wye and bell to some of the other of Colonel Lloyd's farms, if not to all of em.

And it was a choice of yours to work by the day or by the month. You always could hire somebody by the month cause for some people, it was hard for them to get anybody to work for em. You could find a job if you couldn't find where you want to be. It would be someplace if it wasn't right over here at your home where you want to be. Then, sometimes, you get them places between the movin times you'd get somethin that didn't nobody else want. I know they had one man moved from here over in Caroline County one day, and two days after that, he moved back here. There wasn't nothin the matter with the county, it was the man that he was workin for. But things he didn't know when he hired to him, found out afterwards. And I think in three days he moved back. They all had different faults. Was them days lots of poor people worked for men that wasn't able to pay em. That was one thing. And some of em work for men who had to sell pigs or calf before they'd get the money to pay em. Some people wasn't paid their monthly wages on time, lots of em. Some of em left places that the man owed em when they left, and they never did get that. The monthly wage then was ten dollars a month. And you had what they called an overseer, and he got twelve. He was the manager over the ones that he worked. Ninety percent of em was white men. Some of em was black men, but very few. Some of em had old men that was on the farm ever since slavery and they wouldn't get rid of em for no man, and they was good workers, so they put them ahead. Still, that made more work on the man that owned the place, throwed more work on him because the book work would have to be done. And the other fellow, nine times out of ten, he used to do some of the book work. And course, he got some of em that couldn't read or write anymore than the slaves could, I mean white men. I know a white man who worked for Colonel Lloyd for years and years, and he wouldn't know his name if you'd write it down and hand it to him, but he was a good manager, and the Colonel kept him. He know how to get the work out of the men. And what you call an overseer, he was around the men and the majority of em was ahead of the men.

Sometimes bein overseer made a hated man in community. Working class hate him cause some of em carried it too far. But I know was some of em they put ahead of others. Course, foreman and overseer, I think, was two different men. But I knowed of places that had men they put ahead. You take Presqu'ile, there was a man there, he was the head man for years and years and he had been there ever since a boy, and may've been born there. That was Perry Blake. He was just ahead of the work, and everything they went to do them days, they race, see who could do the most. I've heard old people speakin about how much work he could do, and it was surprisin, he was a small man, too. They don't work like that today. Some of em went out to see how much they could do, come down now, they see how less they can do. In them days, they used to work someplaces from can't to can't. From you can't see in the mornin till you can't see at night. That way some of em worked, so they called that can't to can't. That was in free times. You wouldn't expect anymore from slave times, but that was in free times.

My mother used to wash for my grandfather. She lived right in Copperville, too. She used to wash for him and do the cleanin for him. Cause I remember he used to have a black snake used to come, show up in this house every year in the summertime, warm weather. And when she start cleanin for him, he told her if she saw a snake in there not to hurt it, that was his pet. And the first thing he told her when she spoke of comin there doin the washin, he said, "Well," said, "it's all right." Say, "If you don't hurt my pet." And one time he saw a piece of wrappin cords like you used to tie up bundles with was hangin out of this snake's mouth, and he went and cut it out and pulled it out of the snake's mouth, out of its stomach. He was surprised, don't know how the snake swallowed it or why he swallowed it, but it must've been somethin on it to cause him to swallow it. My mother, I don't know whether she ever saw him or not, but she wasn't afraid of snakes either.

My mother would be doing housework whenever she didn't have days work and it was seldom she had days work, cause all around was poor people. And when she did have days work, she had to work for nothin just well say. Fifty cents a day was the highest she got. And some of em used to take in washin and that's what my mother did for years. Go get the wash and carry it home, didn't bring it to you, and got fifty cents for a family wash. She didn't do but a little wash home them days until we moved to Chestnut Lane, then had a dug well right there. And we drank that water open well. But it certainly was good water. But we drank it and then certain times, I don't know whether it was spring or fall, it used to have little red worms in it. They had to pump it off and clean the well out. Then the worms would disappear.

Wasn't work for women, them days. They had plenty of women down on Wye. They had some work at the Wye until they got disable to work, got so old, usually it was the cooks. Bout all that worked at Wye come from Copperville.

Mary Jane Parker had been a widow for several years. She worked days work, sometimes Tunis Mills. She had two sons workin that used to take care of her. William was livin in the place where he was workin. Charlie lived with his mother, but had jobs other places, all were by the month. He didn't get home often. And he worked all the time. So did William. The old lady had a daughter and she had a son in Baltimore.

She married again a man they called Stephen Bidgell. He owned a place up here in the Chapel. That's where they old lady died, up there. And when she went up there, her son, James, went up there with her, naturally. And Charlie, he made his home up there after his mother went there, and that's natural.

Philip Coleman work on the farm, day work. Sam Hinton worked for Colonel Lloyd—I guess that was the first place he worked—before he worked at Tunis Mills. He worked Tunis Mills until he just got disable, but when he was younger man, he was down at Wye. At the saw mill, he was mostly in the bunch that used to go round and cut the timber. When he built that house, he got married and, I think, he had three or four children. His wife died. I don't know how long he was single, then he got married again. His second wife's name was Frances. She came here with the Tilghmans that owned the grocery. They used to go some place, must've been Virginia, every winter, and they brought a lot of help here that didn't go back. That was after the Civil War, that was in my day and before my days, too.

Them that oystered, they did day work, worked on crops, gettin crops, harvestin crops. Like the rest of em, my stepfather worked on the farm summertime, nothin else to do. And John Moody the second, was an oysterman in the wintertime. Sometimes he had a partner, sometimes he didn't. His brother-in-law, Greenbury Gibson, oystered with him for several years. I was with John Moody for awhile. In the summertime, John Moody worked day work on the farms, whatever he could find like the rest of em did.

One time, Colonel Lloyd had some men living on the Glebe, white men. And they stole, I've forgotten now how many shoats. And Colonel Lloyd was comin around Copperville lookin for em. And then my great-grand-mother, she had just a small hog. Somebody give it to her; it was a runt. They give her this hog because said it wouldn't grow, and he fattened it. He had other hogs, two other hogs besides this one, but he killed this little one before regular hog-killin time. And Colonel Lloyd was ridin around Copperville lookin, and he saw him. He rode up in the yard, old man John was dressin the hog. "Moody," say, "where'd you get that pig from?" Say, "I got it." Say, "Master," say, "that ain't none of your business." "Don't talk to me like that. Where'd you get that pig from?" "I got it." Say, "I'll show you, yeah." Say, "If you don't get out of here." He went to the stable and got his pitchfork. It happened my great-grandmother heard the conversation, she went out there and grabbed him, say, "If I hadn't, he'd a stuck that pitch-fork in him." But the Colonel got out from there. But after that, they found out it was the men they had on the Glebe that sold him. They had sold the pigs that Colonel Lloyd had lost. Colonel Lloyd had no right comin there askin such questions like that. Old man Moody told him. "Oh, Massa," say, "that ain't none of your business."

Old man John had a woman was some relation to him that he brought from Queen Annes to live with them. And he told her that his wife and his son treat him like a dog and after the woman got chere, he turned on her and then she told my great-grandmother what he had told her, come up there and told her that all of you all had treated him like a dog. Say, "I found he was the one who treat you all like a dog."

John Moody the second had a horse was down to my grandfather Flamer's and Charlotte Flamer, she was John the second's half-sister, same mother. Old man John wanted to carry it down to pasture in one of the lots that my grandfather Flamer owned. And Will Deshields said he didn't know what to do, said he was half scared to do it. "Go ahead, buddy," say. "You got a son to carry it down there." And when he got it down there, the Flamer boys told him, "Take that horse outta there. Don't turn that horse in here." Say, "Well, Uncle John told me to bring it down." "This ain't Uncle John's place. Carry that horse out the back. Take it out of here." When he carried it back, Uncle John met him to the stable. "Son," say, "you didn't leave the horse." Said, "No, the boys wouldn't let me leave it." And then Will give him some sharp talk, and he got a stick and Will said the old man would've tore him up if he hadn't thought about the little window—in the stable they always had a slidin window, in hot weather you opened it for the horse to get air. And he opened that window and dived right out, right head first.

And then there was a time, I think it was up here to Grosses, and old man John had curly hair. And they had him cleaning up around the thrashin rig, just to keep it cleaned up and throw up what bunch of wheat that drop on a table. And had his hat off and that was close to the machine and his head was full of chaff and stuff. And a woman there, she was cuttin bands, and she got to laughin at him. And after awhile, he got mad and he started to her with a pitchfork. And it was man there that knowed him, got between em, and talked nice to him. Told him not to do it. Say, "You'll get yourself in trouble." "By God," say, "I don't care." Say, "I'm going to kill that big head butcher's dog." And that evening, they had send that woman away from there. They put somebody there in her place because they believe he'd a killed her. But he was a funny old fellow.

There were six of us in Harrison Roberts' house: my mother and step-father, Robert and Birdy and Bessie and myself. They lost one when they was living at Hope fore we moved. I was the oldest of all. Harrison Roberts' house was put up four rooms, two down, two up, and then this shed kitchen—just a low roof was built on to it. That was the style them days. They had just straight up and down boards with a strip tacked over the crack between the two boards and more than half of em that strip had either buckled up or had shifted sideways over the crack and inside they had a sheathin and it'd be cracks in some of that. And sometimes, it runned up where these rafters crossed, wasn't a thing there but the bare rafters crossin. And a lot of em had fireplaces, and a hook come down and that's where you cooked your meals.

The beds were wooden beds with straw tickin. Go out to the shocks right after thrashin wheat, fill your tick up and bring it back. In them days, you had plenty of mice. The mice would get in there cause when you got the straw, you'd always get some wheat and for a long time after you fill it and sleepin on it, you'd hear the mice in that straw. I remember layin there watchin and seeing the tickin move, would be a mouse in there, and I would grab them and squeeze them to death. The old people were in one room and the children slept in a room together.

And I carried the water from the spring. Had to go across the field and carry all the water we used. Sometime I'd have two small tin pails. Mother put a tub to the fence so I wouldn't have to climb over the fence every time I come up with my buckets of water. I'd pour it in this tub, and I had to carry enough to do washin. That was hard. I had to make many a trip cross that field to the spring. Didn't wash every day, but carry water every day. And very often, that would be the first thing I did.

I didn't cut no wood on the wood pile those days, only small stuff. I didn't cut the big wood cause my stepfather, the ax he used, I couldn't use. He was afraid I would dull it up. Poor people was crazy about their axes. He had an old ax there and little things I used to cut, but he did most all the wood-cuttin. I wasn't old enough.

My mother made the most of my clothes. Used to buy material Tunis Mills. They had dry goods and hardware and all that stuff there. They didn't get places like Easton. People like Colonel Lloyd, they would let men have a two-horse wagon and he'd carry all the help was on that farm, but they'd do that about the end of every month.

I went barefooted until I don't know what time, accordin to the weather. I guess we'd start goin barefooted in May. I remember every year when we could take them shoes and stockings off, it'd be just like colts, runnin up and down the road in the mud, sometimes it'd squirtin up between your toes. We wouldn't get in ditches, though, because one the boys got his foot cut bad. Somebody threw glass, broken bottle, in there.

And I was the nurse. That was my job, takin care of the smallest child, the baby. I did that the whole time we was in Copperville after I got big enough. But when we moved to Chestnut Lane, the washin Mother did, they used to bring it to her, and when she commenced doin days work, the children were big and old enough to take care of theirself. Mother would fix the meals even if she was goin away to wash. Fix all the food on the plates, mine and all. I'd eat mine, could eat more and there'd be more there to eat, but I wouldn't touch it.

For breakfast, we'd have sometimes oatmeal and sometimes cream of wheat, and be oftener oatmeal. It wasn't much choice about what you ate just so you got somethin to eat. We had sugar, but I never used sugar on neither one. You might get a piece of bread in your hand for lunch. Course, when I used to visit on the farm that was different because they had lunches on account of the man workin on the farm come home for his lunch. But when you lived in a place like Copperville, you had no particular time to eat, not in the middle of the day. Supper was the big meal. Sometimes we'd eat vegetables, other times it might be fish. One thing I had to eat sometime, it was hominy. I hate that hominy. And in them days, they used to put those little white beans in em, they called em hominy beans, and I fish around and get all the beans out, and most the time, I wasn't filled, I had to go back and eat some of the hominy. But them were hard times, hard on everybody. I was nowheres near starvin, but I could always eat when the meals come. Course, you go on the farm, it was different. You got milk, cornbread, clabber, and at home, you didn't get cornbread. Only time I did have milk, if we went to visit somebody live on a farm. When I'd go with my mother, sometimes I'd get a jar of milk, sometimes get a bucket of clabber. Clabber was a big diet.

We never did have much of a garden. We'd have potatoes, sometime a little corn. We had some that had a better garden in Copperville then, but wasn't many. A lot of em had the land, had an old horse, and what they could've had for a garden, that's be pasture for their horse. Well, we had no horse, but we never had much of a garden exceptin potatoes and corn. Was no place to get vegetables. No place over here you could buy em. And our old people told me, tomatoes, they knowing people afraid to eat em. Some of em said they was poison. I heard one old man said he knowed the time that they used to come up wild in a cornfield. People didn't plant em in no garden them days.

Ninety percent of the people raised hogs. All on the farm raised hogs. And I don't know of anybody, in the country, I mean my range, didn't raise a hog a year. And then you could buy em off'n the scaffold that's killed and cleaned for six cents a pound—six dollars for a hundred. In Copperville, everybody had hogs. We raised two of em every year. They kept em penned up. They didn't have land to let em run out. If they did that they couldn't raise nothin else. Used to have hog killin days. There'd be a bunch of em go round kill God knows how many hogs. They went from place to place. Used to cut a little place cross throat and then stick a long butcher knife down in. If you hit him right the blood would gush out there. My grandmother didn't like to look at em after they was clean, put in the house. They would bring em in for the first night. Then the next day would be the day they'd cut em up. They would read the guts, what they used to call em. They'd take the fat off and I guess bout all of em had hogs they'd eat em. Eat the big guts, didn't eat the little one. We raised chickens. We had about seven or eight hens. You couldn't have much more than that around you, you didn't have stuff to feed em on.

I fished until I went to work. We never caught many fish, but I used to fish durin the summer, fishing and crab. When I went to work, I never got much time to do any a that. We didn't have oysters often. People caught them to sell. Sometimes a storm come up in the evenin, some of em used to shuck oysters and bring em home, but that wasn't often.

In the fall of the year, we'd go rabbit huntin using bricks or stones. My Uncle John Moody had two rabbit dogs. He had about all the rabbit dogs in Copperville, cause they didn't have things around to feed that wasn't no use to em, because they wasn't making the money to buy the stuff to feed em. All I had to do call em. I would whistle for em, and they'd come to me wherever they heard me. And I remember my uncle used to oyster, too, and keep his boat down Bruffs Island and windy days in rabbit season when they couldn't oyster, why, he would go rabbit huntin. And the dogs got so they wouldn't follow him, he had to get me to go along to get the dogs to go with him. They wasn't used to him. I used to take stones and bricks and in the woods, you couldn't do much with an oyster shell, you'd want something heavier, but I have killed rabbits with oyster shells. And the dog would run em. And they'll go in a hollow lots of time and I'd sometimes walk from the woods clear back home to get an ax and go to cut a hole in the hollow so we could get the rabbit out. I run my hand in there and get him and mother warned me never catch them by the head or neck. You did, say they'd rip you to pieces with their hind feet. And the hind feets what a rabbit fight with. She knowed a girl that was her age was settin a rabbit gum and she went to the gum, a rabbit in it, and she reached her hand in there, and caught the rabbit back of the neck, and pulled him out, and he struck her up above her hand. Just bust it open, clear down to fingers with his hind feet, and she had a bad hand for months. So I knowed how to catch em.

Whenever I went to see my great-grandmother, she'd tell me how to get along in the world and what I should do. She'd always give me a lecture, what children to play with, and children not to play with. It wasn't because I was doin something that I shouldn't do, that was for my benefit. And she always did walk with a stick. She used to carry that for dogs—wasn't afraid of no dogs. Used to walk me from Copperville clear down to Wye when I was four and five years old. We used to go to Glebe often as we did to Wye. That was after I got five or six years old. John Blackwell was on the Glebe for years and years. When we'd go to Wye, if his wife was home, she'd stop there. His wife used to cook for the Lloyds.

I was around ten years old and a doctor wanted me to come to him to work in Easton. My great-grandmother wouldn't let me go. Well, I'm glad I didn't go or it probably been just like she said, I'd got in with the worstest ones there, and that'd been too bad. You can always get acquainted with the good-for-nothin ones quicker and easier than you can ones that's decent.

I remember one time was a boy lived up to Gross'. And this boy, him and I was good friends. He was a quiet boy. I used to go up to Gross' to see him. Children used to go backs and forwards after school was out in the summer, visit like that. My great-grandmother heard it and told me not to go up there. Said, "They're bad children." Say, "You know, you've got a brother sent away now," say, "burnin down a straw stack." Say, "Don't go up there." And the children couldn't persuade me to go there after she told me not to go. She had heard about this boy bein sent away and said children them days used to fare bad. Cause he come back and wasn't back so awful long, he died. And he wasn't the onliest one I've heard of doin the same thing. And he had a brother. His brother was the one that I was well acquainted with. He was easy and well, just a good boy. And then, I wanted to go up there to see him. I was only about ten years old.

I know one lecture my great-grandmother give me. I think about it often now, and I haven't forgot it yet. That when you go to anybody's house, take your hat off soon as you step in, or take it off to the door. Now I come in my house that's what I do everytime I come in my own house, cause I got into it—done it from a child. Some people come in your house and keep their hat on if they stay in there half a day. And another one: "Keep away from bad children." And, "Never sass an old person." And that wasn't all of em, cause she'd always brighten my rememberance every time I got around her long as she was livin. When I was small, she used to tell me that I'd want a drink of water, and she'd give it to me. "Well," say, "I'll be gone before you get big enough to hand me a drink." I was married and had three children anyhow before she died.

Whatever they told me to do or not to do, I didn't forget it. And sometimes, if I didn't, I'd get a whippin I wasn't promised. My cousin, he was promised a lot till he got out of hand. And the larger boys had a way, pairin two boys off and make em fight. And Sam Sutton and I was first cousins. They try to get me to fight and Sam wouldn't want to fight and I wouldn't want to fight, and said because it was my cousin. After awhile, I got tired of it, and I said I guess I've got to fight. If I don't, they going to worry me to death. I'm tired of foolin with it. And then next day; we got together and they tried to make us fight. One put a chip on my head. That's the way they used to start you, put a chip on your head and you'd dare the other boy to knock it off. Well, I wouldn't let em put the chip on my head cause I thought he might do me like I did a boy one time. They put a chip on his head, instead of me slappin the chip off, I hit his head so hard until the chip fell off, and I had him whipped. So that day, I wouldn't let em put the chip on my head, but Sam jumped into me and I nailed him right alongside the head, and when I hit him, that was all. Grabbed the side of his head. Never did bother me no more.

But I just got tired of him, thought of a way to break him up. In fact, one of the young men told me, said, "That's the way to do. You fight him once, whip him, and you won't have no more trouble with em." And then I was scared because somebody went home and told my mother. I'd got a whippin when I went home, but she never knowed anything about it. Children them day, I think through ignorance, they'd get together and they'd always have a fight. Some of em would get to fightin and if Buck Copper and I was there, we'd leave.

And then the children'd have a fight, that'd make trouble between the old people. They'd get together and try to find out who start it, and nine times out of ten, they'd ask was I there. Then if I was, they'd either send for me, or the next time they'd see me, they'd want me to tell how it happened, and who hit the first lick and all. And they'd take my word before they would all the rest of the children. And I'd give it just like it was. I wouldn't screen neither one of em. They'd want to know what child was at fault. Then if they had that, then they'd judge whose child was in fault. Never got in many fight myself. I see that brewin, I'd always leave–stop talkin. And wasn't always afraid of the other person, but just didn't want to get in any trouble. But when they crowd me, then I'd know I had to fight then.

Was a boy used to come to Copperville with other boys on Sunday. We'd go to Sunday school, and we'd play together the rest of the afternoon. Never had no trouble. It was one, he lived to Gross'. Whenever he'd come, well, I had no brother to take up for me, and he was a lot larger than I was, older. Well, he'd give me a whippin. He would start beatin on me. That went on for some time, and one time I found a knife. This couple had some family trouble, and they broke up and the woman took her sewin box with buttons and needles and stuff in it, and this little pearl-handle knife was in the box. She took the box and throwed it over the fence and she took her lamp and glasses and broke over the top of the fence post. And I looked down there, there was buttons scattered around, and there was the pearl-handle knife. So I was tickled to get this knife. And I called this boy a name. I said, now, if he come out here Sunday and jump on me, I'm gonna cut him. And I took that knife, when I went home I got a whetstone, a brick, and I worked on it at night. Got it sharper than it was, and that Sunday, he was standin on the road there to Copperville. There was a certain place where the men used to stand in bunches on Sunday, and somebody smokin a cigarette and they throwed it down, and I picked it up. Well, he walked up there, "Put it down!" Well, I didn't put it down, he slapped it out of my hand. And I didn't say nothin. I picked it up again–it hadn't gone out–was puffin her. "I told you to put that cigarette down." Slapped it out of my hand again. And I reached in my pocket, got ahold of that knife, and open it, and I went after him, cuttin him, and I didn't miss him. I know one place, they said, if I had got further over would'a killed him. Dug that knife right through his breast. And I held the knife, not cuttin, but open. And the men standin there, they saw it. Him slappin that cigarette out of my hand and then kickin me–he had on a pair of hard leather boots. And didn't a one say a word to me. They come there and opened his shirt and was lookin at it. It was bleedin. Naturally, I left and went on home. Some of the men know what he usually did when he come out there on Sunday. They never said a word to me. My Uncle John Moody was standin there. And I got scared after I cut him—not from him, but I figured my uncle was goin to get after me, but he never said a word. He knowed he used to jump on me every Sunday he come out there, good weather, summer time, we'd get out and get to playin together. I heard after that through my mother and some of the family, said they didn't blame me. Said they saw it all, saw him start kickin me. Children get together them days, it would always be a fight.

Well, he never bothered me no more, and if he'd get after one of the other children after that, they'd say, "I'm goin to tell Joe." And he'd say, "Joe, I ain't doin nothin to them." He was just scared of me as he was his mother. I never heard any more bother out of him. I remember comin from Sunday school, he used to get after the children if they was ahead of me, they'd slack up. "I'm gonna tell Joe." And he holler to me before the child got back to him, "Joe, I wasn't doin nothin to em." That used to tickle me. That scared him. I never had no more trouble with him.

One time my uncle Joe Flamer had a saplin down in the woods and was ridin on it and called me to him and put me on it in front of him and headed down and he jumped off. And that sapling throwed me—it was just like I was flyin. It was so comfortable, I could've gone to sleep. Throwed me through the woods. And two old ladies was talkin to the yard gate, one was on the inside and the other'n was on the outside, and they saw me. Well, I didn't remember anything for awhile, but they run there, and he flew through the woods, hid hisself.

He cut my forehead with a oyster shell. I was five years old. Throwin at me with an oyster shell. And when they healed, it used to stick out for a long time, and skull would grow in it. You can feel a little of it now, but it don't show like it did before. And my mother, she said she picked pieces of the oyster shell out of the cut in my skull. She took a big safety pin and opened it and took the end that was sharp and washed it in water, and picked the pieces of shell out.

And when he'd do somethin like that, he'd go in the woods, stay in there till night. I never know of him getting a whippin, but he'd go and stay away from home. If he done in the mornin, well, he'd stay from home until that night, bedtime, slip in, and go to bed. Next mornin, the old people had slept it off.

I got the right teachin from all of em. I had learned my lesson when I was a small boy, and all the old people like me. But as my uncle Joe come up, he didn't have many friends in old people. I remember one time he was out in the lot, we called it, it runned back joined another man's property where his house was close to my grandfather's lot. And his wife's mother—what would be his wife—was livin with this other man that had the house that joined my grandfather's. And his wife's mother, she rubbed snuff, and she used to get him sometime. And sometimes some other child would go to the store for her and would get a box of snuff. And one day, Joe was out there weedin the vegetables and she call him. And he figured she wanted him to go to Tunis Mills store and he made out he was crazy. Jump up and he'd fall and roll over and jump up, fall over and lay down and kick, and it scared this old lady and she commenced to hollerin. "Charlotte, Charlotte!" That was my grandmother Flamer. "Charlotte, come here to your boy. Your boy don't know he home!" And Joe said he'd get up and fall, then kick his legs up in the air. Said he only did that cause he thought she wanted him to go to the store for her, and if he'd gone, she'd only give him a penny. And she left there and went in the house. He got up and went to work on pullin weeds out in the vegetables. He stayed up there a little longer, then he come to the house and she didn't come out there no more that day.

One time Joe and another boy and I walked from Copperville to Bruffs Island to dig mananoes. There was a man in a boat and when he got ready to go, he called the man and the man answered him and then he started callin that man nicknames. After awhile, the man jumped in a rowboat, said, "You stay there until I get there!" And he let the man get near about shore and he started off runnin. He run from Bruff's Island to Copperville. That man never caught him. He'd slow down and let the man get a hundred yards or more behind him, and he start out runnin again. Well, that was a man and the man couldn't run as long as the boy. But the man, he know who he was and come to grandfathers. Told my grandfather about it. My grandfather told him, "Well," say, "if you can catch him, whip him." And he said what he would've done if he had caught him. And Joe was out in the woods. He come right out to Copperville, but he didn't cross the road and come home. Stayed out in the woods till that night, late that evenin, come home. And mother or grandfather, one, got after him about it and he said this man called him names. Cussed him say before he called this man names. But nobody didn't ask me. But, if they had, I was goin to tell em the truth. That man didn't call him nothin. He was hollerin at the man.

And Uncle Joe used to jump on me when he'd get out, anybody around, he'd do it. Old people said it was to show himself. Of course, he was five years older than I was. That's a big difference in boys, sizes and strengths and everything. And the man had the store down at Tunis Mills, I used to do little jobs around there and in the back room. And then we both would be there in the store together, and Joe had a way of chumpin in there and makin me cry. His uncle told him two or three times, "You wait till he get a man and he's goin to chump you. And because the way he's built, he going to be a strong man." Well, I broke him up. I used to carry that little pearl-handled knife. One day, I went to Copperville from Chestnut Lane to visit some people, and it was two or three big boys comin towards Tunis Mills, but they come from Unionville. When they got there, my uncle Joe, he thought he would show off. He commenced kickin me and jumpin me. I got a chance to open that knife and the last time he kicked me, I grabbed his leg and hung to his leg. And he couldn't kick me with the other foot good. Stuck his leg full of holes. Never did bother me after that.

My stepfather wasn't so nice at times, but I got along with him till I was grown and after. He never did call my name. He used to call me when he wanted me, "Boy. Come here, Boy." Or, "Boy, do such-and-such a thing." Course, I figured that was lack of intelligence. I didn't take it as an insult, I taken it for a lack of intelligence. I don't remember he ever callin me by name. If he goin to say anything to me, or if he goin to say anything to my mother about me, well, "That boy." I was the oldest.

He called his son Robert "Boy" just like he used to call me. He wasn't so fond of children. Made it rough on children. I feel he was responsible for the boy's death and never feel any other way. Put that boy to work for a renter and work every day and boy the age he was when he went to work, he shouldn't had to work every day. Get up in the mornin light and work till after sundown that night. The onliest day he got off was on Sunday, that was, every other Sunday. That was too steady for a child. And he workin like that for renter, I don't think he was twelve years old.

I did everything that I was told to do and didn't do anything that I was told not to do. I was started out that way. They was positive with me and that's what I looked for. They hadn't promised me like some people do children I guess lots of things. I was told not to do I would't pay any attention to it.

I'll tell you, there was very few things I did wrong cause I knowed what I was goin to get. Whatever I was told to do, I'd do it. I washed dishes till I was about old enough to go to work and never broke a piece of china. And after I was married, I spoke of it and somebody where I spoke of it heard me say that, and they went and asked my mother did I ever break anything. And she told em, "No, he never broke a piece and washed dishes for years." Say, "But others, they'd come along back of him," say, "they broke up everything I had." I never broke a piece cause I was very careful because I know I'd a got a whippin.

Sometime, I was sent over to Tunis Mills store and Mr. Hill would have somethin he'd want me to do and I wouldn't stay to do it. I'd run back to Copperville carrying what I went to the store for and then I'd ask my mother could I go back. But some children would have stayed right there and did what he wanted em to do. But whenever I went over there for that my mother would tell me what time to be back. And I'd better be back at that time, too. Just a little late, I wouldn't get a whippin, but if I was much late, I would and I wouldn't get to go for God knows how long after that. And my mother would let me go down to Charles Copper's house, right down toward the back end of a back lot, and she'd tell me what time to be back.

And I'd been down there several times and would come back, wouldn't stay much more than half the time. Come back and she'd tell me I could go back again, but I'd better be on time. I don't remember bein late. I was always before time.

I got whippin sometimes for somethin I didn't do. She was tight on me. She was tighter on me than she was any of the rest of the children. I never sassed her, never argued with her. It was a little different with the other children. I feel it was a help to me, it made a better child out of me.

And Charles Copper was the same. Always go back in time. He never stayed long like some children would. And if you ever say anything to him bout askin him to stay a little longer, it wouldn't be a bit of use of sayin it, because he wouldn't do it. He had orders like I had. Course, some children them days was raised different, but that's why so many of the children get in trouble today, is the raisin. The parents are not strict on em. You don't have to be whippin a child all the time to make him mind. Just start out with at times talkin to it. That's what I say about trainin a dog. "You've got to have a rule." And stick to that rule with the dog to train it. And the same thing with children. And some people just the opposite. They let do something today and tomorrow, if they did it, they would pretty near kill em. Well, I blame the parents then. My uncle William Sutton was that way.

When I was seven, I was livin with my uncle William Sutton down to Doncaster. He was workin for Howard Lloyd. My mother and the other family was in Copperville. I lived with him a little while then went on back to Copperville again. He want me. He had a boy named Sam near my age and figured be company for that boy. He had two boys, but one got burnt up. Sam was a bad boy. Some of my family didn't want me to play with him. My great-grandmother, she was furious about it, said it was goin to ruin me. But it didn't. And I was livin with him, too.

When Uncle William broke up housekeepin here, he was on Doncaster with the Lloyds. He went to Baltimore and left his son to Copperville with his sister, which was old man John Copper's wife. And my aunt died, old man Copper's daughter come from Baltimore to keep house for him. And Sam was bad livin, always gettin some kind of devilment. She was tight on the children, tighter than necessary, and she sent Sam upstairs. I think she sent him up there to change his clothes, and she went up there with a switch bout the time he got all his clothes off, and he jumped out the window. Say it's a wonder he didn't hurt hisself. It kind of stunned him for awhile from what one of the boys say. He saw him hit the ground, saw him before he hit the ground, saw him when he hoist the window, and he thought he had crippled hisself. Said he was kinda stupid like for a few seconds. When he got hisself together, he hung out from there, right down the woods. He went down the woods, didn't have a stitch of clothes on him. And then when he taken up, he went over to Todd's Store. And the lady there wanted to know what was wrong, why he didn't have any clothes on, and he told a lie. He said the woman took his clothes off sayin for to whip him. And they was talkin strong about getting the law. They wasn't as strict on people being cruel to children as they are now. Anyway, it was a boy there was a little larger than Sam, and she got some of his clothes and give him. And what did Sam do? He didn't come home. It was a man named Pete Blackwell lived down to Wye Town, workin for Colonel Lloyd. And Sam used to live the next farm, Doncaster. So Sam went down there. He stayed there some time. And this woman that went upstairs to whip him, she was the one sent a message down there for him to come home. Sam wouldn't come home. And one day old man Pete Blackwell was haulin logs down to Tunis Mills. That's the way they used to do, they'd get timber wheels from Tunis Mills and haul the logs down there to sell. He's haulin these logs, and he told Sam to get on there, goin to carry him home. He got on the timber wheels with him, and they got to Copperville and stopped to the house and he got off and turned around and flew again. Right down the woods he went.

And this woman sent a bigger boy after him. He said he caught him cause there was a whole lot difference in the size of em and Sam laid down and beg him not to carry him back. Say, "If you do that," say, "that mean woman will kill me." And he let him go and went back down to Wye Town again.

John Copper's daughter was mean to her sisters. Things she'd put on the children, say they did, and they didn't do it. They'd be afraid to tell her that she was wrong. I've heard her tell that. One time she sweeten the coffee and she put salt in the coffee instead of sugar through a mistake. Say, and they set up and drink the coffee and wouldn't tell her it was salt in there. And they used to come out to school, and every mornin they got up they had to clean that house. And they had a certain time to leave Copperville to walk out to school, and it was all the time behind the other children.

Then Sam's father and mother went back together again. They was in Baltimore, and sent him to his father. And, I believe, the first night that he was there, he ran off. They searched for him. Then they went to what they used to call the watch house, and Sam was in there. He inquired for him, a boy, and he had give hisself another name. And told him, "Yeah," say, "we've got a boy here. He's about the same age." Say sent somebody to watch house to get him and brought him in where his father was. So this other man, head man, I guess, said to him, "Is that your father?" Said, "No, sir." Said, "Don't let him have me." Say, "That's my father." Say, "he'll kill me." And then they wouldn't let Uncle William have him. Then Uncle William went back again. They brought him home and when night come, he run off again. When he run off that time, they went to watch house. He wasn't there. He didn't find him. Come to find out where he slept was under the front steps to an old house in the colored section. That's where he slept that night.

Oh, he was a bad boy. He was one them spoilt children, and parents was the cause of him bein that way. Sometimes he could do anything he want— they'd never say nothin to him. And another time, he'd do somethin, wouldn't be enough to get a whippin for, well, he'd tear him up—whip the blood out of him. So you should have rules for children and stick to them, and never use sticks on em. But he'd cut the blood out of him. Well, that's a stupid and mean person.

Uncle William come home one night after work that evenin and ask for this boy. Aunt Rachel told him the boy was over to Richard Blakes. Uncle William asked, "How long he gone?" Say, "He's been over there all the evening." So, he went over there after him and got a whip—what you'd use on mules and things like that. Say, "I'll bring him home. He'll know when night comes the next time." And he went over there and called for Sam. The old man say, "You go on home, I'll tend to you when I get home." And he had to go past the barn, and the barns was built up off'n the ground. Sam got to that barn and crawled under the barn. That's where he stayed. Uncle William got home, asked for him. Aunt Rachel say, "He hadn't been here." Say, "He ain't?" Say, "Well, I sent him home some time ago." "Well," say, "he ain't come chere. I ain't seen him." Wouldn't take her word, he went up the stairs, searched for him. Searched for him around the house, anyplace he could hide. Couldn't find him. And he walked back over there again, and this was cold weather. And old man Blake and his wife told him they hadn't seen him. They got a lantern and they went out and looked for him. Some-body say, I'm going to look under this barn here. He looked and there he was layin back under the barn. And he was so cold, said he couldn't talk. And uncle William pulled his jumper off and put on him, carried him home, talkin to him all the time. "No, indeed, Dad ain't gonna whip you. You come on. Daddy ain't gonna whip you."

And that's the way he was. He could do somethin that he should be whipped for, he wouldn't whip him this time. Next time, wouldn't do as much and pretty near kill him. And Aunt Rachel had a girl there that was a child she had fore she married Uncle William. And he whipped her so bad one time I heard an old lady said that she went to see her, and took her clothes off from her back and she had sores on her where he had cut the blood out of her. And I forgot what it was she did, but it wasn't hardly nothin to whip her for unless he had told her not to do it and she did. But the laws is differ-ent today. They'd send him away.

And I made up my mind, I was bout seven years old, I got mad, I goin to whip him. Didn't get a chance to do it. The children had done somethin, he said he was goin to whip em all. I put my feet in the road and it was pretty near night and walked from there to Copperville. That was some distance for seven-year-old boy to walk by hisself, and it was about dusk when I got home. I said, I wasn't gonna let him whip me.

One mornin Sam got up before I did, and they had a rat terrier, and a hog pen and feedin the hogs on corn. Well, the rat went there and dug burrows around the stage there and this little dog was diggin and Sam had a corncob. She was a little somethin. Put between her back legs, liftin her up on. Only he was tickled, Sam was. And she'd get away and get to diggin again and barkin. And I looked out the window and saw him, so I went out there. I wasn't doin a thing, just standin around—just went out there to see what was happenin. She was barkin. Uncle William was plowin. Across from us, it was a thick place the head of a cove, place they called Chapel Cove. It just had a little ditch for letout to Wye River. And he come across that and he had been hollerin. He said and the dog makin so much noise we didn't hear him. When I looked up, here he come. I said to Sam, "Here come Uncle William." Sam, he stopped, straightened up. He come up there, and he grabbed me. On the way up there had cut a switch—right stiff switch—he grabbed Sam and fanned Sam.

I didn't run, I wasn't doin nothin. And I was standin there, and he got me, and he give me more than he did Sam. Well, I hadn't done a thing. Then, the next Sunday, he come to Copperville. He went to my mother's house, was tellin my mother, say, "I licked that man of yours the other day. I thought I'd tell you." Mother said, "What was he doin?" "Well," say, "he had the dogs out there runnin that white man's stock." That's the lie he told. It wasn't stock. It was nothin in it, onliest Sam was throwin that dog, puttin that cob between her legs liftin her up on her head. And I went to get it straight—dispute it. I told my mother, my stepfather, had nothin to do with that. And my mother told me what, he had been to their house, and told her about havin the dog runnin the stock. And he thought he'd get his tale in first and then by him bein a grown man, they'd believe him quicker than they would me. So he told his tale and mother believe that. And my mother come near whippin me for disputin my uncle. And I had to stop talkin. And after that, I brought it up again another day, told it the same way. Every once in awhile, I'd bring it up and after that, she told me, said, "Well, boy, I believe you." Say, "I believe you tellin the truth."

I said to myself, "When I get a man, I'm going to whip you cause you'll be older. You'll be broke up, and I'll be in my prime." I never got the chance to whip him. He got a job up in Baltimore. He didn't have any when he left here. He had people that he knowed and some relations, he went up there to them, he got a job. And he lived a good many years after that. Still, we don't know just when he did die. We knowed when we got the message, but he hadn't just died. Don't know who buried him. I don't know whether him and his wife were back together again then or not.

And Rachel never interfered with William, cause she'd got somethin more than Sam if she had. She didn't like it, but she didn't interfere with him. He tore me up for nothin! That's what made me mad. If I'd been doin somethin, it would've been different. I wasn't doing a thing. He gave me more than he did his own boy. I was burnin for a long time. If I'd had a gun, I'd a shot him. That's the wrong way to feel about a person though. Have somethin in against him and feel that you should do him harm. I didn't want to feel that way about nobody no more and I haven't about anybody else.

He was kind of barbarish. He had a way of pickin up all stray dogs he find, take em out see if they'd hunt. Didn't hunt, he'd take a rope and hang em. Some of the boys found the bush or saplin where he used to hang em. And he had left his rope that he used to put around their neck and they took it.

And when Sam started that runnin, he never did stop him. He was just that afraid of his father. And that shorten his life. That's what they say. He died when he was about twelve. Mother and father bust up, and then the child had to go stay with somebody else. That's what ruin children, changin homes.

I guess I've spent at least 75 percent of my playin time in Tunis Mills after I got bout eight or nine years old. I started before that goin over there. Then I was a handy boy around the store over there, do little jobs—cleanin mostly around the store, sweepin, dustin—and then I'd have time to play. When I went just for the play in Tunis Mills, I wouldn't spend over two or three hours. But when I'd go over there to clean up the back room of the store, used to get kerosene in barrels then, and you had to pump it out of the wooden barrel and put it in the tanks they had in the store, and that used to be my job. I'd do that and I'd get probably some ginger snaps and a slice of cheese. Still, I was better off doing that for a little bit then be around doin nothin, cause that has got a lot of children into trouble with nothin to do.

And I used to go there and play with some of the boys in Tunis Mills and get along good. Never had a cross word with a white boy over there. And you take the others my age in Copperville, they couldn't hardly get over there to the store, they'd be runnin them.

I remember one time was three white boys was sittin to one side of the store door—had a bench on each side. Three white boys and myself and was two colored boys come down there. They was larger than I was—much larger. And they took the bench on the other side—over on the right side of the door goin into the store. I saw em keep lookin over there. They'd try to get to say something to these white boys, but the boys wouldn't answer em. Wouldn't pay no attention to em. And after while, they called me. And when they called me, some of them white boys looked at me. I didn't know what it meant, but I figured after that, it was for me not to go. So I went over where they was and I forgot now what they said, but I know they kicked me. I don't know why they kicked me, it wasn't anything I said or did. I guess it was just to show off. And I come on back to where these white boys was. When they kicked me, one of these white boys hollered at em and told em not to do that. I come back and we talked together and got after them boys and runned them clear out Tunis Mills. But I was tickled to death and we come on back. It was four of us—three white and myself. Never had no more trouble with them. They was goin to show off they was bigger boys. But if they'd caught me off by myself, I guess they'd a beat me to death.

I never had one minute's trouble. Some of the old people even said they couldn't tell why it was they didn't bother me, tell my mother. I'd go with the boys, but didn't go for fightin. But if they was with me, they wouldn't bother em. Other boys from Copperville couldn't go over there. They couldn't even go to the store unless was three or four of em together, cause the boys would run em. I'd go over there by myself or with somebody. They wouldn't run me. And that was my job. Lots of time the mothers would see my mother and ask me, could I go to the store with the children. And if I'd go with them, they wouldn't bother em, but if they go theirself, they'd have to fight or run. I never was the kind that carried a chip on my shoulder, and I was kind to all of em. And it's just like anything else, some people are liked and some people they don't like.

And that time I was a true thrower. I have killed rabbits runnin with shells. You take stones and shells, I could pick the ones that you could throw the straightest. I remember one time I knocked a woodpecker out of a tree and he was up over my head. Well, that was hot, though. Hit him right in the back and wounded both wings. And the bottom of a big limb reached out and he was under the bottom pickin. And being able to throw like that, I think I saved my life one day. I was round nine years old then. We lived in Harrison house, and right cross the lane, that was Colonel Lloyd's field, and I was on my way over to New Design. Seven, what they called beefs, was in the field, and here they come—all seven of em. They walked close to me and then they commenced makin a circle around me and gettin closer all the time. And you could always find me with somethin to throw. And one of em Herefords had a white head and this brown ring of the color of his body around his eye. I know they were gettin close, and I aimed at that eye, and hit him right in the eye. And he throwed his head up, jumped up front feet off the ground at first, throwed his head up, and went off runnin and blowin his nose and shakin his head, and the others took out after him. That's where I got away, cause they'd a killed me out there. I was small, that's why they was so full of curiosity.

I don't think that I went to school much over two months. Didn't get no schoolin, just as well say. I went to work nine years old and we was livin to Copperville, and winter come, my mother and stepfather didn't get up time enough to get me off to school. Time I got through my break-fast, children'd be to school. In them days, they would whip you if you was late. And two or three days, I walked from Copperville to Millerstown and the last bell would ring before I would get to Millerstown. Then I'd know it was late and I'd stop to one of the houses, rest up, turn around, and go back home. Just messed along like that. And then it got time durin the winter them days, that children couldn't get from Copperville to Unionville to school, but look all the days that they could from time school opened in the fall. And then when it got better travelin in the spring, they used to have to stop oysterin in December and sometime they didn't get back oysterin till the last of March. They could get back to oysterin again, well, I'd have to go cullin oysters.

I got my first start in some call it church school, and some call it Sunday school. I went there every Sunday when we lived in Copperville, and if I hadn't, I wouldn't been able to spell my name. But that was only some things, just readin, no figurin or nothin like that in Sunday school. And I was above a lot of the children was a whole lot older and larger than I was. Some of the bigger ones, it used to make em mad. I read the Bible through twice, *Beautiful Story of the Bible,* cause my grandfather buy all such books as that.

Charles Copper went to school. He'd be up and in the first bunch. All my sisters and brothers used to walk from Copperville to school, and course, the walk from Copperville, that wasn't no walk some of the other children had. Some of em used to come from Presqu'ile. Now that was a walk. And I know a boy was livin in New Quarter. He was round bout seven or eight, and he used to come to school. Say he'd run all the way back home—that's in the winter time when it got dark quick. Say he'd come in give out in the evenin; the mornin wasn't so bad. They had it hard for to get what they did get.

I got some teachin for the little time I went to school, but the most of it, I picked up my ownself. And the last few days I went to school was in Copperville in that old church, and they didn't have many, and they had the third arithmetic on the floor. They had the fourth and third grade together. Course, I didn't have the third and fourth class readers to learn how to read, and no writin. And I was supposed to be in the primer or the first grade. Get on there, that's answerin questions, and I'd be ahead the class. Most anything that the teacher would ask, I was ahead of them other children. They had been goin for years. Well, that's somethin if you miss, you can't make up. But I was happy to learn and willin to learn. After I started sometime, I would carry the book to my mother and ask her words. But I never go any further than what you used to call the primer. I call it neglect. It wasn't need, it was neglect. I couldn't see far enough ahead. Wished I had got the education. This is time it tells, now, when you don't get it.

I'd been a whole lot further advanced if I'd got the opportunity, but I didn't get the opportunity. I didn't read newspapers—I wasn't that high. It got so I could read right smart in the first-grade book. Then, when I come out, I was above some of the rest that went to school for years. I took what I did have and kept readin after I went to work. I read, I remember, one book. I was about fourteen; I read that book through several times. It was

Swiss Family Robinson. And that was the same thing with my grandfather, he never went to school a day in his life cause he was born way back in slavery. He didn't read nothin but the Bible. He was a local preacher. And it wasn't as many people read the newspaper like they do today, or magazines. He did take the Bible and read anythin in the Bible he want.

I went to work nine years old. Always did go to Tunis Mills, and this man picked me out. I heard he told a man there in the store, say, "That seems to be a bright intelligent boy. I'd like to have him." Say, "I've got two men on this schooner, but when I have to load or unload, and one of them men is a cook, and I have to load or unload," say, "I've got nobody to cook. And he have to try to cook and load and unload," and he said, "I'd like to have that boy just to keep the fire up under the food and watch it and put water into it when it need." So then he asked me one day would I like to go with him, so I told him yes. Say, "But you have to see my mother." And he saw my mother, told my mother he'd give me four dollars a month. Four dollars, that was big money them days, and she let me go.

And I went on that bay schooner. He had two men on the schooner and times he went to sailin, he need two men on deck or when he was loadin stuff, and my job was to keep the fire up under the food after the cook put it on the stove. It wasn't no heavy work. That schooner was just runnin itself different places on this side of Chesapeake Bay. It didn't carry any grain while I was on it, and that's what they carried up and down the Chesapeake Bay then. But before time to carry grain, my mother made me quit. We went to Kent Island and made several trips to place they call Piney Neck for Dr. Tilghman. We made two trips or more with just green posts, fence posts. Somebody had a saw mill. We carried building lumber, post. May've been somethin else.

I think I was on there three or four months and never got three cents. Never got nothin. Man never paid my mother a cent. He always had an excuse when it's come to the end of the month. I don't think I got one cent. My mother didn't. He was goin to give the money to her. I was just willin to do whatever she said. One way, it was up to her, and then she wouldn't want me to go if I wasn't satisfied, and I wouldn't go if she wasn't satisfied. And I liked it. I expected everything to happen when I was away. In them months, I should've been goin to school.

My mother took me off and I went cullin oysters and I'd culled oysters until it'd get too cold for me. And the other children goin to school. And then when it'd get too cold for me, why, lots of times very bad roads, and when it got too cold for me to cull oysters, wouldn't be long before the river would freeze up and then I didn't get my breakfast in time then to go to school. And that went all winter. The next spring, I'd go back cullin oysters. If it was warm the last part of March, I would, but every year, it wouldn't be any later than April. There was white and colored men that was oysterin around the same place, was speakin about how good a worker I was. Said the boards never got piled up on me. That meant I worked and worked fast enough to keep the boards clear of shells. When I quit one time about it bein too cold for me, my Uncle John got another boy. "I'll get Annie's Jim." Say, "He's tough." Say, "He can stand it." Carried him out that day and they had a cabin skiff, and the stove in there. And they kept a little wood in there to build a fire lunchtime and Jim got drawed up. He couldn't cull, he couldn't do nothin. And Uncle John told him to go down to the cabin. Say, "I'll light that stove for you." He lit the stove for him and when they got ready to stop for dinner, Jim had burn up a load of wood. So it tickled me. I heard Greenberry Gibson tellin it. That's the one used to oyster with Uncle John, Uncle John's brother-in-law.

And got nothin for cullin oysters—twenty-five cents a day. I give the twenty-five cents to my mother and she saved it for me to buy clothes with. I'd have to work a long time to get enough to get a pair of pants. Twenty-five cnets a day, that wasn't nothin.

And then I carried milk for a child in Copperville over a year. There was two girls in the Deshields family, and it was the youngest girl's child. Her name was Hester, named after old man Solomon Deshields' sister, Hester. And his sister, Hester, was my great-grandmother. And she brought that child home from Baltimore when she was over a month old and had to raise it on the bottle and I'd have to go get the milk every mornin. And them morning, I'd get up and sometime I'd go after the milk before I'd eat my breakfast. You had come up pretty near to Unionville from Copperville. I got the milk at White Hall Farm. I got over the fence at old man Harrison Roberts' house, and went through New Design. White Hall and New Design joins, and that was shorter than goin to Tunis Mills and goin around. The man that was workin on the farm was the baby's mother's brother, so they'd give him quart of milk everyday. I carried that milk well over a year in a fruit jar. Well, that just settled school that day. I had to go every mornin except Sunday mornin. And Sunday mornin, the grandfather would get it. They was expectin that I would do it. They come ask my mother. But I didn't get paid—not what I called paid. And when they weaned the child, he give me two little old shirts, I think cost about fifteen or twenty cents over at Tunis Mills store. That was all I got, and I lost all that time at school.

I remember goin to Unionville once when I was little. I wasn't over five years old. I was seven years old before I ever went to Easton and then when I went back again, I was twelve years old. It was more excitement then than it would be to go to Baltimore. I was seven, I went with my uncle William Sutton. I was livin with him then. I didn't enjoy myself goin to Easton though with him, cause he put me in a store, and I had to stay in that store till he come back, and he was gone three or four hours. I've no idea where he did go, and I wouldn't think of askin him where he had been. If I did, he was liable to whip me. One of the white men said, "That boy must be hungry." Say, "He's been in here." Say, "He hasn't even had a drink of water." Say, "Boy," say, "do you want a drink of water?" I say, "Yeah." He told me where to go to get it. He say, "You hungry?" I say, "Yes, I ain't had no dinner." "Well, I'm sorry, I haven't got anythin to give you. Wished I did have." Course, people used to go to Easton lots of times on Saturday night. I never went anymore till I was twelve years old. I walked there with another boy, older boy. And I never thought a great deal of it, though, no way.

I spend a lot of time at John Copper's. His second wife was my aunt, and he had two girls; we was first cousins. And it wasn't many games that we know how to play them days. About that time a lot of them old people wouldn't let you play checkers in the house. It was a sin to play checkers, and you'd better not show a playing card in there. They'd drive you out of there. Say that was devil's work. They were superstitious.

I'm sorry my mother didn't give me to him. Maybe I'd be better off than I am today, cause I would'a got a good education as was goin them days. He sent his children to school. They went far as you could go out chere. Them days colored had no high school, nothin like that.

I never was scary. I remember one night I went over Tunis Mills—it was Christmas Eve night. And when I left Copperville, somebody told me, said Santa Claus was gonna get me. And lot of the children them days was afraid of Santa Claus, and I laughed at em. I went on over to the store and got what I was sent after. And then one the two men asked me was I afraid to come over there at night there by myself. I told em, "No, wasn't nothin goin to hurt me." And this one old fellow sittin back distance from them said, "No, boy." Say, "That's the way to feel about it." Said, "Ain't nothin gonna hurt you."

Down to Hope, I could look out my window where I slept and look right on a graveyard—I mean a moonshiny night. And I've sat up there in the bed a many moonshiny night to see a ghost come out of the grave or go back. It didn't scare me.

Onliest time I got scared—and that was the onliest time—I went on a possum hunt with my dog. I was about twelve years old, and this dog, where I was huntin, it had been a slave-time graveyard. And the dog got to barkin at somethin upside the shore. Was up the bank in the field. And it looked like a little old woman, and the more I looked at the thing, the more it looked like a little woman. And he was standin there rearin and never thought until afterwards it may've been a possum in the tree. And this was an oak tree that had held its leaves—didn't lose its leaves when the fall come. And looked just like a little old woman with big coat on. So I turned around to go home. When I looked, here come the dogs. I had another little dog with me. Why, he come past me runnin, and then I couldn't keep my feet still. I started, and little while, there they was up to high speed. And that little short-leg dog, I put him behind me. He couldn't keep up with me. And my dog, longer-leg dog, he was ahead of me, and that's the way I went home. And I thought about it, and I said to myself, "I'm goin right back there again tonight, grave-yard or no graveyard." I said, "I ain't seen nothin that I could say was a ghost. I'm goin right back tonight." Next night, I went right back there again, and that was the time I went that little tree that my dog was barkin to that I thought was a woman ghost. So I never was scary.

And I remember when Horace Gibson's father died, we were livin to Hope. He was hundred and some years old. They called him Uncle Kip, and he had what they call the palsy—tremble when he'd talk. My mother and stepfather got the message he was dead and when they was goin to bury him. Then I was only seven years old, and she was fixin to bring me to Copperville, cause she was goin to the funeral. I told her no, I'd stay home cause I didn't like to go no funeral then. Don't like it now. And I stayed home. That day she left Hope come to Copperville early and come home after the funeral, and that seemed like one of the longest days I've ever put in in my life. I stayed there and played around the yard by myself. I didn't get lonesome, but it was a long day to me.

I was down there to Hope in that old house, and a cemetery right close—only a walk between the house and the cemetery. When the moon was shinin, I used to set up in the bed look to see ghosts come out of the graves. I heard old people speak bout that. They come out at twelve o'clock and after. I'd set up in the bed on moonshiny night and watch to see one come out. I heard stepfather's father said a man told him that if you want to learn to play a piece of music, say, you go the cemetery twelve o'clock at night. And I think he wanted to learn to pick a banjo, and he went to the cemetery, and he sit on the fence. And when twelve o'clock come, a little ol woman come out of the grave with a sunbonnet on, and come right past him, and he had to go down the path where she went, that was the direction of where he lived. And when he go off'n that fence, he went runnin down the path and he overtaken her and jumped right over her head and kep on runnin. And that settled him, he didn't go to any more graveyards. He told that story for people to believe because he was scary.

Buck Copper believed in em. And them that believed in em was scary. I didn't believe in em and I couldn't dispute em, cause if I did, my mother would tear me up if I said I didn't believe in em. If I said the old person was lying, she would tear me up.

My mother didn't raise us to believe it, but it was somethin I think she did believe, cause I remember she told me she saw my father and she was livin in Baltimore County then. That was soon after he died, she went to Balti-more. She lived in Baltimore County and she had his picture on her dresser. And some time durin the night, she woke up and there was a man sittin on a chair or stool to the dresser. I think that was all imagination. She went to sleep and was thinkin bout him.

The older people used to make admiration about me goin around Copperville at night time. Sometimes it was so dark you couldn't see your hand hardly before you. But Buck Copper and his brother older than him named Frank, they wasn't the onliest ones, but you wouldn't catch them out nighttime. My Uncle Joe Flamer was scary. If he had to go Tunis Mills store, he used to come up and ask my mother could I go with him nighttime. And we'd get halfway there, I'd ask him, "Did you see that man with that white duster on?" He'd look, say, "Where?" I'd say, "There he is, see him goin across." "You come on here." So one night I tried to show him a woman. I said, "She goin right down this path ahead of us." "I don't see no woman." He slowed up when I said she was goin down the path. He'd carry a stick. He said, "If you see any more things like that," say, "I'm goin to bust your head." So he would've done it, and I was afraid to say anymore. Come home, was tellin my mother, and my mother wouldn't let me go with him no more. Say, "And he'll do it, too." So I stopped goin with him.

And there wasn't another boy in Copperville that'd go out at nighttime by theirself, not another one. And there was several men wouldn't do it. That was borned in em. Quite likely, they heard their parents talkin bout ghosts. They never told them there wasn't anything like ghosts. I heard Buck Copper's uncle talkin bout one time—I forgot now where he said he walked from—sayin he was tired and sleepy and he got up on the gate, sittin up on the gate, said something come along and slapped him clear up off the gate. Wasn't nothin. He got up there and went to sleep and fell off. That'd be in the house, and Buck would get scared then. And I said to myself then, there wasn't a thing, only he fell off'n that gate. But he said somethin slapped him off.

Old man John Copper was the smartest one in town. He was respected. He was more known than any of the rest of em. And him and my grandfather, of the old ones, was the onliest ones that could read. Grandfather Flamer, he could read and old man Copper could read, so that put them ahead the others that couldn't. John Copper could read print, but I don't know whether he could write. He'd read books. I guess he read the Bible. My grandfather Flamer read the Bible. He wouldn't read a book. He wouldn't read the newspaper. He'd get ready sometimes to read the Bible, you could understand him clear far away.

And if people had a fight, they would settle it their own self. They thought fightin was the best way to settle it. I heard of em sometimes goin to preacher about things, takin his advice. The preacher lived Royal Oak, and he just came Sunday afternoons, or he'd come sometimes Sunday mornin. He had three churches—Ferry Neck, Royal Oak, and Copperville. My grandfather Flamer, he was a local preacher. He filled the preacher's place when the preacher couldn't be there. He was what I called a one-horse preacher—not as much power as the regular preacher, so they called em one-horse preacher.

John Copper belonged to Unionville Church. So did Phil Moaney, and so did Solomon Deshields' wife. It would look funny, though, leavin Sunday mornin, walkin, goin to Unionville, goin right past the church where they lived. Cause that used to happen. That was their denomination in Unionville. They had church in Unionville before they had any in Copperville, and them that belonged to it, didn't pull out of the church. Some of em did, I guess. One was African Methodist Episcopal and one was just Methodist. They had different conscience. And people went to John Copper for advice. You see they's right so much trouble then, days with the white man beatin the colored man, didn't have no education and beat him and rob him. And old man John Copper was the one they usually went to.

It was a man there, they built a house for old man Ezekiel Emory and some years after that, well, he claimed old man Zeke hadn't paid him. And old man Zeke went to Uncle John Copper and he carried some papers. And in them papers, it was receipts and it was enough receipts to show that the house was paid for. And old man Copper told him what to do.

They had a case in court about that. And when they had the hearin, he come out all right. Hadn't been for that, this man would have got his home. Had a good judge. The judge told this other man that Ezekiel Emory still owned the place. The man never kick against it, but he come near gettin it, because Uncle Zeke wasn't gonna fight, said no use in fightin.

Well, that's the way they used to rob them, though. There was a time they couldn't count money. Stole they places. Even man that work for used rob em. And that old man that tried to beat Uncle Zeke, when he left Tunis Mills and went up here to Baltimore County, that's where they say a lot of time things will come home to you, went up there, he had a pair of horses to a wagon—no trucks them days—and he was buildin up there, and I guess he was going where the lumber was, to get some lumber concernin the buildin, and the horse run away and broke his neck. He didn't live long after he left here. He lived in Tunis Mills. John Redman was his name. And just to think, he was tryin to beat old man Ezekiel Emory, and he had been the magistrate there in Tunis Mills. That's what I say, some of em carry the law out is just as bad as the criminals sometimes that go before em. Man administering the law is goin to take and do such trick as that. And he'd got the place or got paid double hadn't been for John Copper.

Old man John had an outside son that he got before he got married. I believe his name was Charlie Copper. The mother give him the father's name. John Copper had two girls, that was my first cousins, livin with him when I was a boy. John Copper's second wife was my father's sister. He had several daughters. Henny and Agnes went to Baltimore. They didn't stop in Baltimore, because I saw one of em, I think that was Agnes, she come back home on a visit when I was a small boy about twelve years old. Henny'd come back to visit and then years after that, she came back and got married. Sarah went away, come back, and got married and then stayed here. She married several times. John Henry Gibson was her first husband. He died and she married James Peck, an old soldier. He was as old as her father. He was in the Civil War, so was her father. Then she married Isaac Johnson, and he was an old soldier.

I remember when Sarah got married to John Henry Gibson. He was from Copperville. There was a big wedding. They got married, I'm sure, in Union-ville in church and had the weddin, the reception, in John Copper's house, Miss Sarah's father's house in Copperville. That was a big night for the people there. They certainly had a big time. I can hear them now singin old-time pieces. We was livin then down to Hope House, cause we walked out Hope House, come through the woods and come to it. There was a big bonfire. Everything was all ready to light when we got there. It was built over in Colonel Lloyd's field—New Design field. It was a big pile of stuff they had wood on it—broken rails and stuff like that. I wasn't nothin but a child, bout seven years old, and I was wonderin what it was when we got there. And I didn't know until somebody heard the horse and carriage comin over Tunis Mills bridge. I heard one of em say, "Here they come now. Here they come." And I didn't know who they meant until after that, I'd heard old people say who they thought it was. And then they lit it then. I don't know whether they used kerosene or just lit the straw they had under it, but I know she blazed. And when it got to Copperville, it was somebody else comin to the weddin. But right after that, the bride and groom came. And they got out of the carriage, or whatever they was in, got out on the road, and one of the men grabbed the groom and he hollered for a rail, and got a rail and put him straddle that rail. They carry him on that rail to the house across the road, to the porch. A lot of people was in there doin what they called the promenadin. Then from then on, they had until twelve o'clock or more. I was a little fella, I got in the step where you go upstairs. I got in the step and sit up there, wasn't no room for me in the other part of the house, it was full. And they sang old time songs, some I had never heard before. They had a girl, that was old man John Copper's son John's daughter—she was a great singer—got her to sing a piece. But she was a little larger than I was. Piece she sang was "Mary Don't You Weep, Don't You Moan." That was a new piece then. She could sing, though. She went preachin after she growed-up woman. I call it preachin, it was speakin.

That was one of the houses I used to visit. Never was much goin to every-body's house. There wasn't much visitin went on in Copperville, exceptin one family, and they was close together and lived close together. And that was the Gibsons, my uncle John Moody's wife's people. Her mother lived close to her, and I guess, she was the one that did the visitin. And she used to go to see her often—go every day. They was the onliest place out there. When you get up them families that one can't live without the other, you ain't got much. Mother had no regular visitors, and she didn't do any visitin herself. You take summer time, when the girls got off from their jobs in the city, got a vacation, and they'd come home, them that lived in Copperville that was associates of my mother, well, the most of them would come down to visit her. Her own mother didn't visit her unless sickness or somethin. And on my side, there wasn't many visitors. My great-grandmother, she lived a few houses from us, and she didn't visit us less it was on business, and mother didn't her unless it was on business. She'd come to tell her somethin or ask her somethin. If mother hadn't seen her for two or three days, she'd go to look for her. And her mother wasn't over to visit her. Course, if somebody sick or something like that, she'd come. And her mother never visit nobody in Copperville, only her mother's mother. And I don't remember my mother visiting anybody in Copperville exceptin her mother and her grandmother. And that's a good way to live.

I went to Buck Copper's house a lot, cause him and I used to play together all the time. And that was all the houses that I visited. Buck Copper was the regular one I played with that lived in Copperville. The other boys was boys that come in on Sundays. Other boys, me and Buck, we used to make the same thing. We used to make wooden toys, somethin with wheels on it. And then before it got cold in the winters, I'd make sleighs and I'd shove it under the house until it snowed the next year. We used to make some little things we played in the house out of cotton spools. We used to call them our racin tops—you'd spin it along. And I'd mostly be champion. I'd get a stick to go through the center of that spool and we used to mostly use pine, but I'd always get a pine that the hard grain would come in the center of that stick, and it would rest on that hard grain. And the others Buck used to make, his would come on that soft wood and wouldn't spin as long. And I wouldn't tell im the secret.

And Buck Copper's father, Isaac Copper, he married a woman, I've heard him tell it, he was livin out in Unionville. And he was speakin bout man marryin. He said, "Don't pick a woman for her looks." Said, "The best lookin ones," say, "give you the most trouble." Say, he married one, said she was a clean woman, good cook, keep the house clean, everything clean, keep your clothes clean, say, "But then she give me trouble after that." So he was tellin before me, some other young fellas, say, "Now, don't go by no looks. And remember one time I come home and I was hungry, I went in the table was set, everythin clean and the food was in whatever it was cooked in, the only thing I had to do go to the stove and get it. And I did and I ate my supper and I sat there and I wait for her to come in and I wait till it must've been twelve o'clock. I ain't seen her. By God," say, "I went to bed, wasn't long in goin to sleep, woke up in the night, I felt around for her, and she hadn't come in. By God," say, "I haven't seen her from that day to this. Never did see her no more." And since, I've heard old people say that she was a woman carried herself neat all the time—clean—but they didn't say why she went away from here. And she didn't go with any man. Don't know who she met after she got to Baltimore, but didn't go from here with any man. Several people from here saw her in Baltimore. Isaac Copper never try to find her. Well, he'd be lost soon as he got out of Unionville, somebody'd have to go look for him. But he thought she would come back and he never did see her no more. And then he said, "By God," say, "I'll get somebody I know won't run from me. Won't run away from me, won't leave me, run off from me. By God," say, "I went to see Hon," say, "I married her and there ain't been a day I come home, a day or night," say, "Hon's right there. That's the kind I should've got first." She didn't know where to go. She had never been any further than Easton. I guess it is right bad sometimes, get somebody like that and they don't want to go. The other fella can't go, and the other one like to go, so when that happens make bad gettin along, I guess.

I was ten years old, a white man, James Smith, lived in Copperville. He was in poor class, but nice principles. Old man Oliver that owned Fairview got him and his family right from Ireland. Had em brought chere to work for him, and he worked down there on Fairview for years. And then when Mr. Oliver was sellin that other land and that place for sale, he sold it to him. Oliver was supposed to be the wealthiest man in Miles River Neck or anywheres around in Talbot County. My great-grandmother and old man Smith's wife was very, very close friends. Cause they didn't visit any other white people, cause them days the Americans used to distinguish theirself and felt that they was better than others. I know back in time, the Americans used to laugh at the Germans, wouldn't think about sociatin with em. That went on for years and after that, they found out the Germans had more money than they had.

But the Smiths, I used to go up there to play. I didn't live far from em. I lived in the second house from em. Mother left me off about seven or eight and used to go up there to play. They had three small children. One day I went up there, Mrs. Smith had company, and I stopped on the porch. Was sittin down there on the porch where I could look in the dinin room where they was eatin. And it was a lady in there, she looked out and she kept turnin round lookin. Then she said, "There's a little colored boy," say, "out chere on the porch." Mrs. Smith got up and looked out the door, "Oh," say, "that's Joe." And she went back and fixed me a plate of food. I ate that food, set the plate down on the porch right easy, and watched em. And got up and went around the house and hallowed home. But before that, she said to me, said, "Joe," say, "when we get through, want you to dance for us." I said, "All right'm." But I ate mine before they ever got through and I went around the house and hallowed home. I wouldn't go up there anymore for several days.

In my day, it was two, three poor whites was there. Another man, Southern, was the last white family that lived in that house, because when he lived there, I was about grown. He come here from Baltimore years before that, and used to work in the mill down to Tunis Mills. And he knowed more about that stuff than any man that Tunis had down there. It was something or other that he showed em how to use. They had what it take to cut the sidin, but they didn't know how to use it. They used to bring lumber there, most from Virginia. I never heard, but I think they must've had a mill down there. After I got older, I've helped unload the lumber boats there. They sold that lumber around here. They used to supply places like Easton, Dixon Lumber Yard there. In fact, Tunis sold out to Dixons.

Old man Southern and Ennals Tull had a bet one time and ol man Southern won. Like worried Ennals Tull to death. Them winters, every winter, ice was thick enough to skate on and the men, when they come from work, nights, they used to go down there on the ice and have lanterns and used to skate. Cause up to the store was talkin bout skatin and ol man Southern, he was the one had skates on and Ennals Tull said, "You can't skate fast as I can run." And then Southern bet him that Tull couldn't catch him on the ice. Southern'd be on skates and Tull'd be runnin. So they went down and some from the store, they went down with em. Ol man Southern put the skates on. Ennals Tull was waiting for him. He got em on, started on, and ol man Southern would let Ennals Tull get right up on him and he'd turn, "Scaaa." And then ol man Southern would wheel around and come towards Tull, and when Ennals started towards him he'd "Scaaa." Ennals'd go right past him. And he never got close enough to put his hands on him. And I think the bet was two-dollar bet. And then when Tull give up, it wasn't ol man Southern that give up. When Tull give up, he told him, said, "I'll sell you a load of wood." Ol man Southern told him, said, "I don't want no wood, I want that money." Say, "The bet was no wood." And say it hurt Ennals Tull when he had to take money out of his pocket and give ol man Southern.

Tull was in the low class. Years after that, he bought the place they call White Hall. And he bought it, somebody said, for eight thousand from Colonel Lloyd. And lot of people say he never paid for it. Well, he bought it, and paid for it, and when he left there, he bought a house in Easton. And on that street where he bought was a middle class of people. And he never lived to enjoy it. Soon after he bought it, he taken sick and got so he couldn't walk. Laid in the bed for God knows how long. Cause I went to see him one day. I was in town, on that end, went to see him. But he didn't work hisself to death. He didn't do no work. But he said, "A man works his head, works harder than the man did workin his hands." He used his head, all right. Couldn't read nor write. But say he could count. His wife did all the readin and writin, but when it come to countin, he could beat her countin. And it's another thing to get a wife that'll stick with you, right or wrong. If they don't do it, you'll never get nothin together. You have one that's goin to pull right against you. When he bought this place in Easton, they say he was worth eighty-some thousand. And started with nothin. And got the money with his head, wasn't his hands. And he could figure things, deals. He could figure em out when a lot of the ones that had the education couldn't do it. I know one time a colored man out chere used to work for him now and then. And then, one fall, he told him he'd let him have that field put in wheat. Say, and told him what shares and the poor man worked hard, put that field in wheat. He had to buy the wheat from Tull and Tull got the fertilizer, and he had to pay Tull for that. And Tull hired him the team that put the wheat in. In fact, he hired him the team that plowed the ground. When they got the returns for the wheat, he didn't make as much as five dollars. And all that work he did. Well, Tull had figured that out before hand. He had an idea what it would cost to plow the land, put it in, and what the team was goin to cost. I blame the man, too, for jumpin into somethin he don't know nothin about. He thought he was goin to get rich off'n that one crop of wheat, and he got nothin. Throwed his labor away. God knows how many days he worked at it.

And workin to the mill, they used to give them that worked to the mill slabs and strips—give it to em if they'd haul it themselves. And Ennals Tull kept a couple of horses they used to hire out like livery stable. And he had a cart and them fellows that didn't have a way to haul their slab, Ennals Tull used to get his supper and go down and haul slab until twelve o'clock and after. And load em and unload em. I think it was ten or fifteen cents a load. Then he'd come back and go to bed, get up, and go to work. He'd work Tunis Mills hisself. And that's all he charged em for haulin em. Sometimes he'd make fifty cents a night, and sometimes a little over. No, he was a close man, Tull was.

Ennals Tull was in the low class. That wasn't money enough to make him rich. Another thing was the way he lived. He lived poorer than I live. Anytime anybody goin stint their belly for to save money, well, that's very poor doin. And that's what he did. Old people used to call it stintin it. Wouldn't eat, didn't eat what he should eat. Stuff like that to save money. That's somethin I never believed it. I don't believe in wastin, but I don't believe in not eatin things that's good for you just to save money and lose at the other end of it. I did somethin for him. That was years after that. I think I fired a steam engine from the other side of Easton. Had come around by Longwoods way, and I looked there was a nice lookin cup of coffee sittin on the table. And I was sittin down eatin, I picked it up to take a drink—wasn't a bit of sugar in it. So I said to Mrs. Tull, say, "You forgot to put sugar in my coffee." And he answered before she did. "No, Joe. She didn't forget it." Say, "We don't use no sugar here." That wasn't the onliest mean way he lived, not usin sugar, but on everything, all food. I heard a man say, that was years before the time I was talkin about, he say, "He was so close," say, "he charged his mother board when she come to visit him." That's the tale they was tellin on him. But I never heard talk of him owin anybody he wouldn't pay. So, he wasn't robbin other people, he was the onliest one that he was robbin.

I remember one time when he was on the farm adjoining Tunis Mills, and they start a tomato-cannin factory. And there was no trucks or nothin like that in them days, and he was right there with the team. And he used to do haulin for em—whatever haulin they'd have to do. And one time, they owed him $125 and he went over the office that evening and they paid him $125. And then, he set around over there and then he stopped to the store. Never thought about his money till he got home. He like to went crazy. He walked at night with a lantern. Couldn't find it. Got up and got his breakfast the next mornin, and come down, he walked, but somebody had picked it up and he never did get it. And right from then on, he got in the habit. You'd see him walkin along after he was standin around. If he had any money in his pocket, he'd be pattin on his hip pocket. The man that got the money was the night watchman to the mill. He either got it that night or early that mornin when he was comin off from duty. He lived right in Tunis Mills; his name was Hennings, a German. And just a few days after that, the old man bought hisself a nice milk cow, and that's why they swore that he was the one that found that money that mornin.

Ennals Tull used to beat poor colored people. Course, he'd beat white people, too. He'd beat anybody he could, but he did it more to the poor colored people. And they was the ones gettin hard luck and not knowin any better, too. They mostly got hard luck in the winter time.

He beat William Moaney. They used to shut the mill at that time—there wasn't as much work down there then as had been before, and they used to shut down sometime in the winter. And the old man didn't get enough to put away for the winter, and he just wouldn't have anything. And he, I think, from different times, it mounted up to seventy-five dollars that he borrowed from Tull and Tull took him home. And before the old man died, he had to live wherever he could, cause no social security or nothin, but he had just live in different houses. He lived in the old Post Office there at Tunis Mills for some time. Lived there by hisself. And I don't now whether they tore it down or not, but he went to Copperville and lived there by hisself. He was an old slave time man. At that time, he didn't have relatives—I guess outlived em. He had a couple of grandchildren up here to Denton, but it wasn't much to them. He had nobody down here. I was a young man when that happened. And then Tull wanted to rent the house to somebody before the old man could find a place to go, but nobody would rent it.

People didn't get mad at Ennals Tull, cause they had to get money from somebody to live on. But they knowed they was payin too much, and he couldn't read nor write, but he didn't make no mistake, he knowed who owed him. Nobody else sent in for lendin money. He suffered before he died. Man had robbed as many people as he had, he ought to get somethin to show for it before he died.

But I never know or heard of him owin anybody. He paid his debts and if you owed him, you'd pay him. I know a colored man that owed him a good many years. That was Isaac Deshields. He hired a horse from him, and drove it up here to Queen Annes to a camp meetin that they used to call Joe Georgia Camp and some call it Wye Camp. And he was supposed to pay him five dollars for that Sunday, and he never did pay him for years after that. And when Ennals Tull was rentin Hope, why he had several colored men— I would say two or three from out Copperville, and he got a chance to hire the man that owed him that money for that horse. You see, he worked his head. He figured that fellow had forgot, and he would get it out of him, so he hired him. I think it was seventy-five cents or a dollar a day. And the first payday come, this man made a week, at a dollar a day, and when he went to pay him, he paid the other men and he give this man a dollar. Man looked at it and laughed and called attention to it. "You didn't give me," say, "but a dollar. You made a mistake." "No, I didn't make no mistake." "Yes you did, too. You give me a dollar." "Well," say, "you remember that time you hired that horse from me to go to camp?" Say, "Well, you didn't give me nothin," say, "and I took it out. I took every bit of it at one time." Man went home—only had one dollar.

Solomon Deshields had sons named Isaac, Charlie, and Will. Isaac did some work around the lumber yard. I don't know whether Charlie or Will ever done anything there. Will was livin with his father in 1895, and I remember the night that Will married Priscilla Viney. Then people used to, wintertime it was open or anytime they wasn't doin anything, want a mess of oysters, they'd go out and catch a mess of oysters. And my stepfather and I was out here and Will and his brother-in-law was out, and we went to the same bar in Leeds Creek. And Will's brother-in-law was the one that told my father, said, "Will got married last night." So that was pretty soon after he was married that I heard.

And Isaac Deshields used to carry a stick cause he was afraid of dog where he walked. This man had a dog, well, he'd bite you. And to keep him away from him, he had a stick and a board with him. He was a young man then, but he'd get ahead of the other man, the other man would walk in the back with a stick. This man was livin on New Design, he come out of the house and got after them bout comin through there causin his dogs to bark and growl like that. He got em to where they wouldn't come through there no more. And, "You put that stick down!" Gettin ready to go through a gate that carried him on White Hall property then, well, he throwed the stick down as they told him. This man picked the stick up and hit him in the head with it. It must'a been a terrible blow, cut the man head, busted the hat.

They had a trial over it, didn't do a thing. They let the white man off. Got up there and said men was comin from Longwoods, they sold whiskey at Longwoods then at all time of the night, say, and it just had worried Mr. Lewis. Say and that's what they did, say, prowlin through there nighttime. Cause wasn't nobody walkin from Copperville to Longwoods then, they may've done it years before, but wasn't then.

Right after that, the man went blind. The blow on his head blind him. And he suffered before he did die, because he didn't get what he should have to eat and didn't get as much. He wasn't able to do anything. Didn't do a thing to old man Lewis. And after that, Lewis got off'n the farm and went to Easton and had a run-in with a merchant there. He must've been a mean man. That man had his hat up to the trial, court trial, and showed em where the blow was so bad where until it tore his hat and his hat wasn't a thing but blood. But it didn't do no good. That happened when I was a little boy. Isaac Deshields suffered before he did die. He live a few years and nobody work then but his wife, and she was only getting fifty cents a day and couldn't pay house rent and that fifty cents wouldn't buy clothes and food for em.

There been plenty of cases like that. I had an uncle was workin down to Hope House. The Starrs, they hadn't been here very long, well, when my uncle was one of the first ones that worked for em. And he was head of all the changes and things, on the buildin and layin off plots for some kind of bushes they had in front of the house. And he had two or three men then under him, and they was goin to do somethin with sand. And Mr. Starr had hired a fella they called John Scamble, and he was in charge of all of em. And Mr. Starr told em to take the row boat and get the sand and when they did, John, he, ordered em out of the boat. Uncle John told him, "Mr. Starr told me yesterday to take this boat and get the sand from over on the beach." John Scamble told him to put that boat up. My uncle had his oar just ready to push this row boat off'n the shore, and Scamble grabbed the oar and both of em runned and twist on the oar. My uncle say, "Well," say, "I'll give it to you. I'll put it up." And he let go of the oar, and John Scamble hit him, knocked him down in the head in the water. If it hadn't been for another fella, they was breakin up something down there near the shore, he'd a drowned. He fell in the boat with his head over in the water, and Sam Spence jumped in the boat right quick and pulled his head out of the water. And that evenin, Uncle John went home, after he got so he could walk, and that evenin, John Scamble went to Copperville to see him and tell him he was sorry and all that stuff like that, but that didn't help Uncle John any by him bein sorry. He had to admit he was wrong.

He was mean as a dog. His own race didn't like him. A man told me one time was talkin about him, man told me, said, "Somebody's goin to kill him." He was mean as a dog—mean and a coward. Somebody set up to him, somebody that was able, why, he'd stop talkin! He threatened to lick another man, much smaller than he was, colored man. Colored man set up to him and told him that, "I got a knife." Say, "I'm not as big as you. I'm not as strong," say, "but you try to do anything to me, I'm goin to cut you down to my size." He let him alone, too. And the other two boys was altogether different, altogether different principle. That was Henry and Conrad. And a fine mother, fine old lady. Course, the old man, I guess, he was all right, but he never learnt to speak English. You couldn't understand him. You might understand some words, but very few could understand. He couldn't speak English plain. And that must be a terrible thing, you go to another country and never learn to speak the language.

Part III

And I remember on a Sunday night, I think it was in the fall, for it was cool night, but pleasant, you could look and see in the sky, look like the clouds was red. The clouds was northeast, and I knowed we all was watchin. And then I think my grandfather said we were goin to have another war. And he keep sayin he saw somethin like soldiers marchin on the clouds. Said, "That was blood on the clouds." That's what they called it. And the United States and Cuba and Spain was the head one and they wasn't havin any trouble then. But since then somebody told me it was the light you get from the north and said reflection was from the sun on the clouds.

And we was in Harriet Blackwell's house and we moved out that January and the war start the next spring. We was livin in Chestnut Lane the time of the American-Spanish War, when it broke out. I know just before it did start Cubans sank the *Maine*. We moved to Chestnut Lane the eleventh of January, and Edward Hammond, he moved in middle house just before January. There was three houses. The last house was owned by Sherwoods. They was the onliest ones that kept the lease up. The lease had run out on the middle house they didn't keep it up. The house had gone back to the people owned the ground. But the last house they kept it up for years and years.

I had a little dog. Trained him myself. We moved to Chestnut Lane in January and that spring this dog come to our house and he was a puppy about half grown. Then he would tackle anything. I don't care what it was. I'd see him fight with dog that he could walk under their stomach. And he'd never give up. And then he could run a rabbit. I've known him jump a rabbit and run him down fore he stopped tumbling. I saw him one day he had jumped this rabbit close to the road at the edge of the road, and this rabbit run right straight down to the woods and this dog right behind him. And comin back, a little hitch in it coming back. And then the dog started again. And I walked in the side of the wood. I didn't know the rabbit was there, and stood so I could get a better view when he did come back because the little limbs on the little bushes and trees on the road was thicker than they was in the woods, and I could see better in the wood. And he come on up there tonguing and right straight for this rabbit sittin down. And he saw the rabbit about the time the rabbit got ready to get up and dog if he didn't catch him before he could get his speed up. The rabbit try to duck him, but he couldn't do it, and he caught him.

I remember another time I took him out in the woods, the last woods as you go down to Marengo. I jumped a rabbit up in this end of it, and he went right straight down, tonguing right straight down the way the road run, but not the side of the road. And after awhile he stopped and I called and I called. When I went home I told my mother somethin had happened. I don't know whether he run into somethin and killed hisself or not. She said maybe not. But I couldn't think of nothin but that he had ran into a tree. And I guess about half a hour after, he come home his sides sticking way out. Mother said, "There is your rabbit." I said, "No, that's the dog." "But look at his sides." He caught that rabbit and ate it. And that is why he wouldn't come to me when I would call him. I didn't know whether to get mad with him or not. So I studied. I said to myself, "Well, can't blame you. You wasn't getting as much as you want to eat, and you work hard to get it."

When I'd go out nighttime, I carried a sack, watch for possum. I remember one night I went out, that was on Little Hopewell side where you make your turn to the right, it's a farm to your left there and way in the back part, used to be a slave graveyard. We was goin along, the dog was ahead of me and I had a little dog belonged to the neighbor lived there. And the dog of mine got to barkin. Oh, he'd bark! He just up side the shore ahead of me. He barked, he barked, and everytime I'd speak to him, he'd get worse. When I looked, I thought I saw a little old woman, not very tall, but she was right round looked like. I have seen old women that shape. And right away then I thought about the graveyard. I said, "Go get it, Jack!" And after awhile, he come to me his tail dropped down and he had it hoist up. I've heard old people say when a dog see a ghost, he get scared, he would drop his tail. All that come to me. And this other little dog, she didn't go where he was barkin, she was standin along side of me. And when I got ready to move, you talk about runnin! When we got to the field that run right out where we lived, Chestnut Lane, we was crossin that field I had one dog ahead of me and one behind me. That little dog it was behind me. And my dog was ahead of me. You talk about runnin! I did run! I run the length of more than two fields, the middle field and the road field they called it. When you get scared, well, you don't get tired runnin. That's the onliest time I got scared huntin.

And that night when I thought about it I say I'm goin back around there again. I'm goin back there tomorrow and look see if that thing still there. Went back the next day and looked and it wasn't a thing but an oak bush. I said to myself, "Uh huh, I never believe in no ghost," I said, "Now that's what a lot of people call a ghost."

And my dog got away after I was doin a little work and didn't care him, and I guess food too I reckon. He went to a farm not far from Chestnut Lane. Boys he got acquainted with was white boys I used to play with. After I'd be gone every day, I guess he'd get lonesome he'd go down there.

And I remember the first time I ever went rabbit huntin with a gun. I was oysterin with my stepfather and we was walkin from Chestnut Lane down to Voit Farm joins Hope to where he kept his boat and we'd leave home before light and we'd come back in the evening it'd be dark. So a day or so after the rabbit season opened we went down to go to work. We went to work and the wind got to blowin hard, and I was prayin for it to blow harder so I could get home and go rabbit huntin. We worked awhile, but it got so rough we had to come in. And I went home and the dog was down at this farm. I went out and hollered for him but he didn't hear me, I don't guess. So I took my gun and went out first place I been hearin the rabbits every mornin. I walked in the woods there and didn't go very far, come to a thick place and the rabbit jumped up. I couldn't see him long enough to get a bead on him runnin, kind of thick in there and I could hear him when he was runnin in the leaves and all at once it stopped. I say, "Well, I can't get up on him. If I start walkin, he's going to run again." And I shot through there, right where I thought he stopped and then I went through there, there he was, had killed him. I didn't see him, I just shot where I thought he stopped. Picked my rabbit up and I was tickled.

I went down the road a little further, I used to hear one run in the woods there in the mornin. And I went in there and jumped that rabbit. Instead of shootin I watched for him to stop and then I shot the last place where I last saw him but he wasn't there. So then I come on home. I said, "Ain't no use in me going any further with no dog." And when I come home my dog had come home. So I took him went back there and he got to trailin this rabbit and after awhile the rabbit jumped up and I shot and killed him runnin.

That was my first rabbit huntin. So it was gettin late then and I went to the new ground over on the place where we was livin. I went there, was plenty rabbits in there. It was thick and the dog was runnin. He'd run sometime before I ever saw the rabbit and I saw him and killed him, then it was about sundown and I was tickled to death I'd killed three rabbits. My mother, she couldn't get over it, the first time I had ever been rabbit huntin. I was fourteen. And I skinned em. That was the end of that, though, because I had to go oysterin next day.

And I went to work thirteen years old. Man said he want me to carry milk to the creamer and he was on that farm tryin to work it by hisself exceptin thrashing the wheat and cuttin corn and stuff like that. And my mother hired me there for three dollars a month, and I did a little bit of everything. Thirteen years old, put me in the field cuttin corn. One row of men cut two rows and I cut one row. I didn't plow but I rowed, and I didn't cultivate at that age. I rowed and brambled the whole darn place. At that age, I shouldn't had to do it. And I mean a workin, wasn't just out there, I worked! Some old man told me that I did more in a day brambling than some men, cause I kept goin. I started, be after sun up, but I would go until very near sundown. Wasn't to do anything only to take milk to creamery. Well I blame my mother for that, she should have seen to it, I couldn't do nothin about it. And he paid my mother, didn't pay me. Only had the field in between my mother's house and his house. He didn't trust me with money to carry that distance. I got some of it, but it wasn't much some to it. I used to get a quarter a month.

That man was on Little Hopewell, left Little Hopewell and went to Cook's Hope. Very poor place. The man couldn't get nobody to rent it and talk him into rentin it. It was somethin wrong for a landlord have to go out and get somebody to come on it. If it was any good, he ought to know somebody would'a jumped at it.

He was so poor that he couldn't make a track in ashes. A bug'll make a track in ashes, crawlin through ashes. Them the kind sometime expect more. He was a renter and he was of a low class. And I said to myself then, the next job I got was goin to be with a better class if I had to work for just my board and clothes.

Then mother hired me to an old man in Chapel in December and stayed there until April. That was the first time I worked out of Miles River Neck. Stayed there four months, and she couldn't get the money out of him. He was supposed to pay me four dollars a month. It was more than a month's work that I didn't get paid for. The old man he didn't have nothin cause the next year, he had to get rid of the farm; he couldn't pay for it. It was a little place. What they called a "one-horse place." And I was the onliest one.

And he used to get drunk. He belonged to the huntin club they had in Easton then, that was the poor farmers, and he used to go over there every Saturday, come home drunk. When he bought the place was a peach orchard there, he had the peach orchard pulled up. Until time to plow for corn that was my job cuttin the trees up and only fourteen years old. And one day he come home, come out there where I was, and the amount of work I'd done didn't suit him, and he reared. I wasn't nothin but a boy, and I had been workin whole time I was out there. He come out there, got after me, got to cussin. I took my little ax and start towards him. He commenced backin up. I looked, he had turned around and gone into the house. And I bluffed him. Somethin keep tellin me to cut him and then somethin said no, just get yourself in trouble, he's wrong, but you'll get the worse of it. And I started cuttin wood with that ax.

Didn't have no more trouble with him but I had time set that I was goin to leave. My mother want me to leave cause he owed me money and couldn't get the money out of him. That winter I stayed there, cut all the wood for the house, had the horses to feed. I had cows to milk. I'd milk when it was so cold when the milk would splatter on the bucket and it'd freeze.

And I slept over the kitchen stairs and the kitchen was put up with straight up-and-down boards and strips on the outside. Wasn't fit for a dog to stay up there. And it was places there, I've set in there when the moon was shining and snow was on the ground, and I could see the snow. And I could get in the bed and put the lamp out and I could see broken places in the roof, and I've seen stars. I had to set in that place with a cook stove. Then I got up that winter in the mornin and step out of bed in snow. Gettin up when the stars was shinin and goin till after sundown. And food wasn't good as nothin. Fat meat, hog jowls, and corn cakes, mostly. And I had to eat it or go hungry. Lived a dog's life them days.

And it was cold them days. And you didn't have sufficient clothes, no poor person did them days, not to cope with the weather you had. I remember that winter I wanted to come home get a change of clothes and he loaned me a horse to ride back home and some roads was banked up with snow. I know I went through one place that was near home, I had no other way to get there only goin several miles out of my way, and the snow was up past the horse's stomach.

And the old man I worked for he owed me God knows how much money when I left. I went there the first of January and I left in April and could never get the money out of him. He never did pay my mother. He bought that place, I heard for $2,500. He couldn't pay for it and the next year, they closed in on him and he had to get out. That was tight livin them days. But I bought a muzzle loader from another boy. He had got high enough to get a breech loader. Father owned a farm and was able to buy him a breech loader. He sold it to me dollar and a half. Course that was a lot of money them days for me.

And fourteen, my mother hired me to a man up here on White Hall, next to Tunis Mills. But he only hired me for a month. When his son would be off thrashin wheat, well, I'd be there to help him to milk. He was an old fella. And do feedin round the hogs and things. Well, I got there, I helped to haul hay, I worked in the wheat field there, and that was four dollars a month, and had another boy there. He was seventeen. And I could do anything he did. After he had me a month, he told my mother that he'd like to have me another month, said I was right apt. So he kept me another month. And then when his son-in-law lived here near Easton, when he went to plow for his wheat, he come round and asked my mother could I go up there a day or two days. Mother said yes and I went up there. Stayed three days. Get up in the mornin, dark. Feed the team. Then get on the wood pile and cut wood until breakfast was ready. And then go in the field and plow until you just could see the other team on the other turn row. You'd be up there to this turn row and on the other turn row, you wasn't close enough to make a person out. And I stayed up there three days. And he give me seventy-five cents. That was terrible. Should have been a law. You follow the team and workin that late, you did just as much work as a man did. That's all I got, twenty-five cents a day.

And the way the conditions was, I said to myself, "I'm goin to get a job with somebody that got more money than these people. When I get away from here, I'm going where I'm goin to get better eatin and better treatment." And I went to Rieman's and stayed there for years and years and felt like home to me. Said to myself, I know I'll have a decent place to sleep and decent food to eat. I never even worried about the money, I got good treatment and good eatins. And there I ate just what they did, but with this renter, I didn't always eat what they ate. It was a big difference, and I stayed there. The first opportunity, I went there. The first boy, he had around the house. When he left there, I was pickin peaches. And Mr. Rieman told somebody to tell me to come up where he was sortin peaches before I went home. And I went up there and talked with him, and he hired me.

I was fifteen. Paid me eight dollars a month. I had a room upstairs, over the kitchen. I started doin man's work at fifteen years old. Started cuttin and carryin corn. I stayed up around the house there. Day and night. The first year or so I was there, I used to have to go out and work on the farm and so I commenced complaining about that, quantity of work I'd have to do round the house and then work on the farm, and the same thing about milkin, I had the milkin to do. And they was afraid I was goin to leave and they cut that out. And it was enough work to do up around the house to keep me busy all day. Was one time there, we had, I think it was seven horses up the house stable—that's where the drivin horses was. I used to ride colts. Them days people used to loan some boys colts to ride and glad for em to handle em, that would be breakin em. And I could get a colt to ride anytime I wanted and some of the other older people tellin me, said, they never knowed of Mr. Rieman never lend boys colts. But anytime I wanted one I'd pick out the one I wanted, could always get it. I had them to tend to, and run the errands, mail, sometime in Easton. But I never had any trouble about the work, cause if I had, I'd never been there as long as I was. The old man used to raise a good-size garden, cause the Riemans, then, was a big family of em. Used to be seven head in the family. The old man told me one day, Mr. Rieman said, "Well, Joe," say, "I notice you," say, "you don't rip and run, but you keep steady a goin." I told him, "Yes sir. I want my money stuff, to keep steady a goin." He laughed. He said, "Well, steady pull," say, "is what brought the boat ashore, wasn't it?" I said, "That's what the old people say." Never had no trouble about work.

I trapped down there to Riemans when I was a boy. Then there was so many rats down there you could smell that musk in the daytime. That place was full of em. I caught one down there that was a big rat. I guess it weighed over two pounds. Didn't have any front legs, but he was up in the high part of the marsh. He wasn't out where he was bein in the water all the time. Don't know how he ever got along that way with no front legs, cause I think the front legs is what they dig for the roots with. I remember one time I set twelve traps. Next morning I had eleven rats. I was no boy then. And Rieman's daughter got half the skins, because I was usin her father's time to trap and the father's place I was catchin the muskrats on. If it hadn't been for that, I wouldn't be able to trap. I thought it was fair; as long as you think something is right, if its wrong, its all right if you think its right. It ain't as bad as you think it's wrong and do it, you won't feel as good bout it.

I've sold muskrat hide for eight cents. Them days didn't anything bring very much. Muskrat meat was three for a quarter. I used mostly traps. I had some snares but not many. And it was another trap you could set. I wished I'd learned it. My uncle could set em. You could set it right out here any place, just so you had a pole. It wouldn't look like it was much to it and bait it and soon as he stepped on the treadle, why you'd get him. I never did learn how to set it and he could catch rabbits that way. And he used to use onions, mostly for rabbits.

My mother cooked muskrats when I was a boy. Just cut them up in quarters and put em on the stove in a skillet. And I guess you'd call it boilin em. But they're good. Put them down and put water in it and let them cook in that water until they was done. And let the water cook right down. Boil right down. A lot of people used to fry rabbit. Cook it that way, and then take it out before it was done and fry it.

And I've ate possum. Used to catch a lot of them. I'd catch em in the fall and wintertime. I know one time I had either eight or ten one time. I had them home in a barrel. Kept em in this barrel, used to feed them, fatten em up. Would give em bread, anything like old meat, they would eat it. Course, they wouldn't eat when you was lookin at them. One or two of the barrels was a flour barrel. And it was one, it had been a vinegar barrel. With vinegar, you got a stronger barrel, stronger than a flour barrel. You couldn't use a coal oil barrel, you couldn't get that coal oil out of the wood. And I used to have days when you'd hear me say I was goin hog killing. I used to kill three or four of em. Then you got about ten cents for the hides. Then I would eat em. Sometime my mother'd bake em. I remember one time, this small one, I ate a whole possum myself. I had been sick for two or three days and hadn't ate but very little, and I ate that whole possum, though all but the head.

That's when I was a boy, but after that, I couldn't stomach em. I don't want no more possum. Man said a fellow told him took his two dogs out one night, said they walked and walked, never struck a trail. Then he decided that he would go home, but he didn't go the way he came out. He said his dogs got to barkin and when he got there close enough to see, it was a dead horse. His neighbor had lost a horse and hauled it out to the woods. That's the way they used to do them days. And his dogs was to the back part of this horse rearin. And got a stick and beat that horse on his ribs with that stick. Say when he looked, say he had a sack full of possum. Tale he told, they had gone up in that horse. So that stopped me from eatin and I haven't eaten another piece since. Somebody say that a possum can kill a coon. And then somebody ask the possum why was it he could kill a coon, but when a dog would jump on him, he would just lay there and grin? Possum told him cause the dog was ticklin him in his ribs. That would make him grin.

Sometimes ate some birds at Chestnut Lane. Robbins and blackbirds. Not so many ducks. Nobody to kill them. And after I got to killin them, I didn't fool with them much. Nobody want to pick em and I didn't want to pick em. I start to eat meadow lark, but somebody told me they had a worm in their back and I stopped eatin em. They used to go to roost in fields where it was weeds and, high weeds and grass, close where we lived there at Chestnut Lane and I used to go to that old muzzle loader, jump em and kill em. I didn't eat no crow. People eat em, though. Was the young ones what they ate. And they say they taste just as good as squab.

I left Riemans once or twice on account of too many bosses. One would tell me to do one thing and then another would come along and tell me to do somethin else. I remember one time, old man Reiman got after me bout not doing somethin and I was doin what one of the others told me to do, and I got mad and I quit. And it wasn't nothin bad that caused me to leave, only I wouldn't take a whole lot of foolishness and they'd be glad to get me back anytime I wanted to go back. It wasn't the money question, just left. Some things I don't like to talk about. I might have to go over em again sometime, they'd make bad feelins even with grandchildren.

And I got mad about somethin and went right cross the little cove over to Mr. Will Hall's and worked there. He needed somebody and I worked for him. I'd go over there and stay a while and then go back to the Riemans again. But I could always go back. Wherever I was, I could go back again. And that was the beauty of it. And I could go back and forth to either place after I got young man. Things didn't suit me one place I'd go to the other. And that's good. As old people call it, "Never burn the bridge behind you, cause you might want to go back again." My mother know I wouldn't leave without a cause but she told me not to be sassy. She told me that when I was a boy. If I was gonna quit, quit! And say nothin. Maybe the day I'd want to go back again.

And Mr. Hall was a mean man. He shot a colored man over in St. Michaels. He lived to St. Michaels when his father bought Marengo farm. He was over on St. Michaels side then, before I ever knowed him. Goin across the place, small place he had over there, took his gun, burnt that colored fellow up. Well

I didn't ask him over. Didn't know he was comin. And Monday Mr. Hall said to me, "Joe," said, "your buddy was over here yesterday, I saw him climbin over my fence. I started to take my gun and shoot him, if he ever do it again I'm goin to shoot him." He was that kind of man. But I never had any great trouble with him. Sometime he talk to me just as nice about things and tell me things, sometime again, he'd come out in the morning, wouldn't even speak to me. And I mean he was that way with everybody. He was a dirty man. He'd come out and smile at you like this mornin, and fore the day was out, he'd look at you like you was some kind of beast. You never see him smile. He was just a mean man, and that was when I was workin for him, before I was workin for him, and after I was workin for him. I remember one time when Charlie Hall was a baby, he used to leave my sister, and if I was around the house he'd be with me all the time. And one day Mr. Hall wanted him to come to the house and they was on the porch, and he wouldn't go. He kept callin him, he wouldn't go so he come after him, goin to whip him, and he runned around me and grabbed my leg. And then he'd get away from Mr. Hall and run around the other side. And Mr. Hall said, "Well," said, "I'm goin to whip both of you." And that's the time I bust out into a laugh. And I looked and Mr. Hall was smilin, he turned his head and he went on back to the porch. And it used to tickle Mrs. Hall but she was afraid to say anything cause he was a mean man. And a child know when you love em, too. You don't have to tell em that; it's somethin tellin em. I've been places where children wouldn't hardly say anything to anybody else and if they was goin to say anythin they would always come to me. And, in fact I think animals know who like em and who don't.

But I wasn't goin to work for no more poor class. I mean not to go and work by the month. Rieman was bout the middle class, and Will Hall, he thought he was the highest class, but his father was a ship captain. One of the big ships that runs from here to Europe. And he got seventy thousand dollars. And he wasn't long runnin through that. And when his mother died, he, I heard, got ninety thousand then. In a few years he had runned through that. So he just put on higher than the amount of money he had. That's why he run through it. He went two or three winters to Baltimore to live in a hotel all the winter. Then had an automobile to come down and take his family to Baltimore. And that was unusual here. But whenever he wanted to go any distance, he'd always hire one. And she had her people come to visit her. And if it was warm weather, and in the warm weather, he would get in his boat and go to St. Michaels. And my people he thought he was way ahead of them. That was the Riemans. Just got so after he got the money he didn't speak to em. Just had the money given to him.

I helped to load the Halls' belongings on a boat when they moved from here. I was the onliest colored person they had that did help. Went on the Severn River. He bought an old estate there and we built the house cause they had, I believe, they called a sun parlor, it was all glass at the front, the whole front of it was nothin but glass. And then his wife's people used to visit em, and he got mad and moved to California. And I had a sister, worked for the Halls, the first and only job she ever had until the Halls left here and went to California. She went there for a nurse, she was about fourteen years old. She stayed there with them children longer than anybody had. And they wanted her to go to California with em and she consult me. I was bout grown then, and I advised her not to go. "There may be a time when you want to come home. You fall out and quit and how you goin to get back home. You won't have the money. Best thing you get yourself another job." And she didn't go. So she went to Baltimore to her aunts and got a job up there, and wasn't there long before she was taken sick, and wasn't sick long fore she died.

And he died in California. He went there and got into somethin with the money sharks and lost every cent he had. He didn't know how to take care of money; he didn't work for it.

People had bad stock them days. They kept bulls on Marengo. One bull, he was pretty near grown, and he never made any attempt to run me. But just before he was grown, he got so he had the other men around there scared of him. And then I was workin by the day then, and didn't have a man that would go out and drive em up. Was afraid of that bull. I had been down to the Willows doin some work. Old man Kirsch was always inquirin for me. He stop to my mother to tell me to come down and see him. So I went back and had the same job in the dairy. And Hall was the first one that ever had a dairy in Miles River Neck. And you get up early, milkin in the mornin. They had hours to milk and they say that's the best way to keep cows up and milkin is to have em certain hours to milk.

I was workin in the dairy, I remember one time, the head man left and I had the head man's job and I could call anybody else off'n the farm to help me milk. And this fella was workin by the day. I told Mr. Kirsch I wanted him to help me to milk, so he told him, "All right." So when it come time to get the cows up out of the field, I never thought about the bull, I sent him to get the cows up and I said, "I'll wash this trough out." And I was scrubbin the trough out with an old broom and I heard him hollerin. "Go back! Go back!" I said, "Lord bless my soul." I say, "I forgot about that bull." I wouldn't've sent him out there if I'd thought about that bull, because he would run anybody else on the farm but me then. And I run out there and I hollered at him, the cows was up ahead of him then, come right up and caught the cows and come on in.

And another time I was waitin for the cows to come up that evening and I waited and waited and they was in some bushes down at the edge of the shore on account of the flies. And it seemed like every evenin they'd be as far away from the home in the fields they could get. And I went down there and I hollered at em. They come out and start up and that bull start up ahead of them and something told me, "You better go up and get a brick or somethin, he may have forgot you." And he got me two hundred yards out in the field, he stopped and got down on his knees, rubbin his head on the ground and blowin. Then he'd raise up and look at me and rub his head on the ground again. I looked the distance it was from the fence and I said, "If I start off runnin to that fence, he can overtake me before I get to the fence." I said, "The best thing is just to keep on and out-nerve him." So I kept right on walkin and hollerin at him. When I got close to him he raised his head up and when he raised his head up I hit him right in the nose. He shook his head and blowed and went up and overtaken the cows, went ahead of em. So I said to myself, "Well, that was close enough, that was a warnin for me. I'm not going to take that chance again."

But he got mean, oh, he was terrible. I saw him one day, went out in the river after a man in a boat. I went to drive him up and instead of him comin up, he noticed that boat and he went in the river after that boat. The man liked to drowned him. He didn't hit him but every time he'd swim up to the boat, the man would take the oar and put it against his head or shoulders, and you know, it wouldn't take much to shove him under water. And he'd shove down the whole head and everything down under the water. He did that several times before that bull would give up. Then after that he swam ashore. He must've been full of water, because he was slow walkin after that. He was a Jersey, brown-breast strain. But he was mean. And from then on I'd watch him.

Another narrow escape I had with a male hog. I didn't know even the hog was behind me. This hog was mean and he used to come out to Unionville from Ennals Tull's place. People was always scared to death of him. I don't know why somebody didn't kill him. And he couldn't keep him home, he had sold him to Mr. Will Hall. And he was in the pound with the cows. And Mr. Rieman's cow had gone over there that day. So Mr. Rieman asked me would I go out and see if I could find him. It was about night. Something told me to go over, there see if he was over there and they had put him in this pound, a pound with barbed wire around it. And I saw him when I was comin out. Somethin just told me, just presence of mind, to look behind me. And here come that bull hog. And where the cows had been stocked in the pound, had been eatin through this barbed-wire fence, and had bend it down, made it wider than it should be. And he was so close on me the only thing I could do was do like a frog and I leaped right through that place. And I looked around and that hog was close. Know when they get mad like that they'll commence to choppin their mouth and they'll make a whole lot of foam, and that foam was all out around his mouth, and that was a very narrow escape. And when I went up to the house Mr. Rieman asked me did I find him. I told him yes, they was in the pound over to Mr. Halls. And he said they hadn't been milked. I said I told the boys about it and the boys said they was goin over and get em. But Joe didn't go over there no more. Because them things cut you. I heard the old people say they'll poison you when they cut you. And I've know for em to kill horses. And one time I saw one after the horse was in the pound. And he ruined one ridin mare. She always was lame after that. And he got after the colt and just as I looked, I was comin towards the pound. I looked and this colt had life enough to jump the fence. And I looked again there was mule layin down. Some of his entrails pulled out. Cut him down below his ribs here. The mule was dead. And years ago when I was very small, one cut a colt's throat. Three years old, hadn't broken it. And he to the pen keep puttin his head over there where the hog was. And then he'd pull his head back. He kept doin that and then after awhile the hog made a jump and caught him. And one Sunday night a man by the name of Jake Ockimey was out in Unionville. A man with good age on him. And he was goin from the church property across to this place they call Old Town. And he got over the fence by the cemetery and got a little distance from the church he heard somethin behind him. And he looked, there the hog was. He was tellin me about it. "Buds," say, "throw it in high gear, I blind him from there to Old Town." Say, "I kicked dirt in his face," say, "all the time." Old man Jake say he never run that fast before in his life. When he got to Old Town, he didn't climb over he just went head first right over the fence. When he got up that hog was right there to the fence. Yes said he filled that hog face full of dirt. And somebody said, "Uncle Jake, he didn't bite you at all?" "Well he couldn't see to bite me as much dirt as I was throwin in his face." And if it had been a hog from out Unionville botherin Ennals Tull like that he'd a killed him.

I went back to Copperville sometime. After I got older, I went there more than I did when I was smaller. But thing of it was with me, when I got ready to go anyplace. I didn't want to go back. I would want to get out. I figure I'd lived behind the woods long enough, and I would wantin to go the other way.

When I was seventeen, I went back there to live again because where we lived on Chestnut Lane, it had been other people there but at that time wasn't nobody there but us. It was two more houses with leased land and soon as the people got out of em they was tore down. I had less boys to talk with when I went down to Chestnut Lane. Was only one down there and he was three or four years older than I was.

I moved to Copperville and lived with my great-grandmother. She was by herself. Son was right out in little house right out from the house she was in. It wasn't over two steps from my great-grandmother's house. It was built there so he'd be right there to look after her to see what she wants.

I worked on the Glebe about two or three months. The man that was over me was no good. He was one of the very low class, and I quit. And my great-grandmother said she was glad of it. She said when I went there, she didn't want me to go there. Course, she was older than I was, she had seen more than I had, and she knowed. And she knowed in that class was no help to me. The Glebe was one of Colonel Lloyd's farms. The Colonel was different from a lot of em. He recognized all that was his slaves. And if they got in any trouble, that was after the war, if there was any way he could help em, he'd help em.

Then I worked in cannin factory down Tunis Mills two weeks. That was enough for me. I just didn't like it. You'd work one day and laid off two.

That was all home people then. When they got the other bunch there was very few from here then. They come from Virginia and on down the line. Those people'd do anything—cut your throat. They brought them down, the cannin company did, for the work in the factory, and they carried em back, sent them back to Baltimore. They couldn't get enough of the home people to work. They didn't work regular. Got yourself on the job, Aunt Sally died, they'd stop and lose the whole day so they could go to the funeral. That was right.

And the bunch from Virginia, they all worked cause they ain't got no uncles and aunts here to die. It made a big difference. Couldn't blame the ones own the cannin factory for getting other people cause they'd lose money. They'd rather go to funerals than go to preachin. When they first come, some of em lived in a house out Copperville. And they had shanty down at Tunis Mills. And they had another bunch down there one time, this was while the white people complain about the noise that these black ones made. You don't want that kind of noise day and night. And it was decent white people's house right cross that narrow road from the cannin factory. And they couldn't sit on their front porch. And then the next year they didn't get em, they got Bohemians. They said, "Well, we'll have some peace now, you won't hear all that noise now." And they got so on days they didn't work, sometime after they stop in the evenin, they'd go to them people's porch and set back on the porch, had rocking chairs on it, and sit back and rock. God, they want to get away from that. It tickled me. And they was raising the devil. Then they was afraid to say anything to em. Sometime they'd come there in the evenin or on Sunday. They'd come back down, lay back in the rockin chairs and rock, have a good time.

And I went oysterin. Went by myself. I oystered a while again after I was married but I give it up for something. It was uncertain thing in the winter and I had a long distance to walk to my boat. Course, it had to be done. I went got some other job, days work.

I remember one time went from Wye River to St. Michaels to sell my oysters and come back and was very little bit of wind and I never got back until around two o'clock in the mornin. I never was scary. And I never saw but a few things I didn't make out. I wouldn't be satisfied till I'd make it out and if I didn't make it out that night, I would take a mark of the place and come back the next day and make it out. But a lot of times, you can get to thinkin about somethin and you'll just imagine you see somethin.

And I land my boat on Four Hundred shore, goin to walk across the field, and I got a hundred yards or more from the shore. I walked upon two things. One layin down the other standin up along side of it. Had a head like a sheep and a body like a hog. I carried a big stick on account the stock might've been in the field, and I got close to em I commenced hollerin at em. Slacked up walkin and hollerin at em, and after awhile I said, "If you won't move, I'll move you." And I started walkin right a good gait to em and the one was layin down jumped up. And both of em run to the river bank and jumped down that bank. And I run to the bank and looked both ways. I never did see nothin. I said to myself, "It must be some of them old people." But I don't know, it may've been just imagination, I reckon.

And then I had to go through a graveyard, a slave-time graveyard. And it had growed up with gum saplings. Still it was a path through it I guess stock made. And I goin through and got near the rail fence and it was a cat come up that rail fence just as white as you ever saw a cat, and every time it picked its front feet up, it'd shake em. And I stood there and watched him. And when the cat got past, I got over the fence and went towards home.

And the big stick I had when I was comin across the field, well, I throwed it down, went towards Copperville and got down the road a little distance, I looked, I saw an ox, looked like, sittin right in the middle of the road. And it was so big until it had taken up pretty near all near the road. It was sittin down with its head up. And I stood there and hollered at it, and it still stayed there, horns and all. So I said, "I will move you." I went back and got my stick and come back, I didn't see a thing on that patch of grass in the road. That was all I saw and went on home.

And another time, I was oysterin. Then, I had a boat on up to Tire Top. That was an old landin there, people land boats there in slavery or right after slavery them that was oysterin. I had been to St. Michaels and I had a sailboat and was late gettin back. Well, I land there and the goin home was a gate, Tire Top Gate, they called it. It faced the road that runs down to New Design. And it'd come to me then that I heard an old man say that it was a man got killed, he got out to open the gate and he had either a pair of young oxens or one young oxen, goin to start to run off, or did run off, and jammed him between the hub of the wheel and the gate post. Killed him. I thought about seein him. And I heard some of the old people say you could always see somethin after twelve o'clock, say up there to that gate. And I went through the gate and they say the gate, when you go through it after twelve o'clock and open and shut it, it'll come open and shut again. And I opened, went through and shut it and stood there waitin for to see it come open again. It didn't come open. I went on.

And that spring, I went pickin strawberries up to Ridgely, and I didn't like that. Several fellows over Copperville had been goin every year. Buck Copper went, that was my playmate, and I thought I'd go. But I should've stayed where I was. Course, little better for him than it was for me. he had a big brother there and all. I had nobody, no relation. We went on train from Easton. And we stayed in a shanty with people from St. Michaels. The row boss, the one that got the men together, he brought people there from St. Michaels.

That's the time I surprised all of em. When wasn't pickin strawberries, we'd picked until sometime in the mornin because had to have em to Ridgely for ten o'clock in the mornin. We start just when it was light enough to see the berries. Well, we'd pick till that time of the day and then other parts, you had nothin to do. And it was a young fellow was on the farm there, white fellow. I got in with him. I used to follow him everyday. You didn't eat your breakfast until you come in. I'd eat my breakfast, I'd go out and stay with him. So one day, he was puttin fertilize around tomato plants and he had the fertilize on his sled, horse or mule pullin it. And it'd pull it so far, and then he'd fill his bucket up, go down the rows. And he went in and got another sack and come out and I don't know, takin that sack off the sled or puttin the sack on. I told him I could do it. Say, "No," say, "you can't do it." He was twenty-one years old. I said, "Yes, I can." I said, "Wait a minute." I picked that sack up. It was two hundred pounds, picked it up and put it on the sled. I was seventeen years old. And I was talkin about it that night. Went in the shanty there together, several of em said, "No, boy, you can't shoulder no two hundred pounds." So I say, "Well, they got some up there in the barn." That was the barn belonged to the farm. I said, "I'll get Mr. Porter to let us go in there, I'll show you." So I went up ask him and explained to him why. He said, "Yeah, I'll unlock the barn, go in there, but," he said, "you can't shoulder no two hundred pounds." I said, "All right," said, "I'll show you." And we went in there, he got laughin. We went in there and here are these others standin around, men and boys to see me. And I said, "I can stand the half a bushel. And shoulder two-hundred-pound sack." And you could hear a pin fall. So Mr. Porter said, "Well, boy," say, "you surprised me. I told you that you couldn't do it, but you can." Say, "You surprised me." And the others were standin around lookin right simple. And the row boss told me, said, "Boy, don't hurt yourself." Say, "You're going to be a giant," say, "when you get a man."

I found out that was a man up there related to my father and grandfather. And he went from here either durin the Civil War or after the Civil War, and wasn't any further than Ridgely and never did get down here anymore. And he lived to be over a hundred years old, I heard. His name was George Sutton. And he owned three or four houses up there.

I think we pick strawberries about two or three weeks. Then we left Tuckahoe Neck and that's east of Ridgely and we went to a place west of

Ridgely. Supposed to pick blackberries, and that year, the blackberries didn't turn out, and didn't pick enough to board myself. So I run errands cause some of the people in the shanty made enough to board theirself. That's a dog life. You buy what you eat and cook it yourself. An old lady, she used to cook meals and sell em to the others. And I used to do all her dealin in Ridgely. Course, then I didn't have to worry about eatin. I went there two times in one: first and last. I couldn't stand that livin. I never did go back anymore, and I was sorry I went that time.

And then we went home and I went on to St. Michaels. That old lady, used to bake and cook and sell stuff, she wanted me to go home with her to wait on her like I did when we was up Ridgely. And I was there for awhile, couldn't get no job because that's why the people in St. Michaels went away, to get work. It wasn't work enough down there for em. So then I hired to a man to go sailin and I sailed with him about three or four months, ne'er did pay me right. So then I quit and come back and went to Copperville. Shortly after I went to Copperville, Mr. William Hall, I had lived with him when a boy, he was inquirin for me. Somebody told him where I was, so he sent a man to get me, tellin me come down and he wanted me to help in gettin up hay. So I worked there and got up the hay and worked the flower garden, and stuff like that.

Then I went back to Rieman's. I used to stay there from one end of the month to the other. I didn't go out very often, didn't go home very often. Stayed to Rieman's and had little books to read. Never was crazy about company. I've stayed there I don't know how many night by myself. I'd get some books, sit down to the table, stay ten, eleven o'clock readin. Most of what I read was sport magazines. *Forest and Stream* and *American Field.* And then the Riemans and the Morrises used exchange magazines. If the Morrises bought em, they'd give em to the Riemans. Well, that would be the last exchange, then I'd get em. I never read the newspaper. I got enough to read without em of what I was interested in. I was interested in sports. And the people was interested in em that was interested in dogs. And they used to raise Chesapeakes.

I had a Chesapeake puppy. I broke him to get under the table if I heard any of em comin. At the Riemans' with Miss Martha, that was Mr. Rieman's wife, she didn't like dogs and she didn't want a dog comin in that house, kitchen, or no place. And I used to listen sittin up lookin at my books. He be layin down alongside my chair and I'd be at the table, and I'd hear em when they come in the dinin room—always hear em, had him so that I wouldn't have to say anything to him. I got up and open that door, he'd go out the open door. And then from that, I commenced to puttin him under the table and after that, he learned it and whenever he'd hear that door open, he'd get under that table and stand up and when they would go out, he'd hear the door slam, he'd come back and lay in the floor alongside of me. I named him Beaver; I raised him from a puppy.

After I growed up and was there at Rieman's, I could get off anytime I wanted. I remember when I was twenty-one, all the rest of em in my race would be talkin about Saturday night, Saturday night. They'd go to town. Easton used to be a great place then for poor people to go. There was white and colored. Come back on Sunday and be talking about the things that happened. I didn't have any notion of goin. And worst of all, I was at Rieman's, I'd be there by myself Saturday night. I stayed out in the help's quarters. And if I did go Saturday nights, the most time I'd go with some-body else, either on the Rieman's farm or on the adjoining farm, Marengo. And that wasn't often. Even when I went to Easton Saturday nights, I'd stand around the street by myself unless some come up to stand there and talk to me. West Street and Market Space was the main place. That's the first street we'd hit goin into Easton. I'd go there and stand up there. Course, I'd meet a lot I knowed. And if I wanted a haircut or anythin, the barber shop I went to was on east end. I didn't have many associates. And I was very particular about who it was.

I worked with some Germans fore I was married and some after I got married. And I wouldn't want to work with any better principle, easier people to get along with than them Germans was. I got along with them better than they got along between theirselves. They had two there to Rieman's and they had no way to go out Saturday nights, and I thought so much of em until I used to go home, walk, and come back, and get the horse and durham and take em to town. Then I'd have to bring it back that night, and walk back home. Lot of em said they wouldn't do it. I told em I would. Do anything in the world I could for em. I got along with em for several months and they seem to be very nice people. And it's a person's principle that makes a person. When they left, both of em shook hands with me and told me they was sorry they was goin to leave. Say, "But if I ever come back this way, I'm goin to look for you." But they found jobs some-place else, I guess. Never did come back.

The hottest thing that ever was there was a boy that said he came from Bulgaria. He called it "Bulgatta." He was a hot somethin. Another boy come from Bremen. And I got to playin with em. I couldn't hardly rest after I got through work in the evenin, and one of em, this boy that come from Bremen, he said he wanted to wrestle, just wanted to wrestle all the time. I'd throw him, hold him down, and he'd just wear me out wrestlin. I didn't get mad with him. Only way I break it up I'd go and sit down, wouldn't stand up. But he didn't fool with the others that worked there that'd be white or black. I got along with them all right. Never had no trouble with em. And they cer-tainly thought a lot of me. He used to try to teach me his language. He learnt me several words in his language, but I'd go to sleep, the next mornin, I'd forget em. We'd get on the street in Easton, and we'd get off a little distance from each other, get to talkin, then the people would say, "There's a black Bulgatta and a white Bulgatta." But they certainly liked to see me, cause others would make fun at them and stuff like that. I didn't. And I pitied em, away from home like they was. And one of them was tellin me where they was, kept in a compound here in Baltimore. Say the lice was so thick, say, they could scoop em up with their hands. All of them got lousy, but then that place, put em in there, not much clean, the people say. Course, they wasn't that thick but I guess they was full of em.

Had another fella, old man Kirsch, he was the head man Marengo, and the Halls wasn't livin on the farm that time when old man Kirsch hired some men. He hired one, he come from Chicago, I guess he was American. He wasn't no different. I mean, he would speak plain, but he was one of the bum kind. And he stayed there a month and got his money and then he commenced to drinking and he was terrible. He'd drink like night and tomorrow he wouldn't be able to work. Old man Kirsch had several of em. They'd make a month and quit.

Them others worked all right. Them two I used to carry to Easton, I carry em, introduce em to Germans. I thought they'd be more happier, somebody to talk with, which'n they was. And they told me that one told them, said that they was better than I was, say, "Don't go around with him." Now I was doin that to help them. But I don't know which German told em that, but that's what they told me at night comin home. He told me, said, "I go with you," say, "I like you, you a good man." And I carried em around. I was single, too. Saturday night was usually the time the colored people had their big times, but I let all that go just to carry em to Easton Saturday nights. So they could meet people and better than workin all the week and sittin down in the house. When they left here, one of em give me a pair of felts. The other give me somethin and told me in plain English as he could that they wished they had more to give me. I told em, "No." I didn't charge em anything. I said, "I just figure suppose I was in your country, I'd certainly appreciate it if you'd carry me around, try to help me."

The church used to have entertainment. That was their onliest enjoyment. They used to go from town to town. People from Copperville come out to Unionville and people from Unionville used to go to Copperville. Ninety percent of em didn't have any horses to drive, and if you didn't have things in walking reach, well, you couldn't get to em. And I've seen it so muddy Christmastime that you could hardly get along walkin on the road. Then I've seen it so rough, snow deep, Christmas, you couldn't walk on the road. It worked both ways.

And I remember one Christmas we was livin at Chestnut Lane. Nobody for company, come out to Unionville to an entertainment. They used to give one at the Hall for bout two weeks. The Hall was put up in Unionville right after Civil War. It was a school. And when the old soldiers come out of the service they bought it soon as they could and pay for it. And that was their meetin place. And used to call it the Grand Army Hall. And I bought several little things and got ready to go home. One old man told me not to walk home in all that mud. "You can't see." Say, "You'll find that mud sometime halfway up your shoe top." He was right bout that. Then he called a man asked him would he take me to his house, let me stay that night. So I stayed out to Unionville that night and the next mornin it was drizzling rain. And that was what they called Christmas Week.

Another time, I wasn't grown, I was out to Copperville with my grandparents. Stayed out there that winter. One evening I hadn't cut any wood for em, usually I'd been cuttin in the evenin. Bout time I got through eatin my supper, Charles Copper stopped there, him and his brother. So I told em go ahead. I said, "I'll catch you." And I cut enough wood and I got ready to leave. I went down to Leed's Creek, and I got on the ice and went on across the other side to White Hall field, stubble field. And it was a house down below the big house on White Hall. And the fellow that lived in it, he was goin out to Unionville, too, because they had a contract to play the whole two weeks.

So I went across and I heard the ones that went through Tunis Mills. They was up there by the backgate of White Hall. And this Kellum man, he was leavin the house that was down below, and one of em blowed their horn for Kellum, and he blowed his horn answerin em. And he was comin up along side that rail fence. That was the back way to go into White Hall. Had a long overcoat on, and his coattail was settin out. Then he commenced to hollerin, "Wait a minute boys! Wait a minute. Don't leave me! You can't play till I get there nohow." He had his horn. And then I commenced makin noise like a bull and he stopped hollerin and slacked up runnin. He was comin up the fence. When he'd slack up, first I'd be goin right at him. And then I would bear off and get ahead of him just the time he'd slack up.

One time I got ahead of him like that and while all that was goin on, one these other fellows and Buck, the one I was supposed to go to Unionville with, one of em got to hollerin, "Kellum," say, "go over that fence. It's a wild something coming, don't you hear it?" And he was hollerin back to em, but he didn't understand em. Man say, "Go over the fence." Say, "Don't you hear that wild somethin coming?" And I kept on. And every time he'd come up, every time I'd bear off like I was goin to be ahead of him to cut him off. Why, he'd slack up. And after awhile, I runned right at him. And he wasn't so far from the end of the road, come out on the country road, and he saw a crooked rail in the rail fence, made a hole big enough for a man could get through. Then I was close to him. And just before he got that place, he hollered to one these other fellows, say, "Mister," say, "he's cuttin me off."

Say, "What must I do? What must I do?" And one of the fellows hollered to him, "Go over that fence, man. Don't let that bull get you down out there." When he got to that place where that rail was, well, the snow had banked to the other side of that rail fence, and he jumped through that rail, head first. Jumped right in that snowbank. And when he come out, it was a strip the length of the field, because that's where they had made a backin startin on the other land. And it was bare of snow because the wind had blowed the snow off. It just made a bare strip. And he got on that strip. You talk about goin! And I bust out in a laugh. Then he stopped. "By God," say, "I thought it was a bull." Say, "But it's a two-legged bull."

And then the fellows on the road, they heard him and they felt better. And when they first heard him spoke of it, Greenbury Gibson said Buck Copper commenced walkin around in a circle, walkin around looking both ways. Look over to his left that was Tunis place and they'd look over to White Hall field. They couldn't keep still. And Greenbury Gibson say he said to him, "What's the matter with you, Buck?" Say, "You scared?" Say, "No," say, "just exercisin myself." He called it exercisin hisself. And them was out on the road, they heard, they went back to the lane and they couldn't get the gate opened fast enough. And some of em hollered, "Open that gate! Open that gate!"

And we had a laugh from there to Unionville. Both Buck and I was there. And Will Moaney, he was around our age, and him and I locked arms so we could laugh. We locked arms so one could help the other if he started to fall. We carried that stuff on we got near to Unionville and Bill Kellum got mad. Said, "Ya'll don't cut that out, I'm going to lick both of you." Then when we got down to Hall and some of the others that was stopped there at that gate, they told it down to the Hall. And they certainly did carry it the rest of that night.

But Bill Kellum was a scary man. He went to the store for his mother one time and had three things to get. It was a package of tea, and yeast powder and soap, I believe. And he had two of the things in his pocket and one in his hand. And used to be a wooden bridge where you turn off that Tunis Mills Road to come to Copperville. And he stopped there and got to dancin. The moon was shinin. And one of them things fell out of his hip pocket and hit him on the heel. And he hung out for home and left it. He come in the house out of wind, and his mother asked him did he get the things that she got him to go there after, and this one thing he couldn't find. And it come to him he dropped it on the bridge. But he didn't go down there by hisself. Somebody come along going that way, and he went down with them.

And when he got married, he come out to go to the store and bought a galvanized washtub and put it in the woods. And fellow named Henry Thomas, he heard him comin and when he went in the woods with this tub loaded with stuff talkin with himself, "I'm goin to see Mammy. I ain't seen

Mammy for some time. I'm going to put my things right in here." And he went in the woods and Henry was watchin him. And he come to a low bush, "By God," say, "I'll put you here, and nobody can't see you from the road." And he put it there and went on to Copperville. Well, when he left, Henry Thomas moved the stuff and put it some place else. Well, Kellum come back and he searched and talked to hisself. "By God," say, "I put it right behind this bush. Ain't use tellin me, I know this is the bush where I put it. I wonder what become of it?" Say, "I'm goin to look through here." And he went a little further to another bush, but not as big as the one he had put the tub behind, and he said, "Well, it ain't behind here, and it ain't as big as the one I put the tub behind." So he stopped, studied for a few minutes, and then after awhile Henry made some kind of noise. And he went out of that woods runnin. And he opened up down that road, just runnin. Had left all his groceries and everything. And Henry Thomas, he hollered at him, "Come back here, Bill." Come back and get your stuff!" "By God," say, "who is it?" "That's all right, you know me. Come back and get your stuff, man. What kind of man are you? Got a family and that scary." "By God. I wasn't scary. I just did that see what you goin to say." Well he had run, Henry say, a hundred yards or more.

One night I went out to Unionville and a way back cousin and I was together. And this fella, his half brother, had taken the same name, but he wasn't a Roberts, he was somethin else. The same mother. So we was down here at the Hall, was entertainment there. So this fella, I think he was stayin over to Copperville, and he walked from Copperville with a girl and he asked his brother would he take him to Copperville when he got ready to go home. And say, "I'll give you a dollar and a half." And we was standin there talkin and after a while he come along and said, "Well," say, "you ready to take me?" This fella said, "If you ready to pay me." Said, "But you've got to pay me before I leave here." "Well, I'll pay you." Pulled out fifty cents, he give him. Fella said, "No, you said you'd give me a dollar and a half." "No I didn't. No I didn't." So he turned around to me. He said, "Didn't he say he'd give me a dollar and a half?" I said, "Yeah, that's what he told you." And he walked up to me and grabbbed me, my shirt collars was fasten, he stuck a finger in there and twist it and he cut my wind. And I hit him and looked for him to hit me again and he was layin down to my feet in the road. I knocked him down! Wasn't sure I'd knocked him down. I looked for him to hit him again. Well, he had disappeared. I looked, he was layin on the ground. That's the onliest fight I had after I growed up. I'd always tried to keep away from that kind.

They used to have camp meetins regular in these woods. Out by Dixontown that used to be a big camp meetin ground. And then just out of Easton on Dover Road used to have a big camp meetin there in the woods. And down to Ivory Town. Them was big ones. And then it was one up here in

Queen Annes. They used to call it Joe Georgia's Camp or Wye Camp. And they had a camp there for years and they used to come from New York, Philadelphia, Baltimore, and further away than that. Hundreds of em, they tell me. I was never to that one. I think the old man used to own the woods and started the camp. I think his name was Joe Georgia. Because he left it in his will for colored people to have a camp there just as long as it was a ground there. The white people there, they camped first and then the colored had theirs. For years and years that was one of the biggest ones around but I never went there. When I got grown it was pretty near over. And there used to be a big one to Ridgely.

Some of em there'd kill you as quick as they look at you. And said women used to fight just the same as men did. I heard after I got larger, was talkin up here to Wye Camp, said they sold whiskey. Said the way they did they carried a barrel of whiskey down in the woods, set it down square and bust the head of it. Dip down there with dipper and pour it in your bottle. I don't believe that. They were more careful with it than that bunch was cause whiskey used to cost.

I always went to Dixon Wood Camp. Mr. Dixon gave the Unionville people the privilege to have the camp in his woods. And when automobiles started, well, he cut it out. Stopped em. And a good thing he did. God knows how many would've got killed if he'd kept it up.

One time I got scared there, though. We went down to Glebe Road, nother fellow and I, Walter Moore, he was from Royal Oak. We walked down and saw a bunch of people. And we stood there and talked and waited and thought it'd been an accident, somebody had come to the camp ground. And nobody come up, so we decided to walk down there. And when we walked down there they was shootin crap. That ring was pretty near across the road. And then we stopped there and both got pretty close to it and was a fellow ahead of me they was on their knees and he was on his knees and they had the money down and he'd reach over there to take some of the money. And this other fellow he didn't have but I think was a nickel down there. Said, "Mister, don't pick that money up." He kept on easin his hand. "Mister," said, "I told you not to pick that money up. Pick it up," say, "and I'm goin to leave your fingers workin on the ground." And I didn't pay much attention to him. Neither did this other fellow. So when he got it in his hand I heard this pistol go off right alongside of me. And he shot him through one of his fingers. And then he had to get away from there. And he got a fellow that he knowed from Ivory Town. Both of them from Ivory Town, this fellow had a horse and carriage. And this fellow carried him up the road and he was gone from Easton for years and years. And come back. And the man got shot didn't even have him arrested. He didn't have to run. Because the man he shot in the hand he was sellin whiskey, and he was afraid to have him arrested.

This Moore fellow and I, I turned around when the pistol went off and looked for him, I didn't see him. And I got halfway, more than halfway to the entrance to the camp ground, I met him comin back. I said, "Where you been?" "Oh," say, "I've been standin up here behind that tree." And we'd both left down the road together. And he so often laughed about it. Said he run never stopped runnin till he got in around got behind a big tree.

I know a man, he had bought a new Model T, cost him around three hundred dollars then. And he was carrying people from the camp ground down to Miles River Bridge and back for fifteen cents. And he would bring people from Easton to the camp ground, mostly his family, he put them out, and he would do that for hours. And compared with the wages you make today he was makin right good salary. Fifteen cents apiece. He had made more money than the average years before that as a young man. He was a grain-measurer in Baltimore. You was good at it you'd get good pay. And he saved his money.

But they used to fight down there at Ivory Town. I went down there one Sunday night after some people had got left down there. Person carried em say they couldn't go after em. Couldn't bring em back. Yeah, they got me to go down to get em and I carried another fellow with me. That used to be a tough place. I worked with a white man that lived in that neighborhood that time, I mean come up from that neighborhood, and he said he used to go up there and they was fightin till one, two o'clock in the mornin. Said and he'd be right in the bunch with em. He give me a set of steel knuckles. I asked him did he ever hit anybody with them steel knuckles, said, "Yeah."

I kind of slowed down after I got married; well, I never cared much for em. You could go and do right and then get in trouble. And some people went for the preaching and singin and some people went just to be in the crowd. And I was one of the ones that went just to look and see and be in the crowd. And meetin people. I know I met a young fellow from Royal Oak. Seemed to be very nice. Come from a real respectable family. And the first time I saw and know who he was out Dixon Woods. I guess about a month after that he got killed. Man shot him. And that man went away, spent, I believe, thirty years, I believe, and come back. Served that time and come back.

And was just as mean after he come back as he was fore he went. He lived between Bellview and Royal Oak. Somebody made him mad down there one Sunday mornin, went home and got a double-barrel shotgun and shot right in the house. Put one eye out. I don't know what they ever did with him. I saw him in Easton and had never seen him before. That was a circus or carnival. Somethin about him I noticed I couldn't keep my eyes off him. I said somethin bout that man, that man ain't right. And I got a chance and I asked somebody, asked his name. Said, "Will Thomas." Said, "That's that bad nigger. He'll kill you." But didn't nobody bother with him.

Easton, that's the place they used to have fights. On Saturday nights, some of em walked to Easton and several of em would start walkin, somebody would pick em up that did have a horse. But I kept away from that bunch, much as I possibly could. Graham's Alley was the place. I was a man grown and married some time before I ever was through Graham's Alley. I've heard a fella told me they'd been right in they called it a road, didn't call it a street, shootin crap in a circle. Man wanted to come through there with a team, he'd have to turn around and go back. Some of em would tell him, "Go back, you've got no business through here." And them that did go through there, or attempt to go through there, they knowed what it was and they wouldn't put up no argument. No, it was no place of mine. Maybe somebody out there may have been sellin whiskey. They used to do that out there, Speak-easy, they called em. It used to be several of them in Easton. God knows how many.

I know one old man they say sold whiskey there for years and years. That was old man Ned Rogers. He had picked people. The people over here could go there and buy it, older men, no boys. I remember one time, there was something about him selling whiskey and he went to this man's store on Market Space. Somebody had spoke of him sellin whiskey. And he said, "No," said, "I fought and helped em make the United States like it is now and then you accuse me of sellin whiskey." This other old man, white man, said, "Yeah," say, "he sells whiskey." And Jim Moaney told him, "You better shut your mouth." Say, "That old man will hurt you." And it scared this other man. He never said another word.

But they played a trick on him. That was the time that you couldn't get but a gallon a month. Old man Rogers, somebody warned him about comin to Easton, that was watchin the place. So he had his to come to Bloomfield and somebody notified the sheriff. So he went down there and he got this jug, it was two gallons, and there was the sheriff and deputy there, and he thought somethin was up. Well, he got on the train and they got on and he went to the next coach and got off. And they went searchin for him. They searched, they thought he had gone further up, and then the train pulled off and they couldn't get off. And I think he made it that time. And then was another time, he had it to come to Easton Point. And one side of the road, it was a corn field, and he got up there and two men come out and one struck him and knocked him out and got his jug. Actually knocked the old man out and got his two gallons of whiskey! And the law never got him. Then he got killed. Killed him and took his money. And after he collected that money he should've put it in the bank, but they had heard talk of knockin a person out, robbin him, they hit him too hard and killed him.

And some things they couldn't do any worse in the South. We had a sheriff, he took a buffalo robe out of somebody carriage and he didn't like this colored man, and he carried it to his house. And told this man the chicken house. And the man got dressed and stopped in the yard and he asked him bout this buffalo robe, and the colored man told him that he didn't know nothin about it. "Yes, yes, you do. I knew you got it because I saw you." He say, "I follow you. And you hid it around here someplace." And he went to chicken house and took the buffalo robe out of the chicken house. And he say this colored man goed in chicken house. That's where he was keepin it. And they sent that man away. And he had a young fellow with him, young fellow told somebody, and it was good white people got hold of it, and got this colored man out. Now he had to leave his family, had served some of his time for nothin. But they didn't do nothin with the sheriff. Looked like they'd take his job away from him if they didn't do worse than that. So they couldn't do any worse than that in the South. And all that happened up around Longwoods.

And one time, this Callahan man did me a favor on the fairground in Easton. It was a store opened in Easton and they was advertising, and then they had money in balloons. Somebody said it was two dollars and a half in the balloon in money. And if you caught one of the balloons, of course you could have the money. And we all was watchin for em come over and they had men there, I guess there was four or five of em. Tall men with canes. Time you think it was comin down in your hands, they'd hit on and she'd go up again. And I was in the bunch and everybody was just scramblin. And there was an old white lady, I bumped into her and she got up and reared and the white ones was lookin at her and lookin at me. And that Mr. Callahan say, "That man," say, "is innocent." Say, "A person of her age had no business in the bunch." Say, "He didn't do it intentionally." And I think he saved me from havin a lot of trouble. And she was gettin ready to raise the devil. I guess they'd of locked me up for that. And he said, "Well," say, "woman, you got no business in here." Say, "Your age, you can't get out of the way. What you doin in this bunch? That man wouldn't have run into you if he could help it." And that was the one thing saved me. And I didn't knock her down or anything. Just hit her, not very hard, just light. But she was getting ready to raise the devil.

Old man Callahan, he was a drinker. Still I believe he had a good heart in his body, it wasn't him. Well, he got drunk and he had firey horses and a horse run away with him. And the road passed this colored man's place. It had a little turn, and this colored man, Teats was his name, had a hog pen that was built on his land but right on a turn, and the horses hit the hog pen and tore one side out and turned the hog out. They say he got his neck broke. Callahan died right there. And they say the colored man killed him. And he told them, "No," say, "I didn't touch him." And then they had it, they can put anything in the paper, that this man killed him for tearin his hog pen down. Didn't want the disgrace that he was drunk and the horse got away with him. So they had the trial here in Easton. Colored fellow's lawyer got up and told the jury that it wasn't right. He said, "It ain't no colored man goin to kill a white man unless he really have to do it." And in this case, didn't say he fussed with him. And they was gettin ready to lynch this colored man after he cleared him. And his lawyer cleared him, but he made enemies by clearin him. And told him, said, "Now the best thing you can do," say, "I don't believe you did kill him," say, "if you had, I wouldn't have taken the case." Say, "But someone always believe that you killed him," say, "and the thing for you to do is sell what you got and get away from here. Stay a while, then come back when it blow over." The man went away, I think he went over to Delaware. I guess he stayed twenty years, for nothin. I was a young man the time they had Teats' trial.

And years ago, two white fellows caught this colored fellow layin down drunk and they castrate him. And then went off laughin about it. That was near Longwoods. I remember hearin old people talk about it. That was before I was grown.

Part IV

I got married in 1908. Before I got married we was livin to Chestnut Lane. My wife lived by Hopewell. Place, years after that, I bought it. My wife's single name was Mary Jackson. Unionville was what she called home and the mother called home. They call her mother Sally. Her mother had two brothers, Dan Gibson and Charles Gibson. And Sally's mother was the one they call Aunt Easter. They named her Easter because she was born on Easter's Day in slave-time. And Charles Gibson, he built a house in Unionville. After his death, my wife's mother fell heir to it.

My wife's father come here to Tunis Mills from Virginia. He wasn't old enough to be in the Civil War. But he was big enough and old enough to drive cattle, for they said he was in the bunch that drove a big bunch of cattle from Richmond, Virginia, further down south. And said how they passed Staunton, they was three days makin the trip, and when they come back, some them houses had been shot all through, looked like with cannons.

And then some years after that, after he got about grown, they built a railroad that run pretty much the same place that county road run. And they cut through the hills to level the roads they puttin in. And there was a colored man and a white man plowin around this hill. They was plowin round and round and after awhile say the colored man, "Hello," say, "looky here, look at this. Look at this. Wonder who put this here. Look at this." The white man was ahead of him; he stopped and went back. And the white man pulled off his hat. "Boy," say, "somebody's put this here. Don't know who put it." And he was pickin up money, say, with both hands. Says when the colored man got ready to pick up, he got two or three pieces. White man had picked up all the rest of it. And helpin this colored man out to holler about who put it there. And they say the money was in a stone jar and the plow hit it and burst the jar. And they tell me that's what they did Civil War where they was fightin or goin to fight, they'd buried their valuables, most of their money.

I always said I wouldn't get married when I was younger. I was raised down to Rieman's and some of em get to kiddin about different cooks they had and marrying. I told em I never was goin to get married. But anythin will change. They say a wise man will change his mind and a fool never will. And we decided to get married, didn't ask anybody. It was up to me. The old people used to say, if I made my bed hard, I was the one that had to lay in it. That's what they used to use, that word, when they didn't interfere. And still, I say, don't you want somebody be the judge for you, be your own judge. And if it makes it bad bein your own judge then you've got nobody to blame but yourself. There are some things that you feel about that your parents don't know nothin about. And I know cases where the parents had run the woman down or the man down, he ain't this, he ain't the other. Well, that's the wrong thing to do. Sometime put two people together like that, they gets along good together because a lot of em got intelligent enough have studied each other.

And I was just lookin for somebody could get along with, cook for me, keep my clothes clean. And principle. I've known several men that get somebody on their looks and then find out the looks was all they had. I was old enough to see or know what had happened to so many of em when they get one of that kind. They want em, somebody else want em and lots of times the other fellow get em. Principle is the best thing. And we come up in the same neighborhood.

Then at that time, I was workin on the far down to Marengo and I keep on workin. I workin by the day, got about a dollar and a quarter. Will Hall, the owner, was over at the western shore on Severn River then. And the old man, sometime he was contrary, couldn't nobody get along with him. But he used to get the most of his help from a place here where the immigrants come over from other countries. And he'd put a word in for so many men and he'd get em, and very seldom one of em stayed two months. At this time, old man Chris Kirsch was German manager he had.

And old man Kirsch told me not to have any weddin, said, "You'll need that to live on." He said, "The way times are now, you'll need all you can get to live on." Say, "Don't have any weddin, and I'll give you a hog for a present." And he give me a hog. But I didn't have any idea to have no weddin. I didn't ask him his opinion. I was goin to do just like I did do. I wasn't weak enough in the head to need him to tell me about that, cause I know my own circumstances of gettin along. And I didn't have any weddin. I think it was three or four in the family. Just had a little somethin for the ones that was invited, and I didn't invite them.

We got married in that big old white house right on the corner in Germantown. That's where the preacher named Richard Stepney was livin. I don't guess nobody ever knowed we going to get married, exceptin them that was there. Mother did, I think. Stepfather didn't. The only thing I got was a half a gallon or a gallon of whiskey. That's the only thing I bought.

I got the license at the courthouse. I answered the questions and got the license. I know one thing they asked me: Was she a man or a woman? That's the time I got mad. I asked, "What in the devil you think I was going to marry, a man?" And it wasn't necessary to ask me such a question like that. And he laughed and never said no more. That was the clerk of Talbot County Court. His name was Henry Hollyday. But I didn't like such questions asked to me. I figured if that'd been a white person he wouldn't never have asked a question like that. I was gettin ready to lay him out right there in the courthouse.

When I got married, my mother was livin to Chestnut Lane. They moved that year to Millerstown. They tore that house at Chestnut Lane down soon as they got out of it. And that's the time that they took all that land then and turned into the farm. That was leased land. There was two more houses there. They was tore down. And all the land went back into the farm again. The house my mother was in, it was just somethin to go in out of the rain or cold. The commonest house I ever lived in. And we went there, it was runnin away with chinches. We didn't have any chinches before we went there. It was a house put up with straight up and down boards and wide boards. And if they had any underpinnin they'd just settled in the ground over where the cats used to go under. That was a cold house. The kitchen was so cold until the coldest spell, mother couldn't cook in it.

And then mother and stepfather built a house back of Millerstown. He bought three acres of ground and built that house. They lived back off'n the main road, was the onliest house back there. When I moved to Millerstown, they were right back of where I was livin. I think he was still oysterin and doin other days work. Winter time, lots of time, he cut cordwood for somebody.

I lived in with my in-laws after I got married. They lived round Hopewell. Stayed with them nine months until I found a house around where I wanted. My own mother, they didn't have the room, they had more children. And the house that my mother-in-law and father-in-law lived in was a better house. I know my wife would've rather been with her people, had to spend more time with her people than I would have to spend home there. I wasn't home every day.

There were bout six head of us in the house. We had one bedroom and the parents had the other bedroom. The other children, they was in the other room, too. That house was in good shape then. Wasn't made well but it wasn't rotten. My wife's father stayed there I guess three years. They worked for Dr. Lowndes. He went up around the house that time. He was getting a right good age on him and doctor didn't want him to go on the farm. The old lady, she used to cook there. And then years after that when they left there, they went down to the Willows. And when they left there, they rent to Copperville. That's where the old man died. We was livin in Hopewell. She died later when we was out in Unionville.

And I worked and try to get somethin together to start housekeepin. When I thought I had enough to make out with, I moved out. I was glad to get out. Got out soon as I could. Soon as I was able, like a child walk—soon as I was able to walk, got out. I didn't think it was the thing to do to stay there and have them cramped up like that, anyway. And then I figured it better for us to live to ourself. I was workin by the day most the time and most the time I was workin where I could get my meals. When I was workin at the Halls by the day I got my meals there. And I went where I could get a house to rent. If you ain't got no house, you go where you can get one.

We moved to Millerstown and rent Dobson house. I bought an old sofa from Dobson, and it had been wore out about ten years before I bought it. Bought myself a nice cook stove. It was dirty, greasy. I never see any worse. Whenever I home a rainy day or somethin like that, I'd clean on that stove.

My mother was just a stone's throw from where I lived, but didn't make a practice of goin to visit. They had children big enough to work and help em that wasn't married. In the summer time, I'd go fishin or crabbin. I had more than we'd need, I'd always give my mother some of em. But I never got that far back I had to go to her to get any food. I could've got it through the store without any money at all but I didn't want to do that. And only seldom ever got anything there that I didn't pay for. And some have come to me for help and none of em had a family, not as large a family as mine. And I know all of em didn't pay me back, but was some. They'd take what they did make and throw it away, drink it up. And I should've told em what the ant told the grasshopper. See, the ant worked every day in the week. And winter come, the grasshopper went to the ant and asked for somethin to eat that winter, and the ant ask him what did he do in the summer. He say, "Fiddled all the summer." So the ant told him, "Well, if you fiddled all the summer," say, "now you dance all the winter." And didn't let him have it. That was old joke the old people had. Ant will work just as hard Sundays as he will any other day, layin up stuff. I've loaned em money and my wife give em food.

When I was livin at Dobson house, I had hogs and chickens. That's where I was when I first started raisin Chesapeake dogs. And I had a garden. My wife got a day's work now and then, fifty cents a day or somethin like that. Not over a day a week. But I could always find something to do. Gunnin season, I'd kill a lot of my own meat. Summer time, I'd get a lot of crabs and fish. You had to do it them days to live. I've sold a many a dozen soft crabs, thirty-six cents a dozen. When we lived round by Hopewell, one time there I had four or five nets. I used to go out and it was mostly rock that used to sell, but I'd get a little basket full of rocks and go to Easton and sell em. Times was tight then.

I paid Charles Dobson about three dollars a month rent. When I left Millerstown I didn't owe Dobson nothin. Dobson was livin down the Neck, adjoinin place to the Willows, and he was drivin for Mr. Warden. They used to sell you a car then, they'd furnish a man for so many days to teach whoever was going to drive it. And Dobson had had a man over the time, and old man Warden said to the man one evenin when he come in there, ask him how was Charles makin out. "I can't teach him. He'll never learn. I can't teach him how to drve." And Mr. Warden told him, "Well," say, "if you can't teach him and he can't learn I don't want the car. It's no good to me. I can't drive, my wife can't drive." Man say, "I'll try a few days more." He come back in two days and old man Dobson was drivin. I never had a bit of trouble. Only one thing, I had to get used to turnin like in a gate, slowin up enough. And I don't remember ever havin my hand on a car wheel until that day.

And it wasn't long before I could do some work on the motor, cause I got a little book—several things it taught. And wasn't as much to do on a motor them days. Wasn't no starter them days, you cranked em. The onliest thing that puzzled me, when your magneto wasn't just right or you had three A batteries under the back seat, and I didn't know what. Nobody told me. And I'd been down here like I was goin to Marengo or some place for em for something, and stopped, then I went to start it. Well, she wouldn't start. You had a switch or somethin that run to the dash switch. You had a wire run to the dash switch from the batteries, and I looked around. I found that switch and put it on the batteries, and she jumped right off. But it worried me for some time. And nobody had never told me bout how to start it. Then after that I begin to learn lots of little things about it. I remember one time she got runnin on three cylinders, and carried to the garage and we got in there that mornin around half past nine. And they fooled and messed with that thing until a few minutes of five o'clock. And I watched this fella and he took two wrenches and locked these nuts. "Now," said, "try her." Started up. She drop oil just the same and he did that, put them hours in to make that money. That's what it was. He knowed what it was at first. She drop oil just the same.

I worked different jobs and did just the common work. Did some work on the Miles River Bridge. And I worked for a bridge builder. Never built a bridge, but he built wharfs. And then we had a big job down here at Hope. Mr. Starr had a big wharf built in Lloyds Creek. And we drove double row piles. Then you had to wind that hammer up by hand. Now that was a job! And I've thought about it, seem like they always workin me to a disadvantage. I never did have anybody on my side helpin to wind the hammer. But lots of times, it wouldn't be the same man on the other side, they'd put somebody over there with him to help him to wind. Well, I was able then. Before I was seventeen years old, wasn't grown, and could and did shoulder two hundred pounds of fertilizer. There was men standin there with chin whiskers that couldn't do it.

I worked down the Neck to Mudge's place for contractors. I walked from Millerstown down there night and mornin. And I walked the spring and the whole summer and the whole fall cause I didn't stop until December. And we was stopped in December and at that time the muscles in my legs was so hard until you just could dent em.

Them was rough years. It was no work to do. The most work was just come to seasons like cuttin corn, wood cuttin in the winter and you might get a job in between that, but you didn't get nothin for it. The wages went up gradually when the strange people begin to come in. Mostly come from the North. And the ones here kept the wages down as much as they could. Course they'd tell the people what they was payin but some of em didn't pay any attention to it.

And 1913, I was doin days work. And Mr. Arringdale spoke for me, he picked me out of the bunch. I told him, "Yeah, I didn't have no job." The old man, he thought was nobody like Joe. Say, "He's able." And one day he had been sittin on the porch and I was doin somethin to the hedge each side of the lane. And I never thought about him watchin me. And I don't know whether that evenin or the next day he said to me, "Joe," say, "you keep steady goin." Say, "I was lookin at you; you keep steady goin." Say, "You don't rush and run," say, "but you keep steady goin." And you go to work for him, you had to work. Then after he got acquainted with me, he wanted me to chauffeur for him. Asked whether I'd like the job. He was a hard old man. He left here and went to North Carolina, and that's where he started his first mill. He come back, he was gone twenty some years, and just throwed it away. When he died, he had nothin—owed nothin.

I chauffeured for him for couple or three months. It was too confinin. I goin up to the house in the mornin before half past eight and wouldn't get back the next morning until four and five o'clock in the mornin. I was all night with him. He'd be out drinkin. We'd always stop in Easton. Well, I parked up there front of the courthouse. There'd always be a car, he'd get in with some other men. Then his buddies, I don't know, may have talked to em before, that's where they'd pick him up. Then they'd be out all night long. Went with some of his friends that he knowed before he went down south when he's a young man. I don't know where they went. And I had to stay right with that car all the time. That's what made it bad for you, to leave and tell me he wouldn't be back for such and such a time, why, it wouldn't have been so bad.

I remember one night was right there in front of the courthouse, and he come past, was comin past and slowed up and call me, say, "I'll be back in a few minutes." And then I guess it was two or three o'clock and he never come back until about two o'clock that mornin. And I'd stand around all that time. They'd go from place to place. That night there was four head of em in this car. And Dr. Hardcastle, he was the driver, he was the head of it. That was one of Mr. Arringdale's friends before he left here. And Colonel Tilghman, he was one of em, too. Out several nights like that. And he wouldn't tell me anythin about when he expect to be ready and I'd have to stand by that car and sit in it all that time.

We went down to Tilghman in 1914. The timber on Poplar Island was supposed to be for sale. We drove down there and parked the car and went down there where the oystermens kept their boats. Got a man to carry us out to Poplar Island. It ain't far from Tilghman's Island. So we went to Poplar Island and the old man looked all around and he had his secretary with him, Mr. Edens, he looked all around. So they got ready to go back, they come to the boat. I still stayed in the boat that carried em. And when they got on the shore, got back, Mr. Arringdale ask the man the boat belonged to if was any place that could get anything to eat down here. The man told him, "Yes, sir. Yes, sir." Say, "Place up there you can get nice food, boardin house." And they walked on and I was almost walkin on old man Arringdale's heels cause they was lookin at me hard. He went there and showed the place. There was a big porch and they asked this woman could these men get something to eat chere. She told em, "Yes, indeed. All they want." "Well," said, "this is my chauffer. Could he get something to eat chere?" "Oh yes," said, "he can get somethin to eat chere, too." And they fix the place, old man Eden and Mr. Arringdale went in the house. And on this porch concern was a table. And I got a chair and set down and she brought the food out there nice dinner. I ate it. I was still scared. That Tilghman's Island was bad place.

I give up chaufferin. I don't remember what I was gettin when I was chauffeurin. It wasn't the workin, the drivin, but just too confinin. Kept me away from my family too much. I didn't get the time that I would like with my family, and I don't believe that's the way to raise a family. The old man didn't fall out with me. And some of em was sayin that he had fired me. To show them that he hadn't, well, I went right down to the saw mill and went to work. Cause if he had fired me he wouldn't want me down at the saw mill. And he was tickled. And his boss down there said when he heard that I was comin there to work. I had worked for him on the farm by the day the year before that. And then I worked down on the farm, I think it was around ten years, by the day. Startin in bout April and work all April all the rest of the spring and all the summer up until in December and we got the corn and everything in. The saw-mill bunch was rough. Them days was knife and razors. I never thought about any protection carryin either a pistol or a knife. I wouldn't carry one because I was afraid if I did I'd use it and get myself in trouble. I was workin down at Second Point, Mr. Arringdale's saw mill. He had several of em from down south, colored, and one had some trouble with another one there. And asked me did I have a left-handed wheeler. I didn't know that they had had a fuss. I told him, "No." I did tell him I didn't know what it was. He said it was a pistol. Said she breaks to the left. Arringdale got the help from down south and some of them was criminals when they come up here. Cause that fellow that asked me for a left-hand wheeler, he got into some trouble here, down at the saw mill and then when they had the trial up here, Easton, they asked him where was he from and people from here in Easton wrote down there and asked em was he ever in any trouble there. They did that before his sentencin, and they got a call back. They told the people here they had been lookin for him, say, "He killed a man down here." Say, "We've been lookin for him for three years." So they sent up here and got him.

So you had all them kind of people when you got that bunch from down south here. I never had any trouble with them but I wouldn't let one come in my house. Never invite one to my house, but you workin with em you have to talk with em. Had two sawyers, I believe, and the head man they boarded in Tunis Mills. And the head man went from here to North Carolina. Lot of people do stroll.

Old man Arringdale had the largest saw mill in Wilmington, North Carolina. And down there he tell me they was rough on them colored men. Some of em would treat em like dogs. I heard old man Arringdale said he didn't believe in it. He said one time he was to a place down there they call a boardin house, and he was goin somewhere and he stopped there to get his breakfast and while he was there was two men come in talkin and laughin and spoke of the nigger that they had lynched the night before. And they had to order the fellow's father to get out of there. And one of the fellows spoke of it and the one said, "Well," say, "he's out to the station now, I saw him waitin for the train." Say, "Let's go and get him!" And old man Arringdale said he slipped his pistol out of his pocket and laid it on the opposite side. And old man Arringdale said, "Well it's a damn common shame, you killed the man's son and ordered him from here, and he's gettin out as fast as he can. Common shame to go up there and lynch that man haven't done nothin." One of the fellows got bad and got up to the table to come to old man Arringdale. Old man Arringdale said he reached out and got that pistol, said, "You son-of-a-bitch, I dare you to make another step." Said they went out of there, both of em like a scared dog, tail between their legs. He said they only did that because they had the advantage and everything in their way.

There's one fellow worked at saw mill told me that him and another fellow was trampin, coming to a place up above Longwoods. Said and they saw this man and boy was wrestlin over somethin. One said to the other, "What's boy doin fightin his father?" And come to find out they was wrestlin over a gun. The boy wanted the gun. They got in hearin distance and the boy said, "Give me the gun, Pa." Say, "You told me you were goin to let me shoot the next nigger that come along here." And I said, "What did you do?" Said, "We evaporated!" They went down in the swamp. He said that was the truth.

And another fellow he said that him and another fellow, they'd been trampin several days. Said and they was on the road and they looked and saw a well that had one of them old draw buckets through it. And this fellow said, "We can get some water here." And this other fellow said, "You better not go in there." "Well, they won't mind us gettin a drink of water." Said, "Well, I ain't goin in there." Said and he slacked up on the road. And he went in there. And they used to have a wheel, would squeak sometime. He drawed the bucket forward, got a dipper to get a drink. A little girl come to the door, "Oh, Mama," say, "come here, come here quick!" Say, "What is that thing out chere at the well?" The girl's mother come out looked. She said, "Oh," say, "that's a nigger." Said and the other fellow got scared then but kept on drinkin. The husband, he was plowin in the field and he stopped and come up there a runnin. Asked him what he was doin in there. Told him, "Mister, I just stopped to get a drink of water. We ain't had no water today." "Well come on, I'll give you a drink of water." Said he took one of his mules out and hooked him up with the other mule and plowed him two days like that and then let him go. Course, I believed that'd be a lie, though.

Some people pick up anything, saw-mill bunch, stuff like that. It wouldn't be long before some of em they'd get to fightin, tear up thing. But I never believed in boarders. I never got a house that was too large anymore than that we need. I never did invite one of em to my house. I've had them right out on the road. Some people they had all of em in there.

If I had been takin them people in, associated with em, I wouldn't have been as much thought of down Tunis Mills. And that was my headquarters. For years I didn't do much sociatin out in Unionville. My place was Tunis Mills. I spent 90 percent of my time there at Tunis Mills, summer and winter, sociatin with all the young men—Chas Griffin, Jake Tull, Raymond Tull, Howard Hessey, Councell Blake. I started from a little boy down there. And then Clayton Griffin had the store ever since he was a boy and we was boys together.

I've had white people—fellow from Tunis Mills—drop in for a while. Sit down and talk. One time, it was Christmas Day, one of my friends start passin, walkin, and I saw him and went out to the road and talked with him, and we talked there some time and I asked him would he have a drink. He said, "Yeah, I haven't had one this Christmas." Say, "I come from Oxford on the train and I'm on my way home." We went in and sat down and takin a drink. Set there a while and then he got up to go. I told him to take another one out of the bottle in a glass. He took another one. Then we went outdoor, went out to the road, and we talk there a while. I saw somebody comin I didn't want in my house, and I touched him, then we left and went in the house. I wasn't thinkin about him takin another drink. Dogged if he didn't take another one, and he stop there in the mornin and when he left, was that afternoon. He respect my home. That would be different from some of em. And he wasn't say drunk. It had taken effect on him, but it wasn't causin not helpless drunk. And somebody told his uncle about him bein up to my house and his uncle come after him. First he told his uncle, say, "I'll be home directly." After a while, he did get in and he went home.

All they had Tunis Mills was a good class. Just one in a while maybe some would be a family of lower class get there. And then they wouldn't be there long because they couldn't associate with the others. That was one thing about Tunis Mills far back in my day, and my parents speak of it's been a decent little place. And if you wasn't decent, you wouldn't pay much attention to you. And I guess that'd make a person feel bad and they get out. Course, when that mill was runnin it ballooned, you had all kind of class, and especially in colored. I went Tunis Mills night and day when I wasn't doing anything, mostly to the store. We used to have a little whiskey drinkin, but none of em was bad about it. And I was treated just like one of the boys. And then as a rule lots of things they'd want to know, they'd come to me and ask me about em. Or they'd have an argument about somethin, think I'd know. I'd go down there and they'd get together and try to settle it. I took readin newspapers up in 1914. Before that I read sport magazines. It wasn't many poor people know what they was.

Others wasn't respected like I was respected. By women and men. Then I've heard some of the coloreds, men, say that, "I wouldn't go always stuck around white people like you are." And kept that up until one night made me mad down at the store down the road. I told em, I said, "If you could be, you'd be the same as I am and then you wouldn't have sense enough to handle it like I am." And I think that cut it out. I never heard no more. Who wouldn't want to better their condition? I told him there wasn't one that wouldn't be glad to be able to do it.

After I got married, went housekeepin, that's the time I spent ninety percent of my time Tunis Mills. If I didn't get there in day time, I'd be there at night. And if I had days that I wasn't doin anything, I spent the most of them days Tunis Mills. I did that for years. And used to spend time with Clayton Griffin. Clayton and I come up boys together. Played together. At one time was two stores in Tunis Mills. One when the mill was runnin, was down near saw mill. When the saw mill shut down, why, they didn't do as much business because wasn't goin down there like they was before.

Clayton uncle had the store down by the saw mill. And man named Todd had the store up on the corner where you turn straight down to the bridge. Lot of em deal to both stores. And then with some of the old ones, you couldn't keep them away from the store that was down by the mill. Cause they'd been dealin there since that been a store there. And Clayton wasn't strong and Clayton people figured he wasn't able to do any hard work. And they bought that store and put him in that store at sixteen years old and he stayed there until he died.

Clayton was very good to me. All exceptin one time that I know of. Had a what they used to call a punch board, there with a watch on it. Had a little thing little larger than a match stick and they had little rows of paper put in those, look like honeycomb. Board was made that way. And you punch the one out that you want and open it and it had a number on it. And I used to go in and ask for it. Did several time. I want to see how many more that had to punch out and was left on there, and he'd get the board and show it to me, and I went there, I guess I call for it three or four times at different times, and had gone down to sixteen that many times. And I punched the one with the number. And he put the board back. And I thought it was somethin funny down that low and he had put the board back. I didn't say nothin. Wouldn't accuse im, but some years after that, his sister son told me about it and ask me not to tell him. Say, "You won that watch."

And I don't know whether year or two years, the store burnt down, and he never carried the watch home, and burnt the watch up. And we was speakin about his store burnin down and the nephew say, "Well," say, "Uncle Clayton," say, "did you dirty!" He say, "It come home to him." Say, "You lost the watch and he has lost hundreds of dollars." And I told him, I said, "Well, I wouldn't have said anything if he had told me before," say, "Because he had been good to me." And he had. I remember he had boots, felts, and the government put out a whole lot of stuff after the War. Say he couldn't sell these, and he wasn't going to have it layin around. Said, "I'm goin give it to you," said, "you can sell it." I think it was eighteen pair boots and felts, and I sold em. And every year, used to have a house cleanin. And it was a lot of things he'd give me.

That was the onliest time I knowed Clayton ever got anything off of me. He may've got things off somebody else. Charge em too much. Well, he did that to John Flamer, but John Flamer didn't count after him. John Flamer had too much belief in him. But the old people say, "Praise the bridge that carry you over and let somebody else sink. Praise the bridge that carries you over if he lets somebody else down." They don't shoot down the person for mistreatin somebody else if they treat you right.

I used to go around with Chas Griffin, fellow had a store down here at Tunis Mills. It was the onliest work he ever did do. But he wasn't no rich man. And him and I was boys together. And he said to me one day, "Joe," say, "you know why I like to have you around?" I said, "No." Said, "You are not always beggin for somethin," say, "and I know if you ever ask for anything, you need it." And I got to studyin. I said, "Yes, that will make you unwelcome lots of places, you goin round people beggin." And he done as much or more than any poor person ever done for me, but I never asked him for nothin.

But Chas carried me down Tilghman Island one night, that was November 1913. And that was the night that Jake Tull, that was Chas first cousin, had been to my house and told my wife I say he could get my rabbit dog. And wife didn't know any different, and she let him have the dog. When I come home that night, cause I was cuttin corn, I look for my rabbit dog. Didn't see her and I asked my wife where was she, and she told me Jake Tull had been there and told her I said he could get the rabbit dog. That made me mad. I didn't eat. I'd been cuttin and carryin corn all that day. I went right down to Tunis Mills to get the dog and get after Jake. But I got down there Jake couldn't be found. I went down to his father's store. They hadn't seen him for a long time so I was gettin ready to come home when Chas come along in his car and he come in the store. I believe he got gas. "Sutton," say, "you want to take a ride?" I said, "No, I haven't ate my supper." He say, "We won't be gone long." And they had to go around by Longwoods then in an automobile or a team and we left and we was talkin. I was doin a lot of talk then. I said to myself, Chas going to town after some liquor down to the express office. We used to have somethin drink right often. We got into Easton. I was figurin he was goin to stop there to get his jug or bottle or whatever it come in, and he went right on. And I say, he ain't going to the express office. Didn't ask him no questions. I say, he's going to Bloomfield. Used to be a train station there. Got down to Bloomfield, up the Bloomfield road, God, he never slacked up. I say, I don't know what it is. Said to myself, he couldn't get his boat motor started and that's why he's goin to St. Michaels. I said, "I haven't had any supper and I've been workin hard." "Keep still, set still. You'll be all right."

God, we got up to St. Michaels and went on through St. Michaels. When we got through, I said, "Look here, where in the devil you carryin me?" "Hey, sit still," say, "you ridin all right, ain't you? You're comfortable?" I said, "No, I'm not comfortable. But I want to know where you carryin me." Then I was talkin about this dog and he told me, "Don't worry about that dog." Say, "There's a dog over to my house," say, "Jake brought it over to my house, fastened it up in old milk house." I thought that was a right dirty trick, could cause some trouble.

He carried me pretty near down to end of Tilghman's Island. Turned to his left, and went a distance down that road and stopped to a house, and where he was goin, he was goin to see his girl. Girl was schoolteacher down there. When we stopped there, I said, "Well, well, what'd you stop here for?" "That's all right," say, "you follow me." We went to the house and went on in and told the people that his girlfriend was boardin with, and they all them had a big laugh. He laughed about how he tricked me. I didn't have no laugh because I was about half mad. And Chas told em, said, "Sutton ain't had his supper." And the lady of the house went in the house and come out with three or four great big old hard keeper pears on a dish. Before they put it down, I thought it was something to eat. I didn't want one of them old keeper pears. Then she got some magazines and give me. She had kep me down there twelve o'clock. And I told im, I said, "I have a great mind make you stop and lick you." "No, Sutton," say, "you wouldn't do that." Say, "You wouldn't hit me and I wouldn't hit you." So I changed my mind then.

And fore we got down to Tilghman's Island, he was tellin me bout the boys down there, say they was goin to run him, say comin through there with that car makin a whole lot of noise, had a busted muffler on it. I say, "Well, if they do," I say, "I won't be no good to you against a whole bunch of boys." "Yes you will, yes you will. You set still." But we did see some standin on side of the street, but they didn't say anything.

Well, I wouldn't have been no help to him. I wouldn't go down there and jump on and fight them fellows in their home. I told him after that, "You wouldn't of had no help," I said. Because I'd of been like that fellow that years ago left a drug boat down there. They wouldn't let em go on shore. Kept food and tobacco and stuff like that for em. This fellow, he wanted to get ashore, and they was laying somewhere near Tilghmans Island. And after things got quiet, he took the yawl boat and went ashore. When he went ashore, that was at night, well he stayed in one place around the shore until it got light the next mornin. And the next mornin when it got light, he started and he met a man. He spoke to the man, said, "Mister, can you tell me sir where the colored people hang out down here?" Say, "Yes, sir, well," say, "that's where the last nigger hung that we caught on this island and you better get off'n here." That's the tale the fellow told after he got off. He got off from there.

I don't know what time we left Tilghmans Island cause we didn't get home till four o'clock. And then he got this dog and brought the dog and I both home. But that was all of it. I guess it was three or four days after that I saw Jake. I told Jake not to do it anymore. I said he can cause trouble between you and I and trouble between my wife. Then Jake commence laughin. He laughed so, and he got me to laughin. That was all of it. I couldn't say too much. They was better to me than they was to any other colored person. I said to myself, now, if I make a whole lot out of it, well, I'll lose some friends. And I'll just let it go so as I get my dog back.

I stayed in Charlie Dobson house for seven years. Went down to the Willows in 1915. A man owned it by the name of Durrance. He was from Texas, a big cotton man. It was just a summer home for him. I worked for Durrance before I was married. I worked there several years by the day, from spring until got the corn out. And I went back year after year. This time, I stayed just six months. They had one or two men here in Easton lookin out for things down there and the help and they was just as nasty as they could be. Those men were nasty, the way they used to speak to you. They have had people workin under em, not only colored but white that was afraid of em. I know the white man on the farm, he was just as scared of em as he could be.

I don't think they ever did get somebody that they got settled with. I know the first they got was two fellows from New York—Russians or some other nationality. And they was just as green as they could be. They didn't know what to do. I think they left before the summer was out. And they got somebody else and they made it for the rest of the summer and stayed there all the winter with good as nothin to do and they left. They had a time!

I worked there when they got ready to cut wheat. Mr. Durrance wouldn't let em start in the mornin, start in the afternoon. They had be sure to be dry. And every evenin that we was cuttin he would come out and bring a bottle and get a glass and pour me a drink of whiskey. And we was three or four evenins I know and he didn't miss one, leavin it out in the kitchen for me. And I thought it was funny, was another colored fella there, he didn't give him any and didn't give the white man on the farm any. I used to say funny things to the old man and keep him laughin. That's why it was, I guess. They was afraid to talk to him. I used to talk to him and crack jokes and things like that and get him to laugh. Then when he was workin, he'd come around, he'd always come around me. When he'd start a conversation, he'd start it with me. The white man on the farm, he said he couldn't tell how that was. I said, "You ask him, maybe he'll tell you." I said, "One thing, you all act like you afraid of him." And I say, "You can't talk to a person if you're afraid of him. Well, I ain't afraid of him, just don't like have nothin to say to him." And I used to keep Mr. Durrance laughin but the others couldn't think it was me carryin tales and stuff like that. They couldn't tell why it was he'd come to me or start a conversation, wouldn't even speak to them.

Old man Durrance son came up here in spring. He said somethin to me that I didn't like. Rather than have any argument, I just quit. They came in at night, son and somebody. So I went up the next mornin, the next day I was talkin to em I told em I had some Chesapeake Bay retrievers, and the first thing he hollered, "Well, I don't want em barkin around here and wakin me up in the mornin." I didn't have many then, I guess I had about five or six. But I told him them dogs meant more to me than the job did. Workin for twenty-five dollars a month. Twenty-five dollars a month and boardin myself. That wasn't no money. Them dogs meant more than that to me. I said, "Don't worry, they won't wake you up." And that night I went and rent this house and moved right out. So they didn't wake him up. And it was the way he said it as much as it was what he said. But I heard the old man through his wife both said they were very sorry.

I moved back to Millerstown. It was three houses on the road then and I went to the middle house. I rented from John Deshields and was there, I guess, a year and a half. Paid about three dollars a month. And my wife was doin days work, mostly washin for the poor people. Was not much work them days.

And I was just workin around by the day, but still wasn't many months after I moved I had blood poisonin. Blood was bad. We was cuttin silo corn and that was a little earlier than the other kind of corn. It was in August. In September, the regular corn generally get ripe. And a blister come and it start swellin, puffed up and puffed up. And when I call the doctor, he ask me what I thought was the matter. That was a funny thing to ask me when I wasn't a doctor. I told him I believed I got blood poisonin. Wasn't any skin broken, but it just started swellin. And he come over and looked at it. Said, "Yeah, Joe. I think that's what it is." Then they had to wait for it to get ripe. Couldn't cut it then. And he watched it. I'd see him every two or three days. When it got ripe, they cut it. And they didn't use ether to put you to sleep. They used chloroform and that was a funny feelin. Each one of them made you as sick as what they was operatin on you for. When they put me to sleep with the chloroform, I could hear bells ringing. Big light and bells ringing and a lot of noise and all at once this big light'd explode. Then I didn't know nothin else until I woke up. I lost all the flesh off my left arm. It wasn't a thing but skin, leaders, and bones.

And I was home when it first started bleedin. I was walkin across the floor and it felt like somebody stuck a pin in me. And I looked down and there was the blood. So I went to town and had it dressed and come back. And it started bleedin on me after I'd been to the doctor, on the road walkin home from Easton. I'd hold it down the blood would drip out of the bandage. But if I hold it up, it didn't bleed. A lady and a man come along. The lady knowed me, she was a Miss Goldsborough that lived down at Miles River Bridge, and they wanted to know what was the matter. She told the man to stop. Said, "Joe, what in the world is the matter with your hand?" And I told her. "Well, get right in here, I'll take you home and call your doctor up." And a little after I was up to the house, she said, "I'm going to call a taxi." That was the onliest taxi they had then. "I'm going to get him to take," that was the man and her, "to town." Say, "And we'll carry you right in to the hospital." So before we got to town, I told them I'd rather get to the doctor that dressed it that mornin. And he told me not to leave town. Asked me did I have any my people there I could spend the night with. And I spent the night with an uncle. And didn't have anymore trouble then.

And I begged him to cut the hand off because it's worse dressin it than any other time. When they got ready to dress it they had to shove the gauze back in there, and takin it out was as bad as shovin it in there, because the part that was up to the skin had dried. Then it pretty near set me crazy. So the onliest way to relieve it, I told the doctor to give me some warm water, give me a few minutes, and let it soak. I said, "It won't be as bad." So he used to do that. I'd beg him to cut it off. He wouldn't do it. "It'll be some good to you some day." I'd say, "I wish you'd cut it off." After it got better, I saw him several times there. "Glad I didn't cut that hand off, ain't you?" Told him, "Yes, indeed."

Then I usually shoot from my left shoulder and after that I had to get used to shootin from my right. But I could only kill thing that was sittin, I couldn't kill nothin on the wing or runnin. Had to use my fork, spoon with my right hand. Sometimes I'd hit my mouth, sometime my chin, and sometime my nose for a long time. Dr. Merrick told me it was the worst case he had seen exceptin one. I begin to have chills from it and after I was operated on and all that, gettin better, he told me that was a dangerous period of it, when you get that bad, you're havin chills. But he didn't tell me when I was havin the chills. And that hand smelled so bad. Well, I had put it just as far away from me when I'd go to bed as I could. It was rotten. And that went for some time. I couldn't work. I had to set around until the next spring.

Then I went to work on the road that they was shellin from Unionville to Tunis Mills. When I started, they wasn't quite halfway, they wasn't quite down to Millerstown. Worked a month on the road and got a dollar and a half a day. When it runned out, that was days work. Lot of the time you just couldn't get every day straight. You'd have to miss a lot of days till you get another job. When we finished the road, I went thrashin the wheat, either pitched wheat or worked with the baggers loadin wagons. You wouldn't be thrashin a month unless it come a rainy spell. A wet spell, that would prolong it. Worked all the days exceptin Sunday.

When we finished thrashin the wheat, I didn't have anything to do. And there was a man show up and I got a job down to Bruffs Island, a dollar and fifty a day. Mr. Schuyler was doing a lot of rebuilding. And the plumber's man had the plumbin contract, he was a man short and I got a job with him and stayed until they finished that fall. There was two or three colored fellows from Unionville was workin to Bruffs Island. They was doin a lot of diggin where they was runnin pipes from different places and one of the fellows that was on the job, he quit, and one of the others asked me did I want the job. I told them, "Yeah, didn't have any." And one of the other fellows say, "Get ready," say. "Monday morning, when you go down," say, "I'll speak to the boss and you can get the job. I know you can." So we went down and he had laid the ditch out the way it was to go. And some time during the mornin, the plumber come down, and one of the other fellow tell him he got another man to take the other fellow's place. He got to talkin to me and I got the job.

Then after that got slack, they kept me down there because Mr. Schuyler had a young fellow right out of college, he had put him on the job down there because he had bought thoroughbred stock and he had to keep account of em. And he was the head of it. He was livin in the house when the plumbers was workin there and the plumbers come from Long Island. And when the plumbers got through with me and there was the carpenters and there was fellow that was lookin after the house and he took all of us and laid us off. Wouldn't have anymore to do. Went to me and got a chance taking me back of a little buildin there and hired me over again. Told me to come every day, between the three of em, he'd give me a day's work. So I worked down there a long time after the others was gone.

This young fellow, Mr. Schuyler used to send him the money, and some-time he'd drink it up. I had gone two weeks with a family and I need my money. That must've been December. I know I got my money from Mr. Schuyler. A little after that, Mr. Schuyler fired him. Wasn't no job for him, nothin like that. He was a right young fellow. And Mr. Schuyler, he used to come home from New Jersey bout every other Sunday and I used to go down there and spend the Sunday waitin on him. Nice old fellow.

Wheelock, the plumber, he wanted me to go to New York with him— Long Island, New York. Course if I hadn't a had children and my dogs, I would've gone. I couldn't give my dogs up to go up there with that man that had the job then lose the job. I wouldn't have nothin. If I got stranded and wanted to come home and didn't have the money to come home, I'd be in a mess. At that time, I had four children and about eight or ten dogs—Chesa-peake retrievers—raisin them and I couldn't take that job. I told him I couldn't do it, I had children. He said, "Well, Joe," said, "your children won't be the onliest children up there." But he was a big plumber, what I mean, takin big jobs. And he taken to me. I don't know why, but he did when I first went down there.

I used to carry the keys to the wine closet. Mr. Schuyler and the head man he had there when he was goin out, he'd always give me the keys to keep. Say he fraid to lay em down in the house and fraid to take em with him, fraid he would lose em, and have tear up somethin to get into the closet. I didn't bother the whiskey and nothing else. And I know if they had any idea I'd take things, they'd never let me do that. And I wouldn't get a drink. And the next man above me told me I could get a drink if I wanted it, a bottle of beer or somethin like that. Told him, "No." I didn't care for any and never touched nothin. I carried the keys and a lot of white ones couldn't've carried em. I never bother nothin belong to anybody and I've always had that name.

So just worked around like that, different jobs, no permanent job. But course, I had my dogs to depend on, too. They had a big time down Bruffs Island. One time, stag concern, had over three hundred and some. Knowed a man that was invited and he judged dogs in Madison Square Garden for thirty-five years. They wanted me to meet him so that evening of the party, Mr. Schuyler loaned me the car and somebody to drive it, wanted to go out and see my dogs and see somebody else had some. And I asked this man that had been a judge who he thought had the best type of Chesapeake. He answer me right slow and told me, say, "Well, I like yours better than I do any of the others." Said, "But keep em clean." That's in breedin, not cross-breedin em. Said, "I like the looks of yours better than any the others."

I sold some puppies, eight weeks old, twenty-five dollars. The first one I ever shipped was to a man by the name of Julius C. Peters and that was in Minnesota. Then some time after that, I shipped two more there but not to him.

I sold one to one of the big men in Standard Oil Company. He had his lawyer come down here. I shipped the first one, he was livin in Boston, but this one got hurt after it'd grown then. A boy kicked it and broke his shoulder blade and he was lame. So then he wanted to know whether I had any more. He liked the dog. And he say, "If not," say, "I'm going to wait," say, "cause I know what your dogs are." But he didn't have to wait. I had another one and he had his lawyer from Baltimore to come down to get it. And instead of him shippin that dog to this man, he kept him for the dog to get larger and he could make more money on him. I believe that's what it was. I got two letters from his boss, and that was months after he had come and got the puppy. And he had relations down here to Trappe and was a white man told me when I was talkin about it sometime after that, he say he saw the same dog and said it was in an enclosure, a chicken yard. And he's speakin about how poor it was. Well, I should've straighten that thing out but I was afraid of making trouble between his lawyer and him. It's what I should've done to clear my ownself. I should've explained it to him. And that man had never told him that he had the dog or the dog was down here to either some of his relations or his wife's relations to Trappe.

Some time before that, sold a man to Alaska four female puppies and a male. But he didn't want em any relations, naturally. And one of the Riemans, he was sellin em, too. But I don't know where he got this puppy from. It wouldn't suit me for a Chesapeake. Don't know what it was, but it was some cross somewhere back. And when this man got the puppies in Fairbanks, Alaska, he wrote to me and told me they had reached there well. Said, "I'm tickled to have em," say, "but they look all right. They're fine, but that male." Course, I had a pedigree for the male and he could see it wasn't my breedin. And he wouldn't wanted it if it was my breedin. He wouldn't wanted it cause he wouldn't take sisters and brothers. And I used to get a letter from him bout every month. He went to raisin em, and he wrote to me and told me he had trouble with em to keep people from stealin em.

And was an old retired ship captain that lived in Savannah, Georgia, in a hotel and he wanted a puppy. He said he would pay the price for the puppy. He had a gun. Didn't say what the gun cost, over two hundred dollars, say, "And I'll never gun no more," say. "If you send me a puppy, I'll send you this gun." I sent the puppy, never did hear from him no more. That old fellow was a beat: send the puppy and never got a cent out of it.

Captain Morris gave me the dog that I started raisin Chesapeakes from. After he left the home place, he had no place to go and Harry Rieman took him in. And he owned a little place down here what we call the "back road." And I use to go down and look after him. Cause I know he wasn't use to goin out doin a lot of little things that needs to be done. And I used to go down every day or two get wood in for him, stuff like that. Course I know he had no money. The last he thanked me and offered me the puppy. The one he gave me was a female. Captain Morris and the family as they come up they was the biggest gunners that we had chere. And they had a yacht they called the *Cora*. And then the family broke up. They give me that yacht.

She was aground then. She had broke loose and went ashore. And he didn't have the money to float her. And I sold her right on the ground where she was. She was a sailin yacht. I think I got twenty dollars for it. I give it away. But I wasn't able to float it. And then she need some repairs and I wasn't able to do that or have it done. And I thought that was better than lettin her lay there and rot entirely and do nobody no good. There's a picture of it up to the Harbor Club. And the funniest thing, they give the name of every owner ever owned it, and it come down to me and they skipped that. Didn't have mine on there at all. They didn't want no colored man's name on it.

Part V

And I left Millerstown and moved around opposite Hopewell, a place I was supposed to buy. I stayed there a good many years, twenty some years. I left there in 1935. It was a hard leave, though, cause it was a out-the-way place, but I liked it a whole lot better than I did a town. It was a mix-up there somewhere. I know I lost the place. The sawmill man name Rittenhouse that bought the land, come to find out he never paid for it. It was a mortgage on the place, and if he rent or sold any land, that should've gone on the mortgage. Another man bought the woods and all the property. And I was supposed to own the place. I paid on the place till I thought I owned it. Didn't go there to pay rent. I went there to buy the place. I paid him different amounts. Sometime I'd pay him twenty-five or thirty dollars and sometime it'd be less than that. I saw a lawyer before I finished payin for it and the lawyer told me, "Well, if I was you, I wouldn't pay another cent because he can take the place right back again. The agreement is broke."

Rittenhouse got his back hurt while he was there in the woods and they claim that was the trouble with his mind. He was a hasty man. Always in a hurry. Sometime that works out bad. They cut a tree in Dr. Lowndes woods and it was bigger than a saplin, but it wasn't a big tree; and he went under it to cut this thing. Somebody said it was about six or eight inches, but it was holdin the top up. Wouldn't lay flat and he went under there and when he cut it, the weight of the tree slabbed it, and he started out and the tree rolled. And it caught him and throwed him back and fell right cross his back. And the doctor say that was the trouble with his mind. And while that thing was on his back, he hollered to the men to tell em how many feet to cut it. Say, "Don't spoil the log." And the log was layin on him.

So I stayed there as long as I could. And then they could fix it so that I could get the man, Rittenhouse, to sign a paper but the lawyer told me was no paper he could sign that would be any good, cause he had lost his mind. So there I was. He told me the best thing I could do was just live there as long as I could. Said, "Becuase they ain't no use tryin to get it, cause he can't sign any papers. It wouldn't be legal for him to sign any papers on account of his condition."

And my stepfather and some more of em bought land from him but that was different, that's when he was up and goin. And they got theirs straight when his mind was right. My stepfather, he bought three acres from him and worked it out at the sawmill. Built a house soon as he bought it. Another old man bought two acres. And Charlie Dobson, he bought two acres.

And the fall that I was taken sick I helped cut and carry over a hundred acres of corn and loved to do it. We'd start racin in the mornin. Why I'd get into it and get ahead and I wouldn't let up until dinnertime. I remember one time I was just doin days work where we could get it, a few days, was no contractin work. I had just finished cuttin down to Pascault's, and it was thirty-five or forty acres there I helped to cut. And we had a bunch in the field cuttin corn and there was one fella he had asked Shortall for the full row, and his uncle cut long side of him. Well he started out. Course, I wasn't going to let him just leave my rows. I started out. And his uncle was the fastest corn cutter I ever was in the field with. He cut his and then he'd cut a few hills on Emory's and then keep ahead of me, but I never let up. And after awhile, his uncle, he got tired of doin it, I guess, begin to get back. I never let up. And then his uncle stopped helpin him, he had asked for a full row too, and we got him behind. And I think it was about fourteen or fifteen men in the field, and look over that field, it was a mess the way they had scattered out. I never let up. And that was right after dinner and I cut that way until about twenty minutes till sundown. Never let up.

Emory's uncle was an older man than I was, and he was bout to give out. I never thought then, cause he keep hollerin to me. Said, "You better slow up, you'll cut yourself out of wind directly." And after that, after they were through cuttin, he'd come to me, well, he was the one gettin out of wind and I slowed up. And then we went and set on the fence, twenty or thirty minutes, cause you worked till sundown them days, and the men was all over the field. And one fella when he was goin up said to me, said, "I feel like takin this knife cuttin you right in the face." It was a corn knife. I said, "I wouldn't do that. You wouldn't cut me." "Yeah," say, "I feel like cuttin you." I said, "Don't do it." And I kept laughin at him, didn't get mad. Kept laughin at him, and he was give out.

And we had cut that morning figurin on carrying up in the afternoon and Shortall said, "Going to be hard carryin up." The winds had sprung up. Say, "How about cuttin the evenin." So we agreed to do it and one old man, I looked over in the field, poor old fella, he was on his knees. And somebody hollered to him, ask him what was the matter. Said he had cramps in his legs and he couldn't stand up and couldn't walk. Well, I felt sorry for him. It wasn't my fault, but I just wanted to show Emory what I could do. But his uncle, he was the fastest corn cutter I was ever in the field with.

And my name went all around there then. Lot of em wouldn't even go in the corn fields. Man want to hire em, want to know whether I was there. And said if Joe Sutton was there, they had an excuse. We was down here, place to Tunis Mills, and this fella called hisself a corn cutter. He was cuttin for Mr. Bort that rented the place that Mr. Glen Stewart used to own, and it was two farms and he cut the corn off in one farm and the corn on the second was the last planted and it was a little too green. So, Mr. Bort told Bill, said, "The corn was too green," say, "I think I'll let it stand three or four days. Will you go and help Jewell?" That was Jewell Altvater. Bill was there and ask him, "Did you want somebody else to cut the corn?" And Jewell said, "Yeah." Say, "Who you got?" Jewell say he told him "was nobody but Howard Deshields and Joe Sutton and myself." Bill say, "Is Joe Sutton here?" Say, "Yeah," say, "He's here, he's helpin me." Bill started, "My God," say, "I just thought," say, "I ain't got no wood," say, "and the day that I'm off," say, "I think I'll go over there to Mr. Tull and hire a team and haul myself some wood." It wasn't that—he had heard about me. And he went over there and Ennals Tull was short of men cuttin corn, and he hired him. Went to work; he didn't haul no wood.

When I was kiddin him bout it, Bill said, "By God," he say, "I heard about you." I said, "You ought to've stayed there," I say. "You would've seen what I could do." And got a dollar and a quarter a day. That was from sun to sun. The thing of it is, I liked to do it—cuttin and carryin corn—and anything you like to do will go easier with you.

Then they went up here to Forrest Landing and I was sick. I had one of them attacks to my stomach. Mrs. Thompson sent somebody down to Union-ville to get corn cutters and then they come from there down to Millerstown. They got two or three out of Millerstown. I was in Millerstown just before I moved to Chestnut Lane.

Went up there. And somebody said somethin or the other about Sutton. The other fella there said, "You better let Sutton alone." Say, "He's gonna run you out of this corn field." I said, "No, I ain't goin bother him." I say, "I don't feel well." Used to take my stomach some time to straighten itself out. After awhile I got to feelin good. They cuttin along steady. I got in the field and one got to running. They all cut steady after that.

Next year I went back again. Went up there and that year she had an old man for a foreman and we was cuttin some corn that had the tops cut off and he struck out and he had strung the other men out. So I said to myself, "Ain't no sense an old man runnin like that," say, "Ain't nothin to my credit for to turn rows on him." And he kept on so I started out—I was behind him—and I went up on him so easy I took two more rows and I cut four rows faster than he could cut two. We got to the end, we stopped, and the old man looked, say, "You was cuttin four rows, wasn't you?" I said, "Yeah." I say, "Them other two rows was standin; ain't nobody been here to cut em, yeah, I cut four rows." Say, "Four rows," say, "faster than I could cut two?"

I say, "I guess I did, maybe you wasn't cuttin as fast as you could." "Yeah," say. "I was," say, "I'm goin let you alone," say, "you ain't right."

That's just a habit people had, workin against each other. They'd want to race whether was anythin in it or not. There wasn't anymore in it. The majority of em was doin the best they could. It's an audience, just like anything else. Always find somebody that can do somethin a little better, or a little faster than the others. But I never started it, but when it was started, I'd get into it.

I cut down there to Hope one time. I had helped Mr. Jones to cut his corn on his little place. Him and I cut it and set it up. And then in two days he had to move down here to Hope. He had hired to Mr. Starr. He asked me if I'd come down to Hope and help em to cut corn. I told him, "No, man." I said, "I think I've cut and packed enough corn this fall, and another thing, I'm tired and I don't feel good." "Well come on down. There ain't nothin down there but one day." And I shouldn't've gone, but it was a bunch goin around cuttin corn, I think about eight men, who cut a man's crop off for so much or do it by the day. Well, I went down there and I was surprised when I got there cause hadn't told me nothin about this bunch. When I saw em, I knowed they been goin around takin contract cuttin corn. Had one man was the foreman, and I was cuttin along all right. I was cuttin back of this other fella. He kept hollerin, "Stay back there, stay back." He didn't know me, I mean bout cuttin corn. Cause he had just come from New Jersey. Used to go up there every summer, wife and him worked a hotel there every summer. They'd just come home. He had never been in the field with me. This other man—he was the foreman of the bunch—say, "If he don't stay back," say, "I'll stay him." I said to myself, "You start somethin," I said, "it won't be nothing to my credit." I said to myself, "Because he is a much older man." But he started out and I cut right up on him, and he was lookin around cuttin, lookin, and I said, "Clear out! Give me room," I say, "I'm goin out of here." And I got faster. Went on ahead of him, and I pulled up a weed and got to whippin the knife. I said, "This old knife gone crazy." I say, "I don't know what I'm goin to do. I've got to put it in the water." Say, "It got too hot and gone crazy." He never said a word. But I started out again and I said, "Good-bye." I say, "I'll see you when you come out." We was cuttin the whole length of the field. It certainly throwed under him. He was surprised. But one thing he could do though. He could pick up a turn of corn and we'd start carryin up, he'd beat me out four or five piles. I've seen two or three men do that, but I don't know how they do it. Walk up to a pile of corn, then slack up just kick it like that and long arms, go down, and pick it right up. And when I pick up a turn of corn, I got in the habit of rollin it.

I worked for contractors. And I worked on the farm and I did some fishin, but that was after I was operated on. It helped me make a livin that way. I did anything that come along. And I worked God knows how many years, when they were workin on me. I worked and took medicine every day.

The doctors didn't know what was the matter with me. And they was just givin me medicine. I don't know whether they had any idea whether the medicine was goin to help me or not. And it wasn't helpin me. Did hard work. Lined up a pile driver and hammer and nothin round here was any harder than that. I did that for several years. It was tough. You wind that hammer up and they cut it loose, and then wind right back again. There was many a one that worked there with me that didn't stay long. Some'd stop without an excuse and some would have an excuse to stop.

I did have trouble when I was livin in Dobson house. I would spit a little blood, during the day every time I'd spit. I'd work on that pile dirver, wind that hammer. And had my spoon and bottle of medicine right on there with me. Went through a lot. Hadn't a used common sense, I'd been gone years ago. And then I believe in doin as the doctor say do. But if you don't do as they say—well, you don't know when he is tellin you wrong.

And the last doctor I had just before I got Dr. Travers, well, I asked him did he know what was the matter with me. Dropped his head and looked down and raised his head. "Well, no, Joe, I don't." And he had been takin money from me over a year. Well, I said to myself, I'd better look for somebody else. And I knowed Dr. Travers well. I'd been out on two or three parties that he was to and I knowed him well. I was takin him to town there one time, had to take him to the drug store. It was two drug stores side and side there on Washington Street then. And I got sick and Mr. Percy Cox told the fellow to set me down there on the big chair and then he sent somebody next door to see if it was a doctor in there. And he went and come back, told Mr. Cox, said, "Dr. Travers is in there." And so he sent him back and told him to tell Dr. Travers to come over there right away. And he give me somethin. I don't know what it was but I know I felt better.

And then I was takin this other man medicine then and I forgot now how many months it was. After he told me he didn't know what it was the matter with me, I went to Dr. Travers and he asked, "Joe, you been sick ever since I give you that medicine," say, "in Percy Cox's?" I told him, "Yesir." "Well, why didn't you come to me before?" I don't know what that answer was I gave him. But anyhow, right after that I went back to him. He told me that he couldn't tell me a thing until they take a picture. Dr. Hammond taken em for Dr. Travers. Hammond was the X-ray man. And found out it was ulcers. Told me I'd have to be operated on. Well I didn't ask him any questions at all, left it up to him. Sometime I'd feel all right as far as feelin, then again, I wouldn't. Dr. Travers told me my case was worse that'd ever been in the hospital. Course had I been taken sooner, I wouldn't had to been operated on. Taken sooner you could move it with diet. But she was so far gone, guess he figured he couldn't in my case. After they had taken the X-ray, found what condition it was in.

After he operated on me, I never asked him what did he find or nothin. The first morning he come down here askin me how'd I feel? Course, he had seen my chart I guess up in the office, I reckon. But he always ask me how did I feel. One morning said, "Well, Joe," said, "how you feel this morning?" I said, "Pretty good." I said, "I feel like goin birdin." He laughed. I said, "I'm goin to get up some of these mornings, go home, get my gun and dog, go birdin." He said, "Don't you try to get out of that bed. You fall on this concrete and you'll be worse off than you was before." The places for the colored people was down on the ground floor, cement floor. He cautioned me two or three times not to try to get up, said, "If you have to get up," said, "just call a nurse." That's what they was for. Say, "Don't you try to get up by yourself." But I was only kiddin. The nurses was very, very nice, especially after they found out that I was Dr. Travers' patient. Dr. Travers let me come out in nine days. And he said, "You improved faster than the majority of em." Nine days I come out. Walkin around the hospital in a few days. And old man was operated on for a hernia the day after I was and I was up walkin around several days before he ever fell out of the bed. Course I was young then.

And I didn't pay a cent. That was through Dr. Travers cause he was the head doctor to the hospital. And he never charged me anything. And they operated on two of my boys and never charged me anything. I had a setback and my wife would call him up, it wouldn't be long before he'd be there. And the neighbors closest to me they couldn't understand it. Say, "If we'd call him in the mornin sometime he don't get out here till the afternoon." And my wife told em she didn't know what it was but he would be there. Sometime it'd be one or two nurses would come out with him. They would say that, "Well, I want to see Joe," said, "See how he's gettin along." And I thought that was very nice.

That ulcer operation, I'd went to somebody else I guess it'd cost me more than I'd ever been able to pay. Cause I had a lot of setbacks after I was operated on and he get me come up there nights and try tests on me. Didn't cost me one cent. And I give him a Chesapeake puppy, male puppy, and he raised it. And the dog stayed right in the office or he could go to another part of the house. But I went there one day, after the dog then was a year old or more, and he looked at me and didn't come to me makin friends. Just laid down on the floor and looked at me. Watchin me. After I'd been in there some time I'd decided to come out. He got between me and that door and I'd go back and set down, he'd come and lay down, stay there and watch. And the way I got out, he'd come to the door, got between me and the door and I talked to him. And he let me come out then. But before that I believe he would've bit me if I insist on goin out. And Doc thought a lot of that dog, but after his wife and him bust up, guess he knowed he wouldn't be home much and he give it away. Then he built a little place over Miles River here. And after he went there he tell me he was goin to leave the door open. The door was left open every day. Said I might be down that way sometime and get to feelin bad, want some place to sit down, lay down, said, "Go in," say, "And stay long as you want to." I thought that was very nice.

And then he loaned me a boat and outboard motor, after I got so I could get around. Told me he didn't want me to sit around the house or yard. "I want you to get out and get movin around, fishin, or somethin like that." Say, "I don't mean for you to go no long distance." Said, "You land your boat close, and you get in the boat every day that's fit." Say, "And don't stay over a couple of hours but I don't want you sittin around the yard," say, "all the time."

Then after I got so could get around good, the Doc and I we quail shot together, duck together, built a blind down to Riemans' place. The Riemans people, just as well say raised me, and both of us had the privilege to build the blind there. We had good duck shootin there for a long time until he left here. One time I went down bout three o'clock that evenin before, look to see if anything in the river, it wasn't any ducks of any amount in the river, it wasn't any canvasbacks and wasn't any blackheads. I went down between two and three o'clock and it was a raft of em settin out a long distance from the blind bout halfway I guess to St. Michaels. I went some place and called Dr. Travers up and told him bout it. He said, "I'll be down in the morning." I say, "Well the ducks are here." So I went down there and I waited for Dr. Travers. I waited and waited, wouldn't shoot and I was down there in the blind bout seven o'clock. And some time after I was in the blind I saw a great big bunch of canvasbacks comin my way, I had put out good stool of decoys so I got back in the blind and they come in, I say, "Now I don't want to start shootin till the Doc gets here." And if you stand up they come in and some of em will come back again. So I wouldn't shoot, two hundred or more come right in gun shot, right over decoys. And I stood up and they left and went not so awful far and lit on the Marengo Shore and they stayed there. And I waited until I guess pretty near nine o'clock before I start shootin. "Well," I said, "if Doc ain't chere now," I say, "he ain't comin." And if I had start first in the beginnin God knows how many I could've killed. One shoot in that bunch by God I might'a got five or six fore they got away from there, just shootin in the bunch. And then he cussed his ownself bout not comin down. "Joe," said, "that may be the best day we'd have." I said, "That's what I was thinking."

So we had some good days but never had another day like that for canvasbacks or no other duck. Course they had pretty good shootin the first of the season with blackheads and whifflers. Course you could bake fry em then.

One time whiffler come in to investigate and I let him shoot at him first, he didn't hit him, and I shot at him. Instead of flyin level he went away from there flyin right up. And went almost out of sight over towards St. Micahels and I was about to give up watchin for him and I noticed he was gettin closer and turned and come back and fell within fifty yards from where I shot him. And that shot went through one eye and come out the other, and he was blind.

And it was a teal shot one day out of the blind. And I forgot now who was with me and it was Thanksgiving Day, they stopped to go get their dinner and I stayed in the blind cause I didn't have any turkey at home. And that little duck come in flyin fifty feet or more above me, made a circle and I shot and he went down, and when I shot instead of his wings droppin he went down and hit the water and he was goin so fast when he hit that water he skipped just like a stone and went up. Never did see a duck do that before. But he was movin when I shot him.

And tarpot, they usually fly in a string not far from the water. Seven come in one day and they wouldn't decoy but they'd just come in close enough to look the decoys over is all and I hadn't been shootin at em, so that day nothin else was flyin and I had a pump gun. The old ones held five shells. And I shot five times and killed four of em fore they got out of gun shot. And I give em away cause I wouldn't want to pick em and the feathers stuck to em just like they was stuck on there with tar or glue. That's why they call em tarpots.

And they was one of the commonest ducks that we have. And some people eat em and call em good. I remember one time fellow at Tunis Mills, they struck one of em lucky days, canvasbacks, and they killed them somewhere around seventy-five. And the bunch they had some tarpots and old fellow from Copperville went over there. Well the Daffins, he used to often have em for sale and he asked him about a pair of ducks, he told em, "Yeah, come here and pick out what you want." And he had hung em up and this old man he got to these tarpots and said, "Mr. Daffins," say, "I think I'll take these," say, "I know they nice and fat," say, "they heavy." And there was canvasbacks and whifflers hangin by and he took the tarpots. And all the Daffins laughed at that for a long time. It wasn't right though, he should've told him the difference.

Dr. Travers gave me an old model 12. He told me it was shot out but I didn't see no difference killin birds or ducks or anything. I know the barrel was a little loose. And I guess I had a dozen and half decoys. When Dr. Travers left here I got all his decoys. I think it's about eighty in all. That was canvasbacks and blackheads. And I be dog if I didn't lose all of em. They got away from me. One fella, he leased Bruffs Island, I loaned him all the blackheads and that was thirty some. Never got them. I marked them, too, so I could tell em. And years after that I saw those mixed in with his decoys.

Another fella, I loaned him thirty-five canvasbacks and I never got them. He loaned em to another man or he was duckin down there, left em down there. Man said, "If you want em I'll get em." And they all had been so good to me, so I wouldn't put him to that trouble. Somebody else got em for nothin.

Then after I was operated on, I wasn't able to go out and do a day's work for anybody. I first started puttin on marasco on the houses. And Dr. Travers told he me didn't want me to use that or paint. Neither one of em. Then I got some idea about drivin these shallow wells and I went drivin wells. Didn't get much but it helped me to live.

Children were small. Lawrence, the oldest boy, was born in 1907. And the midwife was my wife's mother, Sally Jackson. That was her job, colored and white. She used to go night and day. It was the same with my great-grandmother, Hester Moody. And them old women didn't get much. My great-grandmother sometime she'd just get some corn meal and meat, somethin like that from some of em. And the second boy, William, was two years after Lawrence. It went along like that. Then Dorothy, and Robert was the fourth one. It was 1914 when he was born. And I was livin round Hopewell, children couldn't get a way to Easton school and wasn't living close to anybody was goin. Dorothy, she used to go in with Cecilia Altvater. Cecilia used to drive a horse. She had been drivin before they put the bus on and she kept on drivin a horse and they'd come right past home. And I've seen them be short of desks in this old school down the road. I've seen em haul desk in there that was ready to fall down. Couldn't use em. I've seen books they'd give me, sometimes several pages tore out of the books. But I do know one thing, the blacks can get better things if they all together. If the children was together, well they'd get just as good books as the white would. They'd get just as good a desks. That's the onliest way I think if they goin to live another way. You goin to separate one, one goin to be taught things different from the other. I heard a man we was talkin in Easton speakin bout a colored doctor some years ago, and he said it should be such a thing, say, "But Joe, I'll tell you," say, "I wouldn't have the faith in the colored doctor as I would the white." I say, "You wouldn't?" "No." And I looked him in the eye. "But," say, "you know why?" I said, "No." He said, "Colored doctor ain't taught what the white doctor's taught." So I believe that's the truth they ain't taught alike. They wasn't at that time. The first time I heard them say that this country was the black man's just as much as it was the white man, well that was when they was in need then. They was gettin pinched then. That was the First World War. Heard em say, "It's just as much your country as it is mine." But course lots of things are done and said on account of ignorance.

And they didn't want you to learn nothin, the majority of em didn't. But I was lucky one or two place I went and they got hard up for labor. The man that owned the place would tell the man that had the contract to put Joe

Sutton in there, "He can do as good as some you got and do better than others you got." That's the way I got to do any carpenter work, and course, if you didn't have intelligence, you wouldn't've been able to do it then.

Now I know one man, place I was workin when I was taken sick. I was workin for Dr. Millard. He was buildin a cow stable, and the contractor, when Dr. Millard'd go back to Baltimore, he would take some of the men, go on another job. And Dr. Millard got after this man about not advancing any faster. So Dr. Millard asked him, "Why don't you put Joe Sutton there? Joe can do as good as some you got and better than several you got." He had been watchin em. He put me in there sawin these great big twelve-by-twelve oak posts. Charlie Hammond marked mine off and he had another fella that he had hired that spring to come out there with him when he started. And Charlie Hammond marked it off. He went and he was gone some time around the buildin, and he come back to see how we was gettin along. Well, he looked at mine, he didn't say a word to me whether mine was right or wrong, and he went to this other fella. "Whoa, whoa, Lee. Whoa, you're makin a mess of it. That got to be straightened up." Say, "Look at Sutt's," say, "Sutt's cuttin the line right out." I was cuttin the pencil mark right out. This fella didn't like it, he didn't say much. And Dr. Millard come in there some time during that mornin. "Hammond," say, "how is Joe doin?" "Oh," say, "he's doin pretty good." Didn't say he was doin all right, "He's doin pretty good."

And I stayed in there till Dr. Millard went back to Baltimore. And Charlie Hammond give me a pick and shovel again like I had. The thing of it was, they didn't want a colored man to learn. They just didn't want him to learn. I heard one say, "If they learn," say, "it'd make it bad on the white one." Say, "They'll be goin round doing for nothin." One fella said, "If the colored man learns," say, "he'll just ruin the wages," say, "because he'll be workin for nothin and you'll have to work for less." And the person of experience knows more than the other person that hasn't experience. And Hammond, right after he finished to Millard's, and then he built another house down Hopewell, and he didn't have men enough to go around. And he never come to look for me and I was right across the road. He went down to Tunis Mill and got the boys right out of school. Put them to work. And he wasn't the onliest one to do that.

Years before, I went down place that man had bought. Contractor asked the colored fellas there for me and they told him they didn't know whether I had a job or not and I didn't. I was livin down here to Millerstown and used to walk night and mornin down and from there and then go to work. And that's every bit four miles or more. Then I'd be so tired mornins. I'd be tireder in the mornin when I got there than I would be in the evening after I had worked all day, and I mean work. And he didn't want you to get hold of a hammer or a hatchet or saw. I remember one time he wanted a hammer to drive a nail for something and I got the hammer. I said, "I'll drive it." "No, hand it chere." Give it to him, he drove the nail. And one time he was cuttin, tearin strips and sharpin one end to make stakes to put in line for somethin, and I got the saw and started sawin. I knowed the length he want em. Come there and took the saw away from me and sawed it hisself.

I knowed I was poor them days; tell that by the conditions of others how much difference. It wasn't all the black people was the same, but they all had the hard time. But you give a bunch of people all a certain amount of money, why it wouldn't be long before some of em would accumulate to it and some again would throw theirs away. That comes from intelligence. Them that didn't know how to provide to get along, they didn't have as much intelligence as the other fella that did get along. It wasn't what they had it was what they know how to spend. I know men from Copperville, when they got married, they accumulate and get a home, and some of the others had homes was left to em. It wouldn't be long fore they wouldn't have no home. They had the opportunity as good as the other fella and they throwed their chances away. Course I got nothin, but I was sick for years. There's lots of people white and black wouldn't got along as good as I did not to have anything, cause they wouldn't know how to provide. After I got so I could do a little somethin—never could do any more hard work—I could do a little bit of anything was to be done. And that must've been intelligence.

When we livin there at Hopewell, buyin the place, we used to put up a lot of preserves, cans and stuff, have a couple of hogs, and had two cows. And some people used to come right often to get a quart of milk, a jar of preserves. And my wife would give them a jar of preserves and jar and all. And they never brought the jars back. And then I'd work durin the summer and buy the jars and buy the fruit. And I have been up workin hard in the day and I've been up till two o'clock in the mornin helping her to put fruit up. When I was taken sick, I think we had put up two hundred jars of peaches. Peaches was my eatin! And that was one thing was against my stomach, against my ulcers.

Two years after I was operated on the ulcer came back bad as ever. Thing of it was, I wasn't on the right diet. And it wasn't as much known them days about ulcers as it is now. And I looked after the Abrey place, joined Marengo. Summer time kept the grass cut. And this doctor, he was down to Abrey place. He was a railroad doctor. And I explained it to him and he told me what to get to eat and I felt better from the first meal. Something in my diet wasn't right because it would sour fifteen or twenty minutes after I ate it. And I could take a drink of water and go about fifteen or twenty minutes and spit some out and it would be just as sour as vinegar. But my diet was pettijohns, cream of wheat, and I forget the other.

Them were hard days, though. The welfare concern they used to give old people, or if you were young and had nothin, baskets of groceries for Thanksgiving or Christmas. And I'd taken the first year and the next year I thanked em and told em some poor people was in worse shape than I was in. Didn't take anymore. Course I was makin some money off'n my dogs. And then I was oysterin and fishin. Wasn't puttin in a whole day of it. I was doin just as the doctor told me, move around and keep doin somethin. Not to set around all the time. I was lookin after the Abrey place and I had an old boat there and I had a pair of nippers, and the creek then was full of oysters. I'd go out and nipper up two or three bushels, take em home and shuck em. When I stopped I had a big pile of shells. Didn't make much out of it though. Sell em in a jar. Had to buy the jars and sell them in the jars and never get the jars back no more. Some of em would promise and I don't know ever gettin one back. I rent the boat from St. Michaels. One season I oystered by myself and then I cut it out. It was inconvenient and a long walk. That was clear down here to Wye House and next to Bruffs Island. And if I had something better when the season opened I wouldn't oyster. Them were hard days, though. I remember one evenin I come in from oysterin, land in a cove they called Ice Pond Cove, right next to Bruffs Island. I had a sail boat and didn't have wind enough to go to St. Michaels sellin oysters and wasn't no buy boats in the mouth of Wye River and this was on a Saturday. And I only had very little bit of money in my pocket. And on my way home, walkin along, I was thinkin of the family and got to get some food and I looked down the side of the road, there was a paper dollar had blowed up layin against the grass, was standin there And then it was dusk, but it come plain to me that it was money and I reached down and got it. It was a paper dollar. And with what I had in my pocket was enough to buy food enough. That was lucky though. Now it was dusk and I saw it. I'd never noticed it layin flat but it was layin against the grass on angle. Well if you try to do, the Lord will always make a way for you to get along. But I wouldn't had enough. Course I could've got food, but I didn't want to go in debt for it. I was a friend of the man who had that store there in Tunis Mills. Him and I was play boys together but I didn't like to get things what they called "on trust." It has been times I had to get somethin there from him and then when I'd go to pay him I'd say, "Well, there's the last of the money." Say, "You don't have to pay for all of it just pay for part." Told him, "No, I'd rather pay every cent I owe you if I have to come back tomorrow." Ennals Tull was man, lived close to Tunis Mills, he'd charge you. Oh he couldn't have good luck the things that man done. He saved his money, bought one of the largest houses in Easton and on the big street. That's where the money people, the most of them was on that street, Royal Street. And then wasn't there long before he got so he couldn't walk. Lot of them things will come home to you.

And my uncle Big Bill was fixed better than other people. He owned three farms. And that old lady, she was handicapped. Her husband had no education. And she had to tend to all the business. It was a good thing, because some men wouldn't a like it, they'd a wanted to get in there and help and mess things up. But he didn't sign nothin without her opinion. I don't know how many children they had. When Big Bill Flamer died, why it wasn't no time fore they had run through borrowin money on the place and the place was gone. And then it was another colored family bought it that went from up there for years and did well in the city, and they come back and bought it and they did the same thing, instead of workin the place, the children come there and had fine horses and runabouts. And they just sported away. And they were the onliest colored ones anyway that had anything like that.

Big Bill Flamer had a son that was on one of the farms and he worked day and night. And when he'd sell his crops or anything like that off em, he had a neighbor, white man, lived next to him that used to go to Easton every Saturday. That was the time that people went to Easton, was on Tuesdays and Saturdays. And when this fellow would sell something, he didn't want to keep any money in the house, and this other man was such a good neighbor to him, why he'd give him his money to bank. And he did that for some time. And he went to the bank to see how much he had but he found out he didn't have a cent. The man kept every cent he give him to bank on. And the man that handled that part of the bank could remember him puttin money in the bank but told him, "He had never put a cent in under your name."

The man like to went crazy. And he had worked day and night and thought he had a good pile of money in the bank. He was goin to buy the winter shoes and clothes for his children and didn't have a cent in there. There wasn't nothin he could do. He had no proof that he gave it to him and they wouldn't take his word no how. It was the colored against the white. He couldn't've beaten him up, cause that'd been worse for him. You couldn't prove it and you're just beatin a man up for no cause, an innocent man, and the colored man that hadn't've gotten lynched he'd have been sent away from his family so he just had to let it go.

I had a man tell me some years ago, I was a grown man and I was praising a man, and this was a money man and he kept smilin and after I stopped talkin, he said, "Joe," said, "You've got a lot of faith in this man haven't you?" I say, "Indeed I have." I say, "He's one of my best friends." He say, "Well, I'll tell you, Joe," say, "You watch your friends just as much as you would somebody that you never knowed." He said, "If you're going to do business or anything, always do it in a business way, don't have too much confidence in the man you're doin the business with." So I found out that was the truth.

One time I run dog, field trial here. Two old ladies come up to me after the dog worked and one of em patted me on the shoulder and ask me not to feel bad. Said, "We know your dog won first prize." Say, "And they didn't give it to you." Say, "But you know as well as we know why they didn't." I said, "Thank you." And I said, "Yes, Mam." I say, "I know why they didn't." And I say, "I feel lucky that I got that good." Second prize. Didn't want a colored man to run the dog in the field trials. And if it wasn't that, it was because the man sponsored the show, the trial, was the one runnin the other dog. And that's why they robbed the dog.

Lot of em made admiration for the way I growed, fast. And I got along fine in Tunis Mills. I always take my hat off to the town people. From a small boy until a few years ago. I spent a lot of time there. I remember one night I was in the store and it was three men come in there from Easton, I believe it was somethin concernin the election. And they had three or four of these theater seats. And I was sittin over there by myself and the three men was to the counter talkin. And man behind the counter turned around, he saw me and he asked me something about gunnin. Well we got to talkin and he come over and sit in one of the seats along side of me. And the other men were up to the counter talkin to the man runned the store. And I noticed one man, Ford Morgan, he keep lookin over there, and after awhile he say, "Look there," say, "he'll get in Joe's lap directly." Man said, "Well, I couldn't get in a better lap." And stopped him from talkin right there. It hurt Ford Morgan to see he was takin that much interest in me, more than he was in what they were sayin.

Ford Morgan was mean man. And he shot hisself. Shot hisself right through the stomach and there was two colored fellows in the next field workin and be dog if I believe they put them in jail. But he told his wife and some more of em just before he died, he shot hisself. Was a stray dog out in the field and he carried his gun backs and forwards to get a chance to kill that dog. And he stopped the team that he had and the dog was in the other field, and then he was gettin through this wire fence and it must've pulled the gun to him by the muzzle and that's the time she went off.

And man in Easton had told me before how he would come in there, Ford Morgan, how he talked about me, "White people around here," say, "just ruined him." I said, "Well, that can happen sometime. The very one that will run you down the most, that's the one somethin will happen to em." He told me, "Don't say much about it because they might think you had somethin to do with it." I didn't know the man, never worked under him. I don't know why he takin a dislikin to me cause I wasn't even acquainted with him. But I guess it was because I was gettin along a whole lot easier than he was. And I could associate with the better class than he could. Sometime that makes a difference.

I had a brother-in-law workin down there under him. And my brother-in-law said he heard him say, "Them people down at Tunis Mills just ruined Joe Sutton. They just ruined him. He goes down there and they treat him like he's a king." Say, "They've just ruined him." My brother-in-law told him, "Well, I guess if that's something they want to do, that's their business." Yeah, he taken a dislikin to me on that account. But he wasn't no good and God wasn't long movin him, either. They say when they was out in the field, they was together somethin like huskin corn, they'd see me come out and turn towards to Easton. "There go Joe Sutton, instead of bein over to work, ridin up and down the roads."

One time, man got lynched or bust his head in the Easton jail yard. Either the yard or right in the jail. And one got lynched in Salisbury. I don't know which was first, they wasn't so far apart. This man they had him for rape. Home was down around Trappe. And they wanted to hang him and one of the officers had a club and busted his head before they put him on that trap. Bust his head and then put him on that trap. And that same officer he killed a fellow right down back of the court house on the street there. For nothin. That's the same time when you couldn't have whiskey in your possession. And him and another fellow was down there drinkin. This man walked up on em and when he walked up on em this fellow dropped the bottle, did it intentionally, down on the bricks and broke it. Well the law had no evidence then. The man told him, "Pick it up." He stooped down to pick it up, shot him and killed him.

And then some of em brought charges against and they had buried him. And the governor, Governor Ritchie, wouldn't let this fellow's people take him up to prove that this officer bust his head. And the way they know it, was two men there. I don't know what business they was on but they was there, they say, up the country. And they never said nothin about it while they was in Easton but after they got home they report it. Well by that time they had buried him. It was too late.

Lots of that stuff has happened. This fellow they killed down here to Salisbury, I heard a white man from down there was tellin it. He told the fellow owned the place where I was in Easton there. That was one of my main places of goin. And the conversation come up. He said, "He didn't shoot that man." And this man that owned the place say he didn't know. Say, "He didn't shoot him." And he say, didn't nobody shoot him but his son and put it on this colored fellow. And the colored fellow had been workin for this man, the man had some kind of lumberyard, I think. "Well," say, "he'd been workin for him ever since a boy," say, "big enough to work." Say, "And, we know him. We know he didn't shoot him. And we know the son was the type to shoot him. He was never made to work and they always give him everything he wanted." And he was spoiled! And they made a mistake and they was trying to break him. And he was the one that killed his father.

And after they had lynched this fellow, well, they say the majority of them then down there spoke of it, they said the same thing, said, "Wasn't nobody but his son." He killed his father and then shot this colored fellow so he wouldn't be there to be against him. Then he said this colored fellow had killed his father and he took the gun away from him and shoot him. They sent this colored fellow to the hospital and when they got him out that night to lynch him he wasn't dead, but they say he was in bad shape critical hurt. And they drug him all through the colored section behind the car.

And, it was another lynchin down there. They sent to Baltimore and got some guards. And had these guards to take I think it was five or six of the white fellows from down there to Baltimore. They did that to show em what they could do to em. Well they didn't do nothin to em. They carried up there and showed em and the fellows come on home. That was all of it. And I know one of the fellows well. Cause he went from up here. Him and I both used to work for Mr. Ed Miller the meat store and he was just that kind of fellow. And his home was down at St. Michaels. And he liked that rough stuff.

Another man, he was on a bicycle and got hit with a car. And he went off that bicycle and head hit that street. And the fellow ran into him, he was driving on the left side of the street and the old man come up Dover Street to Washington Street and he was on his right side. And this car was goin down Washington Street close to the curb on his left side. He didn't see anything, he just come out and the time he was gettin ready to enter the street he see this car come out on the left side and hit him. The old fellow fell off, head hit the street, he kind of staggered when he first got up, then he kept rubbin his head. And they had a town cop, they only had one them days, when he come, "I told him bout ridin that wheel with his head down."

Not less than six months the old man was totally blind and he was that way till he died. "I told him, I told him about ridin that wheel with his head down." They never said a word to the fellow for driving on the left side of the street. "I told him the other day about riding that wheel with his head down." And a short time after that the old man went blind, from that blow to his head. And that was all. Never saw nothin or heard of anything being in the Easton paper bout it. That's the kind of law we had to put up with. I saw one white man shook his head when the officer said that. He shook his head and looked at the other one. Anybody know that was wrong.

And they speak about other places that the colored people treated so bad. In one place in particular is down south. They have it just as bad here as it is down south. Well when they get to talkin about the South I always say, I'll say that openly, it's just as bad here in the way as it is down there. Just as bad. That prejudice, that's the stuff. I had a white man told me that come from down south and I think as much of him as I did anybody here that didn't come from down south. Where you come from don't make you, that stuff's in you. It don't pay to talk about prejudice too much. I don't guess I spoke of it half a dozen times. But I haven't forgot it, though. I still think of it. It don't pay to talk too much cause I could get somethin unjust just as well as the other fella. But as I say, we got somethin comin, we ain't going to miss it. I may be gone, I hope I will be, but we got somethin comin. I don't know how people can see somebody else dirt and can't see their own. They speak of justice. We got somethin comin and I hope I'll live to a ripe old age and be gone. That stuff can't go on all the time. There'll be an end to it someday.

And one time this colored man had been workin for this man. This boy had shot his father and this colored man come in and he shot him. Keep this fella from tellin who killed his father. And he carried im to the hospital and then when he got out well them bad fellows down there to Salisbury, they got together and went to hospital and take him out. Tied him behind the car and drug him all through the colored section. Say they did this just to show the rest of the niggers what they would do if they got out of hand.

Well, I was to this place fixin Dr. Webb pump gun. He had it to some gunsmith and whatever it was that was the matter with it, well, the man hadn't fixed it. Then I was correctin it. And this man come in I heard all he said about it and he said it so I could hear it. And he kept on talkin and talkin loud. He wanted me to hear him and I didn't say nothin. And then he said something and nother man come down and stood alongside of me and nudged me, that was not to answer. And the fella, he kept right on. "Yes," say, "we drug him all through that nigger section let them see what we'll do when they get out of hand." And then he say they goin to get some more of them niggers down there. And then they was gettin close to me, lookin at me. And I said, "Haven't got you." I say, "You're lucky." I say, "You better look out," I say, "they'll get you next then." And that was the time you'd never know it was me, because I had this hammer in my hand. I had made up my mind I was going to hit him right in the head that hammer.

And this poor fella hadn't done a thing, he had worked this man for years and years. I believe it was some twenty years or more he had been workin there. And this man had trust him. Had no trouble with him. And come to find out it was the boy. And she died right down. Never heard no more about it nothin. Nothin in the paper about it. Well, that's what I don't like. If anything bad enough for it to be in the paper about one person, one nationality, it ought to be in the paper just the same bout the other. Then it look like it would be fair.

It was just like the other man killed this colored man down somewheres near Princess Anne. Very little in the Easton paper about it. You got more out of the Cambridge paper than you did the Easton paper. He killed him and got away. And he's way west when they caught him.

That's why I got no use for Salisbury. Had another lynchin down that way. And didn't do a thing only had the fellas to come to Baltimore. That's all they done about it. But still they ought to go by the law. You got a law for a crime, use that law. And then don't use but the same law on both races. Don't use one law on one race and another law on another. It's a law against lynchin. Just as well say both cases was lynchin. Because the man was alive when they took him out of the hospital.

And Isaiah Fountain, he raped a white girl. She was a Simpson. Say he was guilty. I don't know anything about that. But if he was guilty, he should have got the punishment of the law just the same. When they had the trial they wouldn't let her come in the room. Said she was sick. She was in one the other room. I never heard of any say that he didn't get a fair trial, white or black. But he didn't get fair treatment. If he was supposed to be hung, he should been hung. He was killed Easton before they ever put him on the gallows. Man bust his head with stick just as he was ready to go on the gallows. This man was wrong was a friend of mine. They had the gallows put up, just ready to put him on it. And this man took up a stick and bust his head. And it was two white fellas they was from up the country. And they went in to see him hung. And they saw it. And they want to take him up for proof. And one that did it, got in touch with the governor and the governor forbid em takin him up.

And then the same man shot a fella. When you wasn't supposed to carry any whiskey. Walkin, on you, or car. That was the derndest law. And this fella's right back of the courthouse, was under them trees. And another fella was with him and live here in Unionville. And he was goin to give this fella that live Unionville a drink. And he pulled his bottle out and he was goin to take the first drink. And this deputized man, he was walkin up back of em. And he walked up, say, "Hand me that." Well, he dropped it. And all the evidence gone then. He reached and got his pistol, said, "Pick it up." And when he stoop down to pick it up, he shot him. Wasn't nothin to that. And he told the tale, said he dropped the pistol and it went off. Then when come to the day of the trial, the fella that was with him, he was supposed to go up and he went to work. And had it been the other way around, they'd of locked him up. But they didn't do a thing about it. He went on to work. Then you couldn't get him to say much about it even after that.

I was on Washington Street standing up one day and this white man come up to me and spoke. And he smiled. Say, "Well, I don't know you." Say, "You don't know me," say, "but just to look at you," say, "you seem to be a good colored fella." I say, "Well, I was taught to be good and I try to be good." And then he got to speakin about the laws they had here. And I never know who he was or where he's from. He says, "Well, I'll tell you," say, "United States," say, "all right," say, "but they have two laws for the same thing." I say, "How do you mean?" Say, "We got a law for the white and a law for the black. A law for the colored." So I studied and I said, "You're right about that. I go out there and kill, somebody'd lynch me and white man go out there and kill somebody, probably wouldn't lock him up." I say, "You're right about that." Well, I don't know whether he was a spy in this country or not. Talk like this wasn't his home.

I remember one time, was a fella run and hit the colored man with a car comin from Wyc Mills was livin that section up there someplace. It was two of em. It was a younger man and this man he hit must of been around eighty. And they was over one side of the road. And this car come meetin em. And this younger man, he was supple enough and able enough to jump out of the way, jump in the ditch or jump over the ditch. Well, this other man, he couldn't do it. He hit this old man and killed him. And this fella went up the road distance, turned around, come back. I guess, to see whether he got both or em or not. Come back and slowed down and he saw this old man, this young fellow was just standin by the old man then. And saw him layin there and he went down the road and turned around and he come back, say he opened that car up. And some way they found who the fellow was and had him up. And they give him one year. Just one year. And he stayed six months and was back in Easton.

I went to Oxford one time with fella from Tunis Mills, Clayton Griffin. He was goin down to see his girl. She used to be a schoolteacher. And he got me to go down there with him, cause would be night. And I waited for him and waited and waited. I went to house with him and then I knowed a white man down there that kept barber shop. We was good friends. Had been for some time. And I told him I would be up to the barber shop called the fella name. He say, "I'll be goin back in a few minutes." Say, "I'm goin ride in Easton, come back." Well, I waited; the man kept his shop open until ten o'clock. And I waited until ten o'clock and he hadn't come back. Then I went to the house, where he picked his girl up, and her mother said, "No," say, "Mister," say, "not back yet, but they'll be back directly."

And I waited just half an hour or more and then, I guess the devil told me to do it, I got on the road and walked. I say, "I'm gonna walk." And I got out of Oxford, a right good distance up the road. And I was walkin to my left, they say that's what you should do. This car was comin. And well I got far enough over, and this fella was up in the center of the road. When he got to me he cut right cross. And I jump back and then on that old car, there was runnin board. Just brush my leg. Well, if he had run over me killed me, wouldn't have been nothin to it. And why I thought of bein careful, cause two weeks before that, colored fella got killed on the same road. And good thing I did think of it. Cause hadn't, I wouldn't been ready to jump. And he open that car up. Went on down.

And it's been a lot of em killed like that, a lot of em been killed a purpose on the road. I know they tried to run over son William on Easton Road. And William jumped the ditch and run in the woods. They missed him.

And I've heard several of em say that they missed em. They pick John Emory up on the road one time. He was walkin out of the town and he live over here. They pick him up, somewhere out of Easton and he ask him where they goin I don't know whether they told him or not. But anyhow he got in, and he told him if he goin past Pincushion he'd like to get out there. When he got down there, they speed the car up. And they carried him down the other side of Royal Oak. I think it's three of em in the car. And when they got down to Deep Neck Road, well they stop and told him to get out. And two of the fellas was talkin. And John hung out. He got away from em. One of em started behind. But John say this fella couldn't gain on im. And he had to give it up. But they was gonna kill him. They was goin to do somethin like that to him. Put him in the road and claim somebody hit him with a car.

They was bad about killin in them days. They killed a mess of em. And I know a boy, down below St. Michaels. But he used to live over here, not far from where I live when I was around by Hopewell. They killed him. And told a tale that he jumped out and found the car. Was flaggin em down with his hands up. And they struck him. And they don't do any vestigatin. It don't pay to report it. They don't investigate nothin like that. Don't take the time, the money.

Part VI

I lived opposite Hopewell until 1935. The man that held the mortgage on the place was sellin the house and woods all together. We come out to Unionville to William Henry Jackson place. He wasn't livin in it then; hadn't long lost his wife and he was stayin up the road here to his aunt. He was my wife's cousin. His father's father and her father was brothers. And his mother and my wife's mother is sisters. He told my wife that we could go there to live. We lived there about one year.

In 1935, I went down to Colonel Lipscomb's. First time I had lived out of Miles River Neck since I had been married. And moved down there to work for Charles Lipscomb, the son. He had gone in the pigeon business. That was one of the best jobs I ever had or one of the best to work for. And Charles had never seen me I don't guess to know who I was, cause I didn't know him. He had heard about me. My wife was cookin for Charles and his wife. And her sister worked there then. He told my wife to tell me he wanted to see me and when he did see me well that's what he wanted: me for to take care of his pigeons. And Jackson that owned the house I was in was gettin ready to get married and I was workin for man then. And wasn't doin any heavy work or anything like that—dogs, little carpenter work, and stuff like that. And I told him about goin to Lipscomb's and he asked me why. And that's the time he told me, "I'll pay you as much as any other man. I'll pay you as much to stay on." I told him Jackson wanted his house. And I said, "I've got to get out." And I say, "In this job I won't be goin far from home." And after I explained that to him he was kind of downhearted for a time but then I moved down to Lipscomb's.

But that other man was no good. If I wasn't handicapped I wouldn't worked for him for no price. He was a mean man, what you call alcoholic. Had them spells he'd go on drunks. And he didn't know how to talk to you lots of times. And sometime I'd have to raise my voice and I don't like to do it. Don't make me feel so good. Sometimes he'd holler at me, I'd holler at him.

And he was cheap! I was drivin from Unionville down Trippe's Creek, night and mornin and only payin me a dollar and a quarter a day. And when I need a tire, I couldn't save money enough to go and pay for the tire, I had to get it on time. I hardly got enough to pay for my gas and my food. I just quit.

I forgot now what the words we had. But I didn't fuss with him. Just told him to get somebody else. And then he got a boy in my place, less than two weeks after he got the boy, sent the boy on a Sunday to Easton after the Sunday paper and boy tore a brand new car up for him. And one of his associates was tellin me bout it say he didn't know what Jack was thinkin about. "Gettin rid of you," say, "for that boy," say, and one of em said, "I asked him, 'Wouldn't you rather have Joe,'" say, "'than to have that boy?'" And he wouldn't make no answer. He know he would but he wouldn't say. Another one of his associates say he said him, "Joe wouldn't've done that." "I know he wouldn't, I made a mistake." And he tried to get me again I wouldn't go back no more.

I did carpenter work to Lipscombs to finish the buildin. And then he got more pigeons after I got the buildin finished. And I was there two years and I was sick then and on a strick diet and worked every day. I had my work to do Sunday just the same as I did any weekday. Had the pigeons to tend to. Had to feed them at certain time and water em.

I remember a time his wife and Charles went away just for a few days and we had one pen. We had squabs in there wasn't mated. When they'd get old enough to feed theirselves well we'd put them in that pen. And I had one or two old pigeons in there because they had lost their mates. A fellow come in there one day he want to buy a pigeon. He want a hen pigeon. His wife had a rooster pigeon but she want a hen pigeon. And did I have one to sell him. And I studied I said, "Oh yeah, oh yeah." And I went back there and he went back with me. I took the net and caught his hen pigeon and sell it for dollar and a half or two dollars. It what Charles want for them. And he told me he didn't have any money and I kinda held back. I say, well, I don't know what to do about it said, "If Mr. Charles was here, pretty sure he'd let you have it but I don't know what the right thing for me to do." And then he told me he'd leave his watch. Well he left his watch.

And Mr. Charles come home a day or so after that and it was a man went to Mr. Charles that little time and told him said, "Well you know Joe is sellin pigeons." It wasn't but one pigeon. Talked like I had sold several of em. Say, "He's sellin pigeons. He sold a man a pigeon the other day." And it surprised me, that man would do it. So Mr. Charles told him, "Well," say, "he have a right to do it. I give him the privilege to do it. He have a right to do it." And he said this fellow he didn't know what to say. He didn't say anymore. So I say well he's one of them troublemakers. And when Mr. Charles come down to the pigeon house I told him about it. Mr. Charles smiled, said, "Yes, Joe I heard about it." And that's the time he told me what the fellow said. And then come to find it was some relation to me.

And then I was there one year and he said to me one day, "Joe," said, "you remember what happened a year ago today?" I studied. I said, "No, sir. I've been sleep since then. And everything that happened before I go to sleep, I forget the next day. I don't know nothin about it." He laughed. He said, "Well a year ago today you moved here." He said, "The things I heard bout you, I found out that they wasn't true." You see that was somebody that tried to make trouble. That was a poor white fellow. His father had workin there. And he said, "I heard you wouldn't work and you wasn't honest." And I don't know why that fellow wanted to tell that on me, get me out of the job, less he had somebody he wanted to put in there. But he say, "You've been here a year," say, "and I've found you honest, and truthful, and a good worker." Say, "And you keep on like that, you'll get along."

I worked there, it was a little over two years in the condition I was in. And that was too steady, the work was for me, and I broke down. I got so I couldn't do nothin. And couldn't eat much and what I did eat it didn't give me strength enough to work on. Went right back down to nothin. My blood pressure was so low until the doctor wouldn't tell me how low it was. It kept goin down, goin down. But when I was taken there I wrote to Dr. Travers. Dr. Travers was in New Mexico. So he sent me a prescription and his picture. And I never had the prescription filled. Just laid there and looked at his picture. Put it on a stand. And ate what I was supposed to eat and in a few days I could get out of the bed. So Mr. Charles when he used to have oyster roast, I always was there the head of it. He didn't want me to lift nothin. Didn't want me to do no work, just show the others what to do. And then they'd get a crowd together, make a ring, and make me get in the ring and get me to tell the bunch about Dr. Travers. Bout lookin at his picture instead of takin the medicine. That cured me, lookin at his picture. I'd tell it and they'd have a big laugh. Still it was a big help to me. People don't think that something you have on your mind, your life or somethin like that, it do a big part in improving your feelins.

Dr. Travers was in Gallup, New Mexico, then to a government hospital. And in the meantime the head doctor down the hospital at Salisbury, he died and course the head people at the hospital knowed Dr. Travers and they tried to get him. Then they wrote to him. He'd signed up I forgot now for how many years. And when he went to Salisbury they made it just as disagreeable for him they could. And then he left and went to Santa Fe, New Mexico. And then after my wife died he wanted me to come and stay with him as long as I lived. Say, "I'll guarantee you won't have to do a day's work." But that was too big a change. Me leavin here goin to a different climate like that, my age.

Sometime after that I went to Pennsylvania pheasant shootin. And I was so I couldn't eat nothin only whole wheat bread and milk. I was on a strict diet and stuck to my diet. Lost weight, strength, and everything else. I wasn't eatin meat and lots of other things. And then when we got up there that afternoon I set down the table and ate a big dinner. I ate a whole lots of stuff that I couldn't eat home and never fazed me. And I went out a little while that afternoon and when I got up the next mornin I didn't feel a bit tired. And we went out pretty near all day the next day. And I'm up on Blue Ridge Mountain, I felt better than I had felt for fifteen or twenty years. Didn't even feel tired from the bus ride. Then I was afraid to eat too much. I'd rather take a chance around home. Then when the colored went to get their dinners they put us in a place with a tool shed where you got poles and rakes and things set up. You come to a window and get your food and not a thing to sit on. And I didn't see anything in there but a grass mower, just a little place. It was no place for colored people up there. And it was no place for me, I don't care what color I'd been. Never did go back and I never will go back there no more. And I was scared worse coming down than I was goin up. Somebody says, "The brakes goin bad on this bus. Did you hear em squealin?" And that made me mad. I could've busted their head with somethin. And after awhile we got down. Great big rocks hangin up like they're ready to drop down. And they say they would put a notice on em. Well that ain't helping you. You goin to stop under none of them. And Lord knows how much they would tear up down on the low land below.

It was no hard work at Charles Lipscomb's but what I was doin was too steady for a person that was in the condition I was in. I guess I brought some of it on myself comin from Easton after twelve and gettin up at six. That's when I first started playin pool. My oldest boy, he started goin there and would tell me about people he used to meet there and told me about shootin pool. I'd never shot no pool before. I went there and got to shootin pool and I loved it. Played just about every night. My wife used ask me sometimes not to do it but I'd laugh, and got the habit. I stopped work and I'd always wait until she'd come home and get my supper. The pool was on Point Road. I was crazy bout it. I've gone there sometime before twelve o'clock in the day and didn't come out until eleven or twelve o'clock at night. Boys down at Tunis Mills got after me about it and I had cut some of it out. Course, I missed comin down there cause I was sick. They'd think that the colored boys would cut you. "You better stop that before some of them boys cut you." Told em I didn't bother with the boys. I had picked the ones I used to play with. And after awhile I give it up.

I got beaten a good many times. And I beat plenty of em that had been shootin several years. It tickled me one day, that was when I was beginnin to slack up or hadn't shot any, I guess a week or more. This boy come in, "Mr. Joe, play a game of pool?" I said, "Ain't no use in me playin you." I said, "You better pool player than I am." Say, "I won't be so hard on you." Well he kept worryin me and I beat him, five or six straight games. And I said, "Now, I surprised you, didn't I?" He said, "Yeah," say, "and you surprised yourself." Said to myself, "You are right I've surprised myself." Used to get a little rough in there sometime. When it did I'd leave. Was an old man

I started gettin myself in trouble about. He was four-handed. It'd be two other boys and myself. And he saw he was goin to lose the game he'd make out he dropped the cue stick in the bunch of balls. And I told him if he did, "I'm goin to drop you the same way." I say, "You messed this game up." I say, "If you're afraid you're goin to lose, stop!" And some other man say, "Mr. Joe you tell him what's right," say, "I been watchin him," say, "a man like that ain't fit to shoot with. You tell him right." He come from here to Centreville. So I told him, "If that's the way they shoot up Centreville they don't shoot that way down here. You better stay up there and shoot. If you don't somebody's goin to cut your head." Oh, I got good enough to beat the man that owned the pool hall.

And then I'd go into Buddy Taylor's garage, corner of West and Federal Street. The first time I ever went there I was livin around to Hopewell. When he was running a twenty-four-hour service and I was livin with Colonel Lipscomb, I used to go in there nights and sit up with him till twelve o'clock and then go home. It was just a hangin out place, to keep from goin down to Point Road and places like that. I guess that helped to carry me down. I wasn't gettin rest enough. I used to go in there bout every night. I used to bring my wife out to Unionville to her mother's some nights.

And some of them nights I'd be down at the pool room. And then when I went there two or three nights and didn't go to Buddy Taylor's well he'd get after me about not comin there. Said he thought I was sick why I didn't. I told him, "No, I was down at the pool room." And he was one of them told me to keep away from there. Said, "You ain't got no business in that bunch." Said, "You keep going there you going to get into some trouble you're liable to get killed." I used to help out sometime. I didn't have no job there. May might help him to fix a tire or somethin like that. And I worked Dick Renshaw's garage. His oldest boy would be there with him in the summer, when he went to school in September I used to stay there until school closed. One time he hired a fellow and I didn't go back that year and he found out he had nothin, then he fired him. Then I went back again. He was the man said he was surprised what I knowed about cars. The ones I worked on, say, and I never worked in a garage. But my best was the Model A and the Model T. Either one of them come in, Dick would always tell me, "Joe," say, "here's your car." And after I got a station wagon I used to haul his stuff from the wholesale house in Easton. Some time he'd go in with me and we'd go in and load that station wagon up.

And I got in a wreck down by that bend at Doncaster, the other side of the bend it's a big drive to your left. Right there a woman come out, ran into me, come right across the road right into me and knocked me off'n the road. And turned that station wagon bottom upwards. And the floor boards then was removable, and when she turned over, the floor boards fell on the inside and I was smokin a cigar. And I said to myself, "I ain't hurt. I'm goin to look for my cigar." And I was layin there and see a little smoke comin up. And I knowed it would've been my cigar. So a man, he saw when the car hit and he runned there and hollered, "Mister, mister is you hurt?" And I was layin, still lookin for the smoke. "Mister, is you hurt?" I said, "No, I'm lookin for my cigar." And they kidded me about that for a long time.

And I bought a Model T that was dern near as good as it was when the man bought it new. Man in Tunis Mills and he didn't go only when he had to go. And he was a careful driver. He had died. I bought it from his wife. And she had promised it to another fellow, Charles Copper. And she said, "Joe," say, "you and Capt'n Draper," say, "such good friends," say, "I promised it to another man but you and Capt'n Draper such good friends," say, "I know he would rather for you to have it than the other fellow." And I bought it for fifteen dollars and refused fifty dollars for it. That's the time people was havin so much trouble with the heavier cars. Places they couldn't get in you could get in with a light car like a Model T.

After two years at Charles Lipscomb's we come to Unionville to house that used to be my grandfather's when he first started buildin out chere. My wife's sister's husband owned it, that was James Blake, and they was in New York. Stayed there about a year. And Mr. Charles offered to buy me a home in Unionville. The place we was thinkin was for sale, come to find out it had been sold a few days before that. And it was goin to be sold for divide the money up between the children that was left. And the place sold for good as nothing. It cost around three thousand dollars to build it. Them days. And I think it was sold for six hundred dollars. Mr. Bartlett, man that owns the place near Unionville, he bought it. Farm hand used to live in it after that. The house was the newest house in Unionville that time and two lots. And I just missed it.

Never had any money when I was born and then lots of times I didn't have anymore than I had when I was born. I never did go and beg. But always been time that I could always get little money cause I could do more than one thing. And I used to do car work.

I remember one time I fixed a man car, it was seven or eight dollars and I got a dollar and a half and I never did get anymore and I did it cheaper than he could have got it done to the garage. A whole lot cheaper. On a Saturday night, man run into him, wrecked his Ford. Bent it up bad. Fenders. He was out here on a Sunday and I come out the road here and he want to see my brother. Say get him to fix it up. My brother didn't know nothin about fixin no car. And brother asked me would I fix it. I told him, "Yeah." Cause I was doing that thing for a living. And he called this fellow and told him, said, "My brother Joe will fix it for you." Say, "You will, Mr. Joe?" I say, "Yeah." "What will you charge?" I say, "I've got to look at it first." And I looked at it. I said, "I'll tell you what I'll do. I'll charge you seven dollars and I'll fix it up." You will?" I say, "Yeah." I said, "And if you take it to a garage it would cost you about twenty-seven dollars." He laughed. "Yeah, there was a man told me this mornin he got a garage man to go out and look at it. Twenty-seven dollars." And I did it for seven dollars and never got seven cents. Said, "I lost my job." He was workin contractors down to Trappe and lived in Copperville. Told me he had lost his job. Well, I didn't have a thing to do with that. Never got nothin. But it was my fault I should've held it right there until he paid me but I didn't know that he was bad payer.

It's another fellow had a Model A, it was just about wore out. Couldn't get it started, wouldn't run right if he did get it started. And I fixed that thing up, ground the valves, put him in one or two valves. And he never give me a cent. Saw him sometime after that and I asked him for the money. He said, "I've lost my job now." That's all I got out of him. "I've lost my job now."

And I butchered for years. It was a man, he had a meat store over here. The man'd sell meat that was the principalist things he sold. I started with this man's father. And then his son taken the store. The store was in Easton on Washington Street. I started butcherin for him. Then I went from helpin him and I was sent to do it myself. That was calves, lambs. I slaughtered some after I was operated on but I never done much after I was operated on. I killed em and cleaned em. And they cut up to the store. I didn't do any of that. And then we used to kill beefs, they call em. Steers, cows, anything like that. You come to beefs, I couldn't handle it by myself. But, course, that's more than a one-man job.

We was livin in Jim Blake house, but Jim Blake was comin home from New York, they want their house. They had been in New York bout four or five years workin on a job. So we left their house. We had my granddaughter and the youngest boy livin with us. We went to Millerstown to Richard Moaney house. Same as Dobson house we had lived in. Was a man further down the road had lost a rooster. And I was moving like today, and like tomorrow he come down and asked me did I have his rooster. And if I had been well I'd told him somethin.

Left Richard Moaney's. And we come out to Unionville to my wife's mother's house. We went there after my wife's mother died. My wife had shares in the house as much as those other children. My youngest son went to Baltimore, my daughter's daughter was still with us. We stayed there till my wife died. We stayed there four or five years. I wasn't doin nothin then, any particular job, drivin wells, workin on cars, and butcherin.

And time of the war, I butchered two or three horses. One nice-lookin colt three years old. I hate to kill it. This man wanted it butchered, and I need the money. And they say that's what this man did with it, sold it some place. The meat looked good, but somebody said it's a big difference in the taste. And a lot of it was sold right in the stores for beef. And then tellin me in the city in places they got strict law for sellin for beef and they sold it for horse-meat and people bought it. And I butchered a lot of old horses and mules for a man that was raising minks. That's what he fed his minks on. Wonder them things didn't come back and get after me, though. I didn't mind skinnin em but I hated to kill em. I butchered a mule, big old mule here in Easton. It was sold and I'm pretty sure it was sold for beef. One of them things will come back after me. Ain't bothered me yet. People say lots of times things like that will haunt you. And Charles Lipscomb heard of my butcherin. And he got in touch with me and got after me about doin it. I told him I had to do somethin to live. He said, "Well no, you don't have to do that and you ain't able to do it." Say, "I'll find somethin for you to do up home." He was livin up at Forest Landing. I went up there and he studied and he had a lot of paling fence there and give me the job paintin that fence. And I paint there a long time. And then he was tryin to think of something else to give me to do. Oh, I could do several things, and it was a big help to me. And sometime for a period I'd get much as I could do but the trouble was when the payday come. I did work for people there I thought sure I'd get my money. And some of em, I never got a cent. Some of em I got part of it. Somebody come there with big family I got it all. And the ones that had no family them was the ones that wouldn't pay. What I should've done, I should've kept their old cars.

Most of the children was away from home. The youngest one was home, he worked at Lipscomb's one fall from summer. And then of course he was laid off in the fall and he went to work for the Eastern Shore Nursery. And that's what he was doin when he left here. And the oldest boy, Lawrence, left here, went to Baltimore. That was the beginnin of the Second World War. He went to the Provin Ground. And he had a job doin carpenter work. And after that they sent him someplace. And William he went to Baltimore and he worked loadin and unloadin ships. William worked there some time. And you couldn't work white and black together. You'd have to separate em and they used to, when one bunch was workin above the other, the top bunch they'd get a chance they'd drop somethin on the ones below. And they wouldn't work the colored above the white cause if they did they knowed the colored would do the same. But still the colored never did do it but the white did it several times. And they was doin it on purpose. Lawrence, he like it. Somebody told him though, said, "Put you out chere." Say, "Here where you'll stay." Say, "They ain't goin to take you as a soldier, you'll stay here." Wasn't long before he got his notice.

And my wife got sick several days, but not a lingerin sickness. Doctor operated on her last time, if he had taken the pains probably she'd be livin today. I had a colored doctor and she laid home, I think it was three days or more, waitin for him. He was tellin me what to do and what to get. And he come to see her at first. And he didn't find out what was wrong then. And after she didn't get any better I called him up and talked with him. Well he couldn't come that day, he was lookin after these people that come here in bunches to work, goin around to them camps.

And then after she got so bad well I said I was goin to see another doctor. And I saw this doctor and I noticed he didn't talk like he wanted to talk with me. I could see was somethin wrong. I carried her there in the mornin and he never saw her till that afternoon. Then it was too late. I said to myself late that evenin, "Maybe she's better. Maybe she won't have to be operated on because if she did he would notify me." Well they didn't and I got the message eight o'clock that night that she was dead. And called up and say she was dead and asked me what we wanted done with the body. If that had been Dr. Travers, he'd went to work on her earlier that day. And the nurse I knowed her well, white nurse. And she told me say, "We put her down here." Say, "We forgot her." That'd make my case more easier right there. Put her down there and forgot her. And she was taken that night. And the colored ward then you was down on the ground floor and it wasn't a white person down on that floor. Down on a concrete floor as low as you could get. I couldn't've got anymore advice, I don't guess, but it wouldn't've happened if I had been white. But the nurse in that colored ward say, "We put her down here," and say, "We put her down here and . . ." say, "we forgot her." That's why he didn't see her when I first carried her in there that morning. That's what he should've done. I told him how long she had been sick. And I told him her bowels hadn't moved.

Then went there the next mornin after I heard that night, he was in. He had a bunch sittin around the waitin room, I was sittin in there, and he come through the door, looked right at me, said, "What you want?" And I said, "What I want? Want to talk with you. You operated on my wife without consent and not notifyin me for several hours after she was operated on. That's what I want." He shut the door right quick then. So keepin the people inside from hearin it. Well that was a dirty trick. She died from packed bowels. But I didn't ask him any questions. I showed him what I did know that he had no business operatin on her without my consent. And then letting me know she had died the way she did.

And I was told to sue him by two or three of the money people. Say, "You've got a clear case." Say, "He's bonded and you sue him and you'll get your money." But I got to studyin and well I was worried too and just let it go. And one lady told me, "No." Said, "I wouldn't sue him." She was one of my best friends, too. "That won't bring her back." I said, "Yeah, if I go out here and kill him, they'd hang me—that wouldn't bring her back." I say, "Would it?" Say, "No, but Joe, I wouldn't. I'd just let it go." And my druggist, he worked on me several days, "Sue him."

I didn't ask my family questions about it. I was feelin they didn't know any more or if as much as I did. And I wouldn't want their opinions. Cause I was afraid they would be the wrong way, the wrong opinion. Not knowing any more than the majority of em know. But I had a lot of em on my side, the white ones, come and ask me about it and I'd explain. And most of them said I should sue em.

And I never paid for that doctor. Who would? But he heard several times, I'm sure of that. And that was from the lady that used to go to the hospital. Just spoke of it. Didn't run him down or anythin like that. They say he didn't have much to say about it. They told the doctor who I was: say that's your cousin's best friend. Best colored friend—Joe Sutton. We all know him. But it's too late then. Dr. Travers and him was cousins. And when Dr. Travers come here on a visit and I told him about it, well, he didn't want to come out right away and say nothin. He dropped his head. And after awhile, "Well, Joe," say, "you right, Joe." Say, "That wasn't right." He told me with that condition they wouldn't get over it, if it had been in that way so many hours. Course when that happens to a person that's neglect of the person. Course I guess lots of em neglect theirself not knowin. And that was her trouble cause she worked that day and never felt it till that night. But wasn't nothin I could do.

And before she died, the insurance company beat me. Had been with that insurance company I think it was more than twenty years. They didn't pay for what they should've paid. But I don't know whether it was the company or the collector. Cause the collector, they found out after that he had beat several colored people then. And my wife had taken out new insurance or increased or somethin or other. Had different papers than you get just like a deed, she had them, had been payin on them and she was supposed to get more money—seven hundred dollars more. And he went to the house when I don't know who was home and he got them papers. And they couldn't find nothin on the old policy. And then when they paid off they paid by the old one. And I wrote headquarters down there at Salisbury. And got a letter back, if I could tell somethin unnecessary said they'd pay the new premium. When they know or thought I couldn't tell em.

Insurance ain't a thing but a beat. Know the insurance company owed me one hundred and seventy dollars and I don't know how they hid it. As poor as I am. Look like they'd have the government furnish you somebody to look into them cases like that.

And this same fellow he beat so many people until that insurance company had to get rid of him. And this colored doctor in Easton told me that he got a colored woman down at Trappe insurance and she was supposed to be dead. He had it fixed so that he got the money from the insurance. And the woman's still livin. And he had somebody else he wanted to beat and he had papers wanted him to sign as the doctor. And after that when they put him out, they should've sent him to the penitentiary, but they put him out and he bought a man out in a drug store in St. Michaels.

Part VII

After my wife died, I stayed to her mother's place for a while but not long. Moved down to Millerstown to house was Henry Green's daughter's. The one owned that was old man Bill Moaney. And that was the house that Ennals Tull got for seventy-five dollars. And I could have got a better house but it wasn't where I want to be. And Henry Green he stood for the house and the girl dropped it on him. And she told me she said, "You go there, it ain't fit to live in, Mr. Joe," said, "but you go there, you stay there long as you want to." And I asked her what she wanted a month for it. She said, "Nothin." And I stayed in there a few months for nothin. Then after that Henry Green want so much a week for it and it wasn't fit to live in.

But a lot of em was down on me bein in that old house. And the roof was bad and the windows and the doors. I went in there the front door had them two little panels at the bottom, had them out, dern cats was livin in there. They'd go right in there. So I got a door and put a door on there and I had to put a window in it. And it poured down when it rained. I've had to get up at night and turn my mattress on the edge and maybe I could get a place that it wouldn't rain on and then I'd look for a spot where it wasn't leakin! You could lay in there, look up and see the stars. And that's what them boys at Tunis Mills was speakin of, tellin me, "Sutton, that house ain't fit for you to live in." Boys Tunis Mills told me they'd put a roof on it for me. Boys that was doin carpenter work but I wouldn't let em do it because be puttin the roof on somebody else house for me. I could've got the roof on like today and they could take the house away from me like tomorrow. And had a big chair sittin in it and when I got ready to move from there, it was full of bumble bees come in through that window. I don't know how I ever got it out the window, but I got it out the window and left it sittin in the yard. I went there gettin ready to move the chair and could hear them things hummin in there. Know several people, white people, speakin bout me livin in there. I told them, "Drownded man grab at a straw." Some of them had to laugh! I guess I was there a year. It wasn't much more than a year. And that's the time I went down on the farm.

And her father, Henry Green, was tryin to get her to buy it. And she didn't like it because the house was messed up so it'd cost more than it was worth to repair it. And she wasn't able to build a new one. And then she throwed up on it, and it was in such shape. And then her father had to take it. And then I went to pay him the rent. I believe he charged five or six dollars a month. And the last month when I went to pay him he told me he wanted the house. I said, "When?" Say, "Right now." I said, "Well you will not get it right now." I say, "I got to have thirty days or more." I'll be durn if he didn't go in town here and give it to the sheriff for the collection and get me out. And I saw him the day when he went in the jail. And I said I bet that was his business. So after that I saw the sheriff and he said, "Joe," said, "are you livin in Henry Green's house?" I said, "Well I guess it is, I've been payin him the rent." And he say, "He wanted me to put you out. Said he had a sale for the house. You got a place to go?" I said, "No indeed." Say, "Well, you stay right there long as you want to till you get a place. I ain't goin to put you out." But he went up there to the sheriff, give it to the sheriff to get me out the house. Dirty man do somethin like that.

I saw Mrs. Glenn Stewart sometime after I had moved to that old house in Millerstown. And Mrs. Stewart said, "Joe," said, "where you living now?" I told her, "Millerstown." And told her what house. "You living in that thing?" I said, "Yes'm." Said, "Well, Joe, you too good a man to be livin in anything like that." Say, "I've got a house down Tunis Mills," say, "I had it repaired just two years ago and it ought to be in good shape now. You go down there and look at it and if it's fit to live in you go there and stay as long as you want to. It won't cost you one cent." She said if it wasn't fittin to live in, say, "I own seven farms on Wye Island and seven house." Say, "And you go there and pick the best one and stay there just as long as you want to." I thought that was very nice but I couldn't live to Wye Island because my back there I wouldn't have nothin to do to make a penny. And I wasn't able to go out to work like I had been years before I was operated on.

But that house was all messed up. Mrs. Stewart had a colored man was livin up here to Rich Neck. And then she wasn't going to farm Rich Neck any longer and she rent it out. She had this colored fellow to move down here to Tunis Mills and take that house. Then that colored fellow moved out of it. After he moved out, somebody had messed the walls up. Took looked like a two by four and went along the walls just picked the plasterin full of big holes all around. And had shelves put up, nice shape in the kitchen, they went there and mashed all them shelves right down. Just messed it up all around. Well they did the same thing with Mr. Schiller house over here at New Design. I'm pretty sure it was boys, I don't think a man would do anything like that. They used to use the house and they locked the house, when they come to get it, they couldn't get in, and they broke the door open and went in and just messed the walls up. Some of them walls had been plastered ever since slave time.

But I wouldn't have the money to fix that house up. And I wouldn't ask Mrs. Stewart to. She told me where I could go if it wasn't fittin to live in. It don't pay to ask too many favors. And those people at Tunis Mills didn't want that colored man livin there. But I could live there! Cause the boys didn't call me "colored." Used to call me a "white man." Say, "Sutton's a white man only they made a mistake paintin him." Well, I used to live around them—ninety percent of my associatin when I was up and around was down at Tunis Mills. And lot of colored people I've heard had things to say about it.

And I went down on the Rieman place in an old house wasn't fit to live in. I went there and stayed there a year or more. The Riemans raised me. And the ladies they was tickled to death that I was down there. She even told me I could come up to the house and get my breakfast every mornin. I thanked em but I didn't do it. I got enough to eat cause I used to get two meals a day down to Schiller's.

And after awhile man say he wanted that house but it wasn't that he wanted it, he just wanted to burn it down. And I didn't have no place to go. And looked like he would've thought about the favors I had done for him. So I had to get out and I went to the next farm to the Riemans. There was an empty house there, and the caretaker he had the say of the houses, say he would ask this man. He say he turned down some of them want to rent it. He wanted to know who wanted it, told him Joe Sutton and he told this fella, "If it's Joe Sutton, tell him yes, he can have it and stay here as long as he wants to." So I went there.

Then after awhile my daughter bought this place in Unionville, had the ground, bought this shack and she wanted me to come out to Unionville to live, which'n I was glad of. And when I come here to live, I was tryin to find a outbuildin so I could bring all my things here. Place was small, well, I had no place to put all my things. Was a farm house next to mine and I didn't worry about my things, left everything in the house. After awhile, said to myself, "Well, I've got to go down and see bout my things; somebody will take em all." And went down there they had broke the door open, had taken what they want. Everything that was movable. Things I had had for long as I had been married.

I had an old antique wardrobe, somewhere way back in the Rieman family some of the Riemans owned it. I had presents people had give me for birthday and Christmas for years like ties and stockins and handkerchiefs, I had piled up high in that wardrobe. They got every one of them. I had at least three suits of clothes hangin up in there and they had got them. And I had some clothes that people had give me, was mostly shirts that I had never wore. And I had a big old-time bureau and I think it was three drawers. And they had taken them trays out and they had got everything. And that's where I had all my dogs' pedigrees and pictures in there and whoever got the clothes well they carried all of them off and all the pedigrees. And I thought that was safekeepin puttin em in there but it was no place in the house safe. And they got some dishes. I know one thing it made me sick. Stuff my wife and I had had that long. We had pillow cases, sheets, and towels that I had never used. And we had several salt and pepper shakers and I had put the dishes and glasses on the table and some of em went there and picked every silver piece out of the bunch. And they finally got pretty near all the glasses. And I had a box of tools, saw and a hammer and a hatchet, planes and things like that. Had em in a nice box. They didn't have to put em in no box, just take the box and all. And I had made a box had my fishin tackles in there. Lines and reels. In a nice box. Had made a handle for it and they just carried it on home where they want to go. And an old draw knife. Handle on each end and blade in the middle. And you could sit and cut, whatever you want to cut down with it just as same as you would a plane. And I had had that for years and the man that I bought it from, well, he went way back in his people's time.

And these were white men who were painting in the house. And the painters come from Easton. Painters and one carpenter. He come from Easton. This man that rent the place then when I saw him he told me about these fellows had the stuff and he spoke to em about it. And he told me he told Herbie Anders for to tell me that the fellows was takin my stuff. And Herbie never told me a thing. And come to find out he had had his mother there and had his daughter there. He told me hisself his daughter's mother had been in the house, say, "But they didn't want nothin," say, "they just come to look." Well why in the devil did they go out of their way to come down to go in the house and look?

And then after that, this man that owned the place had told me, said had spoke to em about gettin the things out of the house. Say he saw two or three of em. Say that things comin from over that way, and asked em where they'd get em and they told him. And he asked em didn't they know that they wasn't theirs, belonged to another fellow, a colored fellow. They say, "Yeah, I know him." Say, "He don't want em." When I went down there they had busted the back door open. And I nailed it up. When I went back the next day with a truck to get what I had in there they had busted it open again. It made me sick—one time I felt like I was better off if I was dead. It made me sick the stuff they'd got from me.

And then I went from Easton right down there and that's where I caught three or four head of em in the house then. But it wasn't nothin I could do. They had carried the stuff out, the most of it, I judge before that. But I've thought since then I should a give it to the law, but still I don't know. They knowed each other and they had been a long time doin anything about it. They all come from Easton. So I just had to let it go. And I wasn't acquainted with man who owned the place. Afraid he didn't want any trouble on his place. That's why I didn't see the sheriff. It's some people don't like anything like that happen on their place. If it had been a white man things gone the colored man was known to get em, well, he'd been locked up right away. But I didn't say much about it, just said I was better off for them to take the things than it would've been for them to come there some night and kill me.

So I stayed with my daughter. She heard talk of this part of the house and got in touch with the owner. And she bought it, they moved in here. And after that she bought that part that joined on, bought it from a contractor up here at Queen Anne. And had it moved down here. She paid so much for it moved. And the land belonged to her uncle, Charlie Jackson. He died up in New York, Long Island, I think some years after. And my granddaughter and her husband, they bought right next to my daughter. She bought from my son. My son had bought it, started increase his nursery down here but they want a piece of ground then got him to understand he couldn't take care of it surrounded by other people like it is here. And then my grand-daughter and her husband, they bought it from him. And then my daughter bought this little strip.

The Moody house Copperville could have been mine. That house still standin, well, that's where I was born. It's the oldest house in Copperville. Great-grandmother want to give it to me. And said it hadn't been changed in the courthouse from her husband's name. It was in John Moody Senior's name. When old man John died, well, it never changed at the courthouse. And young John just went paid taxes as John Moody. He was the first one took over, and he had as much right then or anytime as I had. He took over right away and wherever I was livin at that time, I wouldn't want leave to move there. And John Moody died, his wife, I forgot now how long, she died. And one of my uncle's sons got it. My uncle John Flamer went right over and taken possession of it. And he did it for get a place for one or more of his children to live. That would have been a battle right there. And rather than have that, I'd rather stay where I was. But if my great-grandmother had got what would like to had, I would owned it today. She wanted to go up to the courthouse and change it in my name. And I guess that's all she'd had to do, I reckon. I don't know nothin about the law. Maybe she would have to do a little more than that. But I may have some right to it. I think that anything that is taken over like that it should have to get consent of all the heirs. And there is the home place, Flamer place, that ain't nobody on it. Tore the house down and I don't know what—somebody tilled the piece of ground, I guess. Somebody's paying taxes, don't know how they ever fixed that up but I guess he got it fixed up all. And it's a place down the road here, mother's place. Down back of Millerstown. Pretty near three acres of ground it, but I don't say nothin about it. Haven't any idea own my share of it. Got a half-brother that lives there.

Well there's a piece cross the road you could buy once and say you can't buy it. Say it's a mess, people been trying to get it. It was goin once, it was ninety-eight dollars or one hundred and ninety-eight. Now you can't buy it. It's all mixed up. I had one brother that had a tomato patch in there. He married a woman, that man's daughter that owned the place. And she got a brother livin and he's the one makin all that noise and cuttin up about the place. And my brother's wife thought she was goin to get it but she come to find out that she couldn't do a thing. And he ain't done nothin with it.

When I moved to Unionville, I wasn't able to do nothin only little light jobs. I was still handlin dogs but I wasn't able to go out chere and do any heavy work but I was lucky I was able to do any kind what I had gone through. I went twenty years before I eat any meat. Livin on whole-wheat bread and milk and crackers and milk. And it ain't many who would survived, especially of my race cause they'd been eatin something they shouldn't and it would've killed em. But I stuck to right what the doctor told me.

I was going back and forth to Mr. Peter Thompson's for several years and never asked for a favor. And I could have got most any kind of favor that I asked for I believe but I didn't do it and some people would've wore theirself out asking for favors. I was eatin different places. I used to get the cook at night at Mr. Peter Thompson's and carry her home. Mrs. Thompson told me that she would go get her in the morning if I would come take her home at night. And say, "You can always get your supper." So I'd always get my supper there. Eat my breakfast home, get supper there. I always had enough to eat. And then I had a job lookin after dogs up to Forrest Landing, Mr. Thompson dogs and Mr. Schiller dogs.

And I did that I didn't know what year that Mr. Schiller moved from Pittsburgh. I went down to Wye to him. Some of em was sayin he was a hard man to work for. Of course I was into just what he was, like what he did. He liked quail and doves and duck shootin. I liked the same. And I know more about either one than he did when he taken me. At first I used to go down one day a week I believe. Take the dogs out and exercise. And after that it start every day. He was a nice old man. He had his funny ways. Everyone of us have ways different. Well, he must've thought more of me than he ever told me he did but I got up with people that class would tell me that "Mr. Schiller thought a lot of you," and all that stuff like that. He didn't give me the roses but he told other people about me. And was goin to buy me a place here but he was just a little too late. The place had been sold, hadn't been a week. Him and I had been to Easton and out Unionville together and he knowed the house was empty. He said, "Joe," said, "that's a good place for you." Told him, "Yes, sir, but it's sold." He said, "What?" I say, "It's sold." Say, "It is?" I say, "Yes, sir, sold about a week ago." And by that I think he was thinkin bout buyin it and givin it to me.

I made more than I could have got gettin social security. And then I think you only could make so much beside what they was givin you. I never put in for mine until I was seventy-two. I know when I put in for it I had to work for a year and a half before I could get it. Then when you did get it you didn't get much them days.

And I was operated on for a hernia. Hadn't long moved to my daughter's, cause my son, William, heard I was sick. I think his wife told him he better come down here and look for me. What brought it down on me as soon as it did it was pullin the boat up. I knowed I had a little puff there, I felt somethin sting like somebody shot a pin in you. And I noticed from that it begin to get larger. I knowed the thing hadn't broke. It was gettin larger all the time and this night it was larger than it had been. Then after awhile it woke me up. And I got my son with me to call Dr. Cox. Somebody said they wouldn't come in the country to you, tell you to come to the hospital. But he wasn't long comin out here. And that was I guess between six and seven o'clock. He come right out chere and then he examined me. Saw where it popped up and told me to get ready. Say, "You've got to go to the hospital, and you've got to go right away."

And man operated on me, he did all the operatin for Dr. Cox when his operatin came. They carried me up to the operatin room and it was a nurse walkin alongside the chair, and we had to wait to go in the operatin room. I guess they don't carry you in till you go to sleep. Well, outside, colored fellow pushin the wheelchair and she was walkin along the side next to me and she had somethin in her hand. We was there waitin, so I looked up at her. I said, "Are you goin to operate on me?" She smiled, said, "No, Joe," say, "I ain't goin to operate on you." I said, "I was goin to tell you if you did and I didn't wake up, I'd come back to haunt you." And she laughed. And I must've went to sleep sittin there cause I don't remember goin in the operatin room. And she had somethin in her hand and I believe that was what put me to sleep. And I saw her two or three days after I was operated on, I was in the hall. She said, "Well, Joe," say, "you did wake up." I said, "Yeah," say, "If I hadn't it'd been too bad on you." And she laughed.

But I paid when I was operated on for a hernia. It had been I think around fifty dollars and I had to pay that man one hundred and twenty-five. Course it was worth it, I just had to be operated on. I was glad I didn't stay in there so long. Glad I was able to pay him. I was workin down to Wye then. Wasn't much work but I got paid for it. When I went in Mr. Schiller was away and when he heard it he went to the hospital and when he went to the hospital I was out chere. I had come out the day before he went to the hospital. And he stopped in my son's there to see me and I was up walkin around.

And had a son, Lawrence, in Baltimore. That was the oldest son. He used to come down every two weeks to see me and I told him not to do it because the dangers on the road. He didn't have to come that often. The more he was on the road the more he'd be apt to be in a wreck or somethin. He told me, said, "You looked after me when I couldn't look after myself. And now I'm goin to look after you." So I told him if anything happened to me that somebody'd let him know. He said, "When I was little, you looked after me, when I couldn't look after myself." Well, I was awful good to him. I wasn't rough on im like some fathers, but still I taught im the right way to go. I had rules for em. But never was rough on em like some people with children. I taught em things they should know. That was be honest and have manners and them the two most important things in any child's life. Honesty and respect others. Have manners. And that's for all. That's for colored and white. And that's the way I came up. The person that I didn't want to associate with I wouldn't get where they was and argue with em. I just kept em around treat em like I'd want them to treat me but still didn't associate with em. I always told em what was right and what was wrong. Just like goin to school you take a teacher teaches children all alike. Some will learn and some won't. And some will learn quicker than some others. Lawrence was easier to control and you'll find that most all families.

I encouraged them to go to school when they was able to go and only had the one school over here and that wasn't called a high school. And none looked to go to any high school. Not then. And that just started I believe Lawrence and William both was out of school when it started. When they start going to Easton. And they put on a bus. Wasn't like the bus they got now. Wasn't as many white ones went. And I forgot now how many school sessions they runned it but there was several. They wouldn't carry nothing but the white. Wouldn't carry the colored. And then the colored got a bus of their own. It looked like an old truck concern. That used to carry em.

And Lawrence lived in New York awhile. Then come back home, wasn't long after he come back home that I moved down to Mr. Charles Lipscomb. And then they draft him for service. He was workin Mr. Lipscomb then. He left and went to work Aberdeen provin ground.

And he was in the service and then after he come out they give you free schoolin. He got that through Uncle Sam. Well he went into this frigeratin business. And he got a job with a man that had so many ships, ships of that freight line I reckon. Overhaulin them big freezers. And he liked the man he was workin under or just well to say workin for and the man liked him but the man retired at twenty years service. And then after he retired I don't know whether Lawrence say he told him he'd better stop and get hisself another job. But anyhow he was in favor of it and because he know the whites didn't want to work with the colored. Even some of em was immigrants here, they didn't want to work with colored. So he left and he went out for hisself. And he did that some time. And another fellow got around him and told him that he'd go in with him and that fellow didn't know nothin about it. And I told Lawrence before that happened to watch for such things as that. I said, "Somebody want to go in with you and he want you to do the work and he get the money." And wasn't in there long found this fellow was collectin the bills and he wasn't gettin anything. Found that what I told him was the truth.

Somebody said Lawrence should come home but he couldn't make a livin on the shore. He'd have to have somethin else to make a livin, he couldn't make a livin just doing that. I know a man used to do it and had a helper for eight or nine years with him. And the business got so poor he had to let this colored fellow go. He had to try to make out by hisself. And the colored fellow made it worse for him after he let him go. Colored fellow went into business hisself. And he was taken up by some the people that knowed him that they had worked for. He got business enough to live on in Baltimore but he wouldn't've got it here.

And he never got married until he was gettin old and only married about two years before his wife died. And never had any children. Both of em was gettin along in age then. And she was very smart, workin I mean. She had a job. Think she was a nurse in the hospital. Had that job several years. She was from Baltimore. Well that's where he met her in Baltimore. I don't know where she was from. Somewhere in the south anyhow. I don't know whether it was Virginia, North Carolina, or where. Course, Baltimore is runnin over with them southern colored people now. And a good many southern whites. Just running over with em. And percentage is greater in Washington than it is Baltimore. And always has been. That's their first stop. The majority of em come up here that's their first stop in Washington. Then comes Baltimore. Not all of em but the majority of em. Then they go from there to New York.

And when Lawrence was comin regularly, he was single then. He had lost her then. Then he was sick and died. He had a stroke and then went on with that stroke for some time and then he had another one. I don't know why Lawrence had the second one unless he did what he shouldn't do or somethin or other or didn't get the right attention. He went to the hospital up there and they put him in the hospital. He couldn't get in Reed's and he just laid there. They didn't do nothin for him. And then they worked on him and got him down here to Deerhead but that was too late to do him any good. But he went to this other hospital the one up there near Baltimore they say they didn't do nothin for him only just laid there. I think if he had gone down there when he first had that stroke I think he'd straighten up enough to get around. But he had a stroke and then he was doin somethin with his car. Doin somethin and they think he must've had another one. And he hadn't long got this car. And it belong to his sister now. He give what he had to his sister. And that's what he told her before he died. He told me. And he buried down here in Unionville.

Have got another boy, Robert. And he come down now and then. He lived in Baltimore. He's workin for the Salvation Army now. Drivin truck for them. Cause he's been down on the Shore here several times. And he drove a truck for years for the people that makes this asphalt. Cause he had one of the trucks that brought em down here to Talbottown. That was a right good drive, too, from Baltimore. But he did that for a long time. He's for a long time been workin for contractors. Drivin a truck. And then he had a job landscapin.

And the other son, William, is livin Unionville. He bought that place I think it was the end of the Second World War. He worked in Baltimore as a stevedore durin the Second World War. He didn't go in the service. He just worked there like hundreds of em did. Unloadin and loadin ships.

And daughter, Dorothy, we both live here together. She lives in one part the house and I live in the other. We're close together. I see her every day. Several times durin the day.

Some people ask me, "Don't it get lonesome?" I don't get lonesome. Listenin at somethin over the radio or lookin at somethin on television when I ain't readin. Oh, it could been better. If I had got to school like I should've got. I wouldn't been sittin down here. I'd've been some place making a decent livin. That's water over the dam. No use to worry about it, or think hard of somebody else that they didn't get it. Cause I was offered two jobs that you had to have a fair education. And each one of em was better than any job that I ever did. One was drivin a fuel truck. A colored man never drove any fuel truck around here, nowheres around here. Wasn't another colored man had a job like that and didn't get one like that for years I guess afterwards. But you got to have the education to do that. You've got so many papers to sign and stuff like that. I turned it down, had an excuse and turned it down, cause I didn't want to hurt the person's feelin, was a friend of mine that offered it to me. And it was two or three that I turned down on account of lack of education.

The other one was judgin Chesapeake Bay retrievers. In the dog show. That would've carried me out of the United States. And one man was tellin me all through Europe. Civilized part. The American Kennel Club governs show over there as well as the United States. I know sometime I would need to be readin and writin and I never answered the letter. But the reason they knowed about me is the dogs I sold and give pedigrees why the breeder's name had to be there. And that's the way they got hold of it. I was talkin to a man down at Bruffs Island, used to have dogs showed down there now and then. I was speakin bout the job that I turned down. An this man said, "Well, why didn't you take it?" Well, I didn't want to tell him nothin bout the education. I said, "Well, I was a colored man, I don't guess they'd be satisfied." He said, "Well, we don't care whether you're black or white if you know and that wouldn't have been any trouble. And you should've taken that, probably the best offer you'll have in your life." I said to myself, "I thought that when I turn it down." If I'd had the education I'd been big man up in there now. Well this man, I forgot now what breed dogs he had and he was only doin it for a hobby. He had somethin like a station wagon or a panel truck and that thing was long or longer than anything like that I ever saw. And it had different compartments for the dogs. An he had several of em in there. Some of em was tellin me he didn't have to do that—they say he was worth forty million dollars. Well, that's too much money for one person.

Well, I'm happy livin this way. Don't get lonesome. Whenever I ain't lookin at the television, I'm readin, and I can get a better conversation readin than I can listenin to a bunch in my house. I ain't livin like I'd like to live, but I'm happy. If I had money the onliest thing that I'd change is my surroundings better in the home. I don't like no bunch of people. It's so many different classes can get in one bunch, I don't care who they are, I'm particular bout who I associate with to a certain extent. And I guess that's from being around the Riemans from a boy but mostly Tunis Mills. No other colored person could've associated with em like I did. And I went to some of the homes. I didn't want all kinds of people associatin with em comin to my house, rather not have em. No other colored person could go down there and get the treatment I got.

But I do know color don't make man. Don't make in principle or nothin else. And color nothin to be ashamed of. Some say the blacks have got the original color. And who knows any difference. Things that you see in the Bible, colors and stuff like that, people just put it in there, they don't know what color them people are. They claim Adam was a black man. His two sons was black. Cain and Abel. Course ain't nobody can dispute that. What I feel about it as the old saying go, "That's water over the dam." Ain't nothin can be done about it now. And that's something I have never worried about. What bad treatment the black man had I reckon they got used to it. Like they cuttin up there in Africa. When it wind up the ones want Africa are goin to get it. Its wrong but you just have to take it. And they say the majority rules but not always. But they just stand around do nothin and let it be taken. Never ask for help. And I think it's three or four times more blacks in their own country, that's what God give em and still they goin to take it and give it to the whites. England said when she did give it up, that was South Africa I think, Johannesburg, and she said the islands and things, possessions she controlled, she'd give them up and give up her hold in Africa. Well, she could give it right over to the colored. That's their home. Didn't do it. England's just as dirty as any the rest of em. And Africa was a rich country but it ain't helpin the black people there. I don't know why they didn't take possession of the mines and things. And then I read where they was workin in mines, the help. They can't bring no families there and it was two or three times a year the men can go home, stay so long and come back. And just have to take what they offer. That's goin to straighten up after awhile. I may be gone.

And when I was a boy I didn't know nothin bout prejudice. But I learned about it. Still I haven't found as much as some people have but what I have found has been in the lower class. Know the better class give me a good name and we got some there to tell a lie on me in the lower class. It's prejudice, that's all. That was like that poor white fellow down here to the Wye. He used to call me Mr. Schiller, Mr. Morgan, and all the stuff like that. Prejudice, that's all. One day we was passin the carpenter shop and they had been doin somethin in there, and had dirtied it up. And Mr. Schiller said he was goin to let the farm men clean it again. Him and I walked past the door one day and he was in there and he hollered, "Joe ought to be doing this." And Mr. Schiller didn't say a word, kept on walkin. Then he come to the door. "Joe ought to be doing this." And Mr. Schiller never turned his head. Mr. Schiller said, "Joe can't do it." And that would made me feel like a fool and he turned around and went back in again. Come near causin me one mornin to wreck my car. Met him comin out in the truck. And I was over to my right side and he was comin right down the left side. He recognized my car, right down the left side. And I slowed right down, goin slow and I was just gettin ready to pull the car in the ditch cause I figured goin in that ditch wouldn't hurt me much as he would hittin me with that big truck. And he pulled off right quick. Just missed me, pulled off. And looked over and laughed. You see them things is hard to swallow, but you got to do it.

He was the one that I heard used to kick when he'd see me goin out in my car. "He's never workin. You see him every day drivin around in his car." Well, that was my business. And he didn't see me every day. It was just prejudicy.

And two or three occasions, when I got in a bunch of my color, I heard some of em to say, "I wouldn't want to be stuck around white people all the time." So I told em, I say, "If you could you'd be stuck right around there. Right around there and tell em everything you know and things you didn't know." But course I couldn't judge all the whole bunch by one. I'd only judge the one by what I heard him say. I heard one of em out there say one time, "I can't tell how it is that these people," say, "with money, some of them," say, "Sutton won't work, but seems like these people all with money like him." Well he didn't know what it was, it was prejudice, that's all. And it was only the low class they'd be black or white. I heard one said something about, up here to Safeway store, fellows and girls were there talkin with me. Well, they don't talk with nobody else. I said, "Well, that's their choice. You can't make em have a choice, they know who they want to talk to." It tickled me. I just laugh at em.

And when I die will leave where I'm buried up to the family. They'll do it where it's the most convenient place. I wouldn't like to decide on that. Still they have got a private graveyard, too. Family graveyard, Copperville, on the family's land. I think that's where they'll bury me. That's where they buried the rest that's died in the family but I don't like that private graveyard, somebody else get the place they gonna tear that up. Someday it'll be plowed up, somebody else own the land. Like down to Wye, they've got a colored graveyard down there but nobody knows where anybody's buried, just know they in there somewhere. And Mrs. Schiller I heard was talkin about fixin the graves up the ones that have sank down, they have them in there. And then somebody told me said right smart of that graveyard had been plowed, too. Plowin the field. And them that did know where different ones was buried, you see they gone theirself, it ain't nobody else here that ever knowed. Well, I'd rather for the family to decide that sometime accordin to the convenience and then that's the one thing you ain't gonna worry nobody, when you're gone you're gone.

Appendix A

Historical Notes on Talbot County

In this appendix, a brief and selective background for Joseph Sutton's oral history, based almost solely on a variety of documentary sources, is provided. Both primary and secondary sources have been examined. Where possible, particular focus is placed on Talbot County and, within the county, on Miles River Neck. Although information on blacks is scanty, especially for the seventeenth and eighteenth centuries, Miles River Neck is fortunately not neglected in documentary sources, mainly because it had been favored by whites as a residential area since the mid-seventeenth century. Also, and more importantly, the eloquent and influential nineteenth century abolitionist Frederick Douglass spent and recorded part of his youth as a slave on the Miles River Neck estate of Edward Lloyd.

These notes are arranged in four parts: first, a period beginning with the first grants of land in the mid-seventeenth century and lasting through the eighteenth century; second, the antebellum nineteenth century; third, the period of the Civil War and its aftermath; and fourth, the years beginning with Joseph Sutton's birth in 1885 and ending with the major portion of his narrative in 1940. Each period will be treated more fully than the preceding, a reflection of the amount of material available and its temporal relevance to Joseph Sutton's oral history.

Not appraised in this appendix is the divergence or overlap between histories of Talbot County blacks constructed from documents or from oral sources. In Appendix B, the reliability of parts of Joseph Sutton's oral history is assessed and the problems encountered in taking documents at face value are mentioned in a different context. The systematic comparison of documentary and oral versions of history should be undertaken, but the oral version must be constructed from the testimony of two or more informants, among whom there is sufficient agreement on specific versions of events.

The Seventeenth and Eighteenth Centuries

By the time that black slaves were imported to Maryland's Eastern Shore in the latter half of the seventeenth century, white planters had been settled on granted lands for several decades. Labor demands were met at first by white indentured servants, and slaves did not figure in the economic strategies of whites until the eighteenth century. This is reflected in the growth of the Talbot County slave population, which numbered only 500 in the early eighteenth century but which increased ten-fold in the next eighty years.[1]

In 1658, thirty-five whites were granted land in what would become Talbot County. Each man received from 100 to 3,000 acres, the total varying directly with the number of indentured servants imported.[2] Edward Lloyd, who had arrived in Maryland from England (via Virginia) in 1649, received the largest grant. In 1658, a 600-acre parcel called "Linton" was surveyed in Miles River Neck. "The Grange," an adjacent 150-acre piece, was soon added, and these would become the core of Lloyd's vast Miles River Neck estate.[3]

Land was the basis of wealth in Talbot County. The economy was based on a single crop, tobacco, until the mid-eighteenth century. Most planters were farmers who lived in one-room sparsely furnished houses and who leased forested lands, cleared them for tobacco and subsistence crops and fenced them against their few cows or horses. They purchased goods on credit from local merchants, and they hoped that the tobacco crop they later traded would cover their debt. A bad year, caused perhaps by drought, pests, or soil exhaustion, left many planters in debt; some became discouraged and left the area.[4]

There were very few rich tobacco planters on the Eastern Shore before 1750; only a handful amassed estates worth more than £1,000. These wealthy planters were merchants and land speculators also. They received an initial push by having brought indentured servants to America and on this basis (and perhaps because of influence with the grantors), they received proportionately more land. Some of this land was leased to tenants who had to improve the land in addition to paying rent. Other lands were worked by servants for their indenture period. Most importantly, these great planters were merchant-creditors who ran the county stores and extended dry goods, tea, spices, liquor, and other goods on credit to the mass of planters. Lloyd was in this group of rich planters. He cultivated his lands with indentured servants, sold small parcels to other planters, and, as an entrepreneur-merchant, probably supplied Miles River Neck planters from stores on his estate.[5]

Miles River Neck was the geographic center of Talbot County's population in the seventeenth century, and court was held here in the homes of Edward Lloyd and other planters. By the end of the century, Talbot was organized as a county, with a local government, commissioners, civil divisions, and a sheriff. The county's population was settled mainly along the rivers, which remained the major routes for communication and transportation until the twentieth century.[6]

In the eighteenth century, a local aristocracy emerged, as distinctions in wealth and influence became more marked. A series of events affected tobacco planters after 1670: tobacco prices dropped, transport costs and English import duties increased, and wars eliminated the French market. Careful investors in Talbot County and elsewhere received only a marginal return. Small planters did not survive the competition. Many sold their lands or left their leaseholds, and their wealthy neighbors added these contiguous plots to their expanding estates.[7]

For the first time, slave labor became important. Planters who survived did so because of labor advantages. Tobacco is a labor-intensive crop that quite literally exhausts the soil, divesting it of its nitrogen and potash content and necessitating a length fallow after two or three crops, and so clearing new plots was a continual task. Estates were developed only by leasing parcels to renters or by owning slaves. Landowners favored the latter, as just the overseer received a share of the crop. Still, only a few men flourished in these hardships of tobacco culture. In 1733, only one in ten whites owned slaves. By the end of the century, only 135 men owned ten or more slaves. This was a small group of wealthy slaveowners, and Edward Lloyd was at its apex: his 305 slaves in 1800 represented the largest total in Talbot County and on the Eastern Shore.[8]

The late-seventeenth-century events that adversely affected tobacco prices changed Eastern Shore agriculture. Substantial diversification had occured by 1750, when wheat and corn were being grown and shipped to New England and Philadelphia. By this time the average landholding in Talbot County was 330 acres, and county affairs were controlled by the Lloyds and other families related to them.[9]

This shift away from tobacco and in favor of corn and wheat lessened the demands for labor and the slave and free population of Talbot County would decline in the first half of the nineteenth century. However, the basic slaveowning character of the county did not alter, and Talbot County remained one of the northernmost regions where slavery was essential to the economy.[10]

The Antebellum Nineteenth Century

Talbot County remained rural and agricultural during this period. Flour mills, lumber mills, and boat building were the main industries, and all were extensions of agricultural pursuits. Boats were instrumental in moving grain to markets. Miles River Neck grain was moved to market by boats built in St. Michaels, a center also for oystering, which was a winter pursuit for many men.[11]

Most improved land was devoted to agriculture: one-quarter to one-third to wheat and corn, the rest in meadow for cattle, horses, sheep and hogs, and some still in tobacco. The typical Talbot County farm consisted of several hundred acres, divided into small fields separated by split-rail fences. A three-field rotation among wheat (the major crop), corn, and pasture was used. The location of estates and development of land continued to reflect a riverine orientation for transportation and communication. By 1817, a steamboat came thrice weekly from Baltimore to Miles River Bridge and Saint Michaels.[12]

The population of the county was scattered on farms. In 1790, the population was slightly over 13,000. The largest town was Easton, with a population of only 700. Almost one-half of the total population was black, including roughly 5,000 slaves and 1,000 free blacks in 1790. By the outbreak of the Civil War, there were over 3,700 slaves in Talbot County, almost 40 percent of the county population. The largest owner was Edward Lloyd (VI), who in 1850 listed 355 slaves on the Miles River Neck farms and who in 1862 still had over 200 slaves.[13]

The slave population declined in the early nineteenth century, in part due to manumission. A manumission-inclined Quaker population began to petition as early as 1785 in Talbot for the abolition of slavery.[14] There had been large numbers of free blacks in Maryland since the early 1700s; in the preceding century, free blacks were able to hold land, borrow money, and sign legal documents in some parts of Maryland.[15] In 1790, Talbot had more free blacks than any other Eastern Shore county, and by 1860 this number had tripled.

Some owners manumitted slaves in their wills. In 1798, Jeremiah Banning, who owned twenty-nine slaves in 1790, died and declared in his will that he "hope[d] the period not far remote before, first in part, then totally, slavery will be abolished." Banning manumitted six slaves on his death and set provisons for the other slaves to become free at specific ages. Banning said that his sentiments "no man would dare to have published 40 years ago."[16]

Most Talbot County slaveowners willed slaves to their offspring rather than manumit them. For example, in 1829 Edward Lloyd willed his farms to his several sons, ten slaves of her choice to his wife, and to each daughter "a negro girl, such as each of my said daughters may select, after the selection made by their mother of the slaves given to her." The eldest daughter was to choose first, the next-eldest second, and so forth. All remaining slaves were willed to his sons.[17]

Agriculture diversification, runaways, and slave traders also contributed to the nineteenth-century decline in Talbot County's slave population. Slavery was less compatible with a mixed wheat-and-corn economy than it had been with labor-intensive tobacco. In some counties, slaves were encouraged to escape because they could not be supported any longer. Others ran away during peak labor demands at harvest or cultivation times. Blacks who could not prove that they were free were jailed and, if unclaimed, sold after sixty days. In the 1830s, at least six slave traders were active in Talbot County, buying slaves and speculating on higher demand and profitable resale in the deep South. They undoubtedly bought and sold unclaimed slaves in jail. Slaves escaped from their Talbot County owners during this period; in 1849 alone, twenty-two fled Talbot County, more than from any other Maryland county.[18]

The sentiments and attitudes of the Talbot County white population were predominantly southern. This was a slave economy. Proslavery voices remained strong even after the emancipation. Runaways were sold out of the state. Near the end of the period, insurrection rumors from Talbot and neighboring Dorchester counties affected a skittish white population. Still, there were whites who called for the abolition of slavery. In the 1790s, Edward Lloyd (IV) was accused of treating his slaves inhumanely. This affair attracted some attention, perhaps due more to Lloyd's political aspirations than to any differences between the way he and other slave-owners treated their slaves.[19]

In his autobiographies, Frederick Douglass has provided the best firsthand account of Talbot County life in the antebellum nineteenth century, and one from the standpoint of a slave.

Douglass offers intimate details on slavery in Miles River Neck during the 1820s and 1830s, when he belonged to the chief clerk for Edward Lloyd (V). In the mid-1830s, he lived on one of Lloyd's farms in Miles River Neck.

Douglass was born in 1817, twelve miles east of Miles River Neck in a section of Talbot County known as Tuckahoe. He spent his early years with his mother's mother. He did not remember his mother very well, as she made only several visits to him in 1824–1825. She had been hired out by her owner to a man twelve miles distant and was seldom able to make the trip to see her son. She died in 1826, and although Douglass said that he was not strongly affected by her death, for he had never really known her, in later life he reflected:

> The practice of separating children from their mothers, and hiring
> the latter out at distances too great to admit of their meeting, except
> at long intervals, is a marked feature of the cruelty and barbarity of
> the slave system. But it is in harmony with the grand aim of slavery,
> which, always and everywhere, is to reduce man to a level with the
> brute.[20]

Douglass never knew who his father was, though he suspected that he was a white man, and perhaps his owner; he met his brother and sisters for the first time when he went to Miles River Neck at age seven. Douglass concluded that slavery had made his mother a myth, his father a mystery, and his

brother and sisters strangers, and had "left me without an intelligible beginning in the world,"[21] although he was absorbed into a network of kin in
Miles River Neck.

Frederick Douglass presented a strong counterpoint to the view, perhaps
prevalent at that time, that slavery in Maryland was very mild. If this opinion
did prevail, it was due in part to Maryland's position as a border state and to
a belief that abolitionist, humanitarian influences from the contiguous North
had an ameliorative effect on conditions of slavery there. According to
Douglass, however, the Miles River Neck plantation of the Lloyds was one of
those

> secluded and out-of-the way places . . . seldom visited by a single
> ray of healthy public sentiment—where slavery, wrapt in its own
> congenial, midnight darkness, *can* and *does,* develop all its malign
> and shocking characteristics; where it can be indecent without
> shame, cruel without shuddering, and murderous without appre-
> hension of fear of exposure.[22]

The Lloyd plantation consisted of roughly 8,000 acres and was subdivided
into farms, each directed by an overseer-manager. The Miles River Neck farms
were named Wye Town, Wye House, 400 Acres, New Design, Hopewell,
Woolmans, White House, New Quarter, and Davises.[23] The affairs of all the
farms were coordinated at "Great House Farm" (Wye House) on the Wye
River, where the Lloyds lived. Frederick Douglass' owner managed all the
overseers and was in charge of shipments of grain and tobacco, of goods in
storage, of the cooper, blacksmith and wheelwright shops, and was the inter-
mediary between Lloyd and the various farm overseers. White society was
stratified: the Lloyds communicated only with their well-to-do neighbors,
many of whom were also kin; Douglass' master, an owner of thirty slaves
and three farms in Tuckahoe, was not considered rich and had no social
interaction with the Lloyds; and the overseers, "a class by themselves,"
rarely talked with the Lloyds and had no social communication with
Douglass' owner. These distances were rigidly maintained.[24]

The plantation was practically a self-contained community: all staple
foods consumed were gathered and processed there; raw materials were
fashioned in shops, and tools and equipment repaired there; and in the
formulation and execution of sanctions, the plantation was in many respects
autonomous.[25]

Douglass depicted emotionally, and in detail, the life of the Lloyds in the
"Great House," where "the toil of a thousand men supports a single family
in easy idleness and sin." He contrasted "the close-fisted stinginess that fed
the poor slave on coarse corn-meal" with the dining table of the Lloyds,
which "groans under the heavy and blood-bought luxuries gathered with
pains-taking care, at home and abroad." Douglass left no doubt how he

viewed these "evidences of pride and luxurious extravagance" that characterized the life of the most wealthy of the Lloyds.[26] Douglass' sentiments were clear in his pointed contrasts:

> This immense wealth; this gilded splendor; this profusion of luxury; this exemption from toil; this life of ease; this sea of plenty; age, what of it all? . . . The poor slave, on his hard, pine plank, but scantily covered with his thin blanket, sleeps more soundly than the feverish voluptuary who reclines upon his feather bed and downy pillow. Food, to the indolent lounger, is poison, not sustenance. Lurking beneath all their dishes, are invisible spirits of evil, ready to feed the self-deluded gourmandizers with aches, pains, fierce temper, uncontrolled passions, dyspepsia, rheumatism, lumbago and gout; and of these the Lloyds got their full share.[27]

Edward Lloyd (V), Governor of Maryland and then a member of the United States Senate, had to retire from the Senate in January 1826 because of gout. From that point until his death in 1834, he managed agricultural activities and introduced new breeds of cattle, sheep, and horses and experimented with strains of wheat on his Miles River Neck farms.[28]

Most slaves at Douglass' time were born on Lloyd's plantation; the parents of some had been brought from Africa, and still others were "direct from Guinea." Almost all of these slaves worked in the field on the various farms; a very few—fifteen—worked in the Lloyd house. These fifteen "constituted a sort of black aristocracy," separate "in dress, . . . in form and feature, in manner and speech, in tastes and habits" from those who worked in the fields. In addition to this cleavage in the slave population, there were differences in status associated with age. Older men and women were called "Uncle" and "Aunt" by the young, "according to plantation *etiquette,* as a mark of respect," a custom rigidly adhered to.[29] There were also differences between the slave populations of different plantations, and slaves argued over the qualities of their masters: "To be a SLAVE, was thought to be bad enough; but to be a *poor man's* slave, was deemed a disgrace, indeed."[30]

The daily existence of field slaves was filled with monotony, sorrow, resignation, hardship and discomfort, and fear. Slaves went to fields, some three miles distant, "at the first grey streak of morning" and worked "often as long as they can see," returning to cook, mend, or wash and to sleep, covered with a blanket, on a clay floor in a compartment within a slave quarter. Daily food was portioned from a monthly ration. This ration, or allowance, was received at the end of each month, when slaves chosen from each farm (and thereby gaining in prestige) converged on the Great House to receive the next month's food. This consisted of eight pounds of pickled pork or herring, one bushel of unbolted meal, and one pint of salt, or one-quarter pound of pork per day and a peck of cornmeal per week for an adult slave working six days a week, morning to night. Each year, a slave received two coarse tow-linen shirts, one pair tow-linen trousers, one wool jacket and trousers, one pair of yarn stockings, and one pair of shoes. Children who were not old enough to work in the fields went naked in summer.[31]

Slaves working in the fields sang often, songs of sorrow, not joy, songs designed to "make themselves happy." Slaves who were punished physically "bore it patiently" more often than not, believing both that "'*God up in the sky*' made everybody; and that he made *white* people to be masters and mistresses, and *black* people to be slaves" and that a better time would come,[32] all signs of resignation and orientation to the future against which few rebelled. Douglass, of course, was one who did.

Slaves lived in continual fear of physical punishment or of being handed over to slave traders. Douglass himself was "seldom whipped—and never severely—by my old master." He was under the constant vigilance of a black cook, Aunt Katy, who was "ambitious, ill tempered and cruel" and who, being responsible for the allocation of food (coarse cornmeal) to children in the household, favored her own offspring to Douglass. Hunger and cold were Douglass' "two great physical troubles."[33]

Slaves were charged frequently with "impudence," an offense that might be interpreted in numerous actions: "in the tone of an answer; in answering at all; in not answering; in the expression of countenance; in the motion of the head; in the gait, manner and bearing of the slave."[34] Slaves were whipped by other slaves, by overseers and by their owners, including Lloyd. Slaves were accused of being impudent, of undesirable intimacy with another slave, of finding fault with their owners, and of refusal to obey orders.[35]

Punishments varied, but tended to be severe. Oversleeping, impudence, unwanted intimacy—all prompted cowskin and hickory-stick whippings of thirty lashes and more. Although there were overseers who "seemed to take no especial pleasure in" whipping, there was always the fear that if punishment was not immediate and severe and if a wayward person was not made an example of, then others would rebel. Whipping, then, was necessary to the slave system:

> The whip is all in all, it is supposed to secure obedience to the
> slaveholder, and is held as a sovereign remedy among the slaves
> themselves, for every form of disobedience, temporal or spiritual.
> Slaves, as well as slaveholders, use it with an unsparing hand.[36]

And some overseers were feared for their cruelty. One overseer "could torture the slightest word or look into impudence; he had the nerve, not only to resent, but to punish, promptly and severely. He never allowed himself to be answered back, by a slave."[37] There were a very few slaves who did answer back, but they were exceptions. Most bore their punishment, either fearing worse or with "the fear of God, and the hope of heaven . . . found sufficient to sustain" them. Douglass noted, however, that "he is whipped oftenest, who is whipped easiest," an observation that led him to take a strong stand later in life and that led to his successful flight to freedom.[38]

One of the ultimate reactions of overseers and owners to slave "offenses" was murder. One Lloyd slave ran into the river when he was being whipped, refused to come out, whereupon he was shot and killed by the overseer. Lloyd took no action against the overseer, whose fame spread with a heightened fear of him. The murder was justified on the grounds that if one slave so openly defied authority, others might follow the example in a general uprising. Douglass mentions several other murders and suggests that "killing a slave, or any colored person, in Talbot County, Maryland, is not treated as a crime, either by the courts or the community."[39] Slaves could not testify and accused killers could argue self-defense even on the basis of a hand raised to ward off a shot, an argument "fully justified by southern, or Maryland, public opinion."[40]

Another ultimate sanction was being sold to slave traders who dealt in a speculative market in the deep South. This might be the fate of those who were critical of the plantation regime or who were impudent. The fear of being "without a moment's warning . . . snatched away, and forever sundered from his family and friends, by a hand more unrelenting than that of death" ran deep, and it surely permeated all aspects of slave life. Douglass said that "scarcely a month passed without the sale of one or more lots to the Georgia traders."[41]

It is small wonder that Douglass left the Lloyd plantation (for Baltimore) in 1827 "with inexpressible joy."[42] He remained in Baltimore until 1833, when he came back to St. Michaels in Talbot County. He stayed there, in slavery, under increasingly trying conditions for five years; in September 1838, he escaped north to freedom.

The Civil War Period

On the eve of the Civil War, the Talbot County white population, with its large slaveowning proportion, was very Southern in inclination. There did exist pockets of Union strength that prevented unanimous opposition to the North. Still, the philosophy of the slaveowners, who had so much to lose by emancipation, dominated county sentiment and policies.

There was some agitation in Talbot County on the eve of the war, when a "letter of an insurrectionary character," found in St. Michaels, prompted white residents to become "ready and equipped for any ordinary emergency."[43] There was increasing difficulty with the growing population of free blacks. In 1858, a convention of slaveholders met in Cambridge, Maryland, where they resolved that because of the vast increase of the free negro population of Maryland, their vicious habits, their refusal to labor, the incapacity for self-government . . . the State should present the alternative to this class of population, of going into slavery, or leaving the State."[44]

One of the delegates appointed by the Talbot County slaveholders to attend this convention was Edward Lloyd, Jr.[45] The general reaction to this resolution was that it was neither humane nor (especially) practical, since free blacks were a labor pool for poor whites. There were a number of laws keeping free blacks subordinate, and if they were enslaved or given the choice to leave, many of the best would go, the worst would remain, and foreign immigrants "infinitely worse than the free negroes" would take their place as laborers.[46]

Newspaper notices advertised the sale of slaves following the settlement of estates, the hiring of blacks, and the actions of slave traders. One slave trader, active in the late 1850s, advertised:

Negroes Wanted: I am again in the market, and still pay liberal prices in Cash, for any number of likely NEGROES, that are slaves for life. I can be found at the Brick Hotel in Easton. Communications promptly attended to. Wm. Harker.[47]

Slaves were sold upon the settlement of some estates:

ADMINISTRATOR'S SALE OF VALUABLE PROPERTY. By order of the Orphan's Court of Talbot County, the undersigned, as Administrator of Richard Dorsey [of Miles River Neck], will offer at public sale to the highest bidder, on Tuesday, the 28th of December, between the hours of 2 and 5 o'clock p.m. of that day, at the front door of the Court House in Easton, the following Negroes to wit: Four Valuable NEGRO MEN, aged from 20 to 25 years; also a NEGRO WOMAN, aged about 54 years; also a NEGRO WOMAN, aged about 25 years, and her girl child aged one year; also one NEGRO GIRL, aged about 14 years; and two NEGRO BOYS, aged about 3 and 5 years, respectively children of the second named negro woman, and slaves for life.[48]

These other advertisements were typical for this period:

FOR SALE: A NEGRO WOMAN—slave for life—is one of the best cooks in the county; also a good washer and ironer. No one need apply out of the county. Apply at the Gazette office.

FOR SALE: A NEGRO WOMAN, a good cook, washer, and ironer, 34 years old and healthy, who has three children, one, four, and nine years old, all healthy and sound, and slaves for life. Apply to the Editor.

WANTED TO HIRE FOR THE YEAR 1859. TWO WOMEN, slaves one for chamber maid, who is neat in her appearance and honest and industrious. The other for washerwoman and ironer. She must be competent to do this kind of work, in the best manner. Also a girl from 12 to 15 years of age for nurse. Apply to the subscriber at Brick Hotel, Easton, Md. J.Q.A. Hardaway.[49]

At the outbreak of the Civil War, the stand taken by many whites in Maryland was ambiguous and indecisive. In general terms, there was a split between the Southern-sympathizing, homogeneous, and agrarian Eastern Shore (and southernmost Western Shore counties) and the more pro-Union, heterogenous, and industrialized Western Shore.[50] Sentiment in Talbot County and on much of the Eastern Shore is illustrated by this 1860 proclamation from Easton:

That Maryland is essentially a Southern State in association, in feeling, in interest and in her domestic relations; that her destiny is interwoven with that of her sister Southern States; and that her action will be firm and unyielding in the maintenance and vindication of her Constitutional rights.[51]

Maryland's geographical position was too critical to allow such sentiment to flourish, and as loyalty was essential, military law was declared in Talbot County.[52]

State politics in the 1860s reflected the general split between the Eastern and Western Shores and the Southern inclination of Talbot County whites. In 1861, pro-Union Governor Bradford was elected with the aid of loyalty oaths on the Eastern Shore; four counties, one of them Talbot, voted against him. That same year in national politics, people from Maryland signaled their support for the war but not for the abolition of slavery; these were perceived as separate issues. Although the proemancipation candidates won congressional seats overwhelmingly in 1863, many potential voters were excluded as "unqualified" (pro-Southern) and the military presence at the voting booths made these results predictable. In Talbot County, the pro-slavery representative, who was also against the recruitment of blacks and in favor of compensating slaveowners in the event of emancipation, was narrowly defeated.[53]

More illustrative of the North-South split in Talbot County was the fact that many Talbot County whites moved secretively to Virginia, along the

Chesapeake, to fight for the Confederacy, either with Virginia regiments or as the first Maryland Confederate Regiment. And Talbot County whites fought for the Union in Company H of the First Eastern Shore Regiment of Volunteers.[54] From time to time, "Rebel Soldiers" in Talbot County were arrested, as in 1863 when "George Valliant, formerly of this county, but has for some time past been in the Rebel service" was captured in Talbot County. Twenty others were believed to have been with him, their mission to sabotage Baltimore-bound ships from the Eastern Shore.[55]

During the 1860s, three significant things strongly affected Talbot County blacks: the recruitment into the Union Army of free blacks and slaves; emancipation; and the notorious apprenticeships following the emancipation.

Recruitment into the Union Army of blacks in Talbot County began the year before emancipation. Free blacks first were recruited, but by late 1863 slaves as well as free blacks were boarding steamers for Baltimore. There were protests and general confusion on the Eastern Shore, as recruitment interfered with the corn harvest,[56] and considerable impressment occurred, although a Baltimore-based claimant board theoretically compensated loyal slaveowners.[57]

Many slaveowners stood to lose a large part of their wealth, and the potential for change as a result of recruiting was great. The evaluation of slaves had declined by 1863, and that August, twenty slaves sold at the Easton courthouse brought prices ranging from $80 for a five-year-old boy to $300 for a forty-two-year-old man, "one third" the prices in the late 1850s.[58]

Slaveowners like Lloyd and other wealthy men in Miles River Neck lost a lot by recruitment. Miles River Neck remained an affluent part of the county in the early 1860s, when one observer remarked:

> April 20, 1863—Today I went through Easton . . . to attend upon the sale of a farm, owned by one Redman, who is in the South and probably in the army. This farm is situated in Miles River Neck, one of the most fertile portions of our [Talbot] county. This neck of land when compared with the remainder of the Co: illustrates the influence of Slavery upon the people, and upon property. This neck of land is owned in great measure by large landed proprietors, and large slave-owners. Southern plantation life, and agriculture, slightly modified, is here illustrated. The property holders are few, and the whites taken together are very largely outnumbered by the slave blacks. The wealthy are generally refined to their manners, very proud in their bearings, and very exclusive in their social intercourse. They have the ordinary intelligence of our people at large; neither more nor less well informed, but as a body, are probably more polite and accomplished in their manners.—The negroes live in quarters apart from the white family—that is to say, they have no

intercourse with their superiors, except thro. the overseer. In this their situation differs from that of the negroes in other portions of the county, where they live in the family of the master, and where, though they do not sleep under his roof, nor eat at his table, they sleep in the same tenement and eat of . . . food provided for the master, where, they make a part of the family—and come in immediate and constant contact with the master and his family [and thus receive some civilizing influences which Negroes under the other system do not get] . . . . Under the one [system] labor is associated in their narrow minds with degradation, while in the other, if it does not acquire a dignity, it is not humiliating, for the slave often works beside his master in the field, and shares the toil of the master's son. The effects upon the general comfort and wealth of the community of these two systems [are] very remarkably contrasted. The few land owners of Miles River Neck—have proverbially all that can be had, but the other few whites are very poor, and destitute. But the aggregate wealth of this section is very far inferior to that of any similar section of the county of the same extent and fertility . . . a gradual change is taking place there also—farms are dividing, new men going in, old families dying out, slave property diminishing.[59]

In September 1863, the recruitment apparently affected Lloyd, who "lost at one time as many as 84 able bodied hands and . . . enough have not been left him 'to black his boots' as a low fellow remarked."[60] There was a great deal of confusion at this time: only free blacks were supposed to have been recruited at first, but slaves were carried off "by boat loads"; there was some immediate concern by pro-Union men that slaveowners would profit by the recruitment of free blacks, as they would be able to hire out their slaves as labor; when slaves were recruited, "it seems to give great satisfaction to the laboring whites that the non laboring slave owners are losing their slaves, and they too will be reduced to the necessity of going into the fields"; many farmers failed to harvest corn or seed wheat because of a loss of labor; and when 200 black recruits came to enlist but found no recruitment officer, they disappeared and an armed posse patrolled the county.[61] In early 1864, the enlistments continued, when a company of black soldiers arrived to enlist free blacks and slaves.[62] In Maryland, over 8,000 blacks enlisted or were recruited; they were organized into six regiments and suffered 1,500 casualties.[63]

Lincoln issued the Emancipation Proclamation, declaring freedom for slaves in all rebellious states, in January 1863. In Maryland, the beginning of abolition occurred in late 1863 with the election of a proemancipation legislature, and a new constitution proclaimed that "all persons held to service or labor, as slaves, are hereby declared free." The new constitution went into effect on November 1, 1864, when slaves were emancipated.[64] There was a substantial amount of violence directed against blacks in Talbot County on the eve of emancipation. The slaveholders expressed "great bitterness . . . against those who accomplished the work of emancipation"; many whites feared that blacks "will be placed upon a footing of social equality. The lower the rank of the white the greater the fear."[65]

There was no celebratory announcement in the pro-Union *Eastern Gazette* on "the day upon which the new Constitution went into effect, by which universal freedom was declared throughout the state"[66] reflecting perhaps the feeling in the county that emancipation "has not been from high principle, but devotion to liberty . . . but party spirit, vengeful feeling against disloyal slaveholders, and regard for material interest. There has been no expressions, at least in this community, of regard for the negro—for human rights."[67]

This lack of regard for human rights was apparent in an ominous note in November 1864 of "several instances in which persons have refused to deliver up children, who have heretofore been slaves, to their parents, and continue to hold them in possession because they have applied to the Orphans' Court to have them bound."[68] The apprenticeship period had begun. The problem was more serious than "several instances." A federal marshal wrote from Easton in early November 1864: "Many . . . citizens are endeavoring to intimidate colored people and compel them to bind their children to them under the old apprenticeship law. . . . Boys of twelve and fourteen are taken from their parents under the pretence that they are incapable of supporting them, while the younger children are left to be maintained by the parents." Two judges of the Orphans' Court were said to be "so prejudiced against these poor creatures that they do not regard their rights," and "justice has become a mockery."[69]

The apprentice system kept many blacks in a state of virtual slavery. The apprentice code itself was not unconstitutional, but the way that it was applied to blacks was. White children could be apprenticed, but they had to be educated and taught some trade; they could not be bound to another person without their parents' knowledge. Black children, on the other hand, only had to be taught a trade, could be sold if they ran away, and could be bound to another white without parental consent. Anyone accused of enticing away a black bound child faced an eighteen-month jail term (compared with a $20 fine for enticing away a white child).

More than 1,500 black children were bound in Talbot and three other Eastern Shore counties in the first month alone following emancipation. State law allowed binding minors "if the parent or parents have [not] the means [or] are [un]willing to support them"; yet, as one black woman testified in Talbot County in December 1864, "I have four children. . . . I can by their assistance maintain them ... [but] John Baggs has held my children as slaves since the first of November."[70] The Freedman's Bureau made slow headway against the proapprenticeship attitudes of local judges, but in 1867 indenture was declared unconstitutional and, by the following year, some bound minors were being released and no new cases of binding resulted.[71] The apprenticeship reaction to emancipation, although short-lived, reflected the predominant Southern sentiments in Talbot's white population, and foreshadowed the emergence of black codes, of Jim Crow laws and moves toward disfranchisement, and finally mob violence that erupted in the next period, the lifetime of Joseph Sutton.

Talbot County in the period 1885–1940

This final section focuses on Talbot County during the years covered by the major portion of Joseph Sutton's oral history. Sutton was born in 1885 and he was fifty-five years old in 1940. Talbot County during this period remained rural, with an economy focused on agriculture; in almost all facilities it was segregated, and blacks were portrayed in county newspapers stereotypically, as less than human and unintelligent people. The economic climate was in general severe, and this was reflected in interracial tension, which peaked on the Eastern Shore in the early 1930s. These and other aspects of life in Talbot County will be detailed.

Economic Patterns[72]

Agriculture was the base of the economy throughout the period, although oystering in winter was also an important source of cash. Wheat was the most important cash crop; corn, hay, and tomatoes became increasingly important supplements. Wheat yields varied substantially from year to year and from one form to the next in any given year. In the late 1890s, some farmers achieved 30 bushels/acre, others only 4 bu/a. In 1925, yields were 12–15 bu/a, and in 1926, up to 25–40 bu/a, the best in ten years. Although fertilizer increased the yields, fluctuating and generally downward-falling prices were constant problems. In 1915, the price per bushel was over $1.50; in 1920, over $2, but then it fell steadily to $1 in the mid-1930s Depression and to 70 cents in 1938. The outlook in the 1930s was very poor, with wheat barely paying for fertilizer, twine, threshing, and freight to Baltimore markets. The market had been flooded by farmers increasing their wheat acreage, and prices plunged.

Corn became increasingly important throughout the period, although it was used mainly to feed stock on farms. In 1900, farms averaged 250 acres (some of which was in woodland), prices ranged from $25 to $125 per acre, and land was portioned among wheat, corn, and stock (including pigs, sheep, horses, or mules and cows).

Most farms were worked by renters or tenants.[73] This was particularly true in Miles River Neck, where a 150-acre farm was sold for almost $15,000 in 1918 and where land prices were high throughout this period. Buying a farm here was out of the reach of many Talbot County residents. No blacks owned farms in Miles River Neck, and, with one exception, none rented directly from landowners. Tenants were white, and they hired in turn other tenants who were black and white.

The tenant-landowner relationship could be unstable. Tenants had the security only of a one-year agreement with landowners. Some tenants quit and others were fired for a number of reasons. Some landlords were difficult to work under; some never trusted their tenants. Some tenants wanted to work for a larger farm; some couldn't be trusted; others didn't get crops in on time because they devoted too much time to their dairy herd. In fact, their stock was often the burning issue. It was owned solely by the tenant and provided income for him (which he needed in order to pay the men he hired). Crop profits, on the other hand, were split with the owner. Tenants who planned to move gave their notice by July 1, and actually moved just after New Year's. If they knew where they were going, they worked the ground on the next farm, planting wheat in October.

Farms averaging 150–300 acres were divided into five or six fields of between thirty and fifty acres, each separated by ditches and hedgerows. One or two fields were allocated to corn, one or two to wheat, and the remainder to hay and pasture for the fifteen to twenty milk cows and other stock (horses, pigs, sheep).

The cycles for wheat and corn differed. The wheat cycle began in August, when the fallow field was plowed for later wheat planting. In September, one cornfield was plowed for wheat. In October, wheat was planted. The following June, it was cut, reaped, and shocked in the field; in July, it was threshed. The corn year began in March, when the pasture or hay field was manured; it was plowed in April, planted in May, and cultivated in June. In September, corn was cut and carried and shocked in the field, and in October and November it was husked and put into cribs. Other chores centered on stock, which required care (and milking) all year, peaking in midwinter; cutting firewood in December, January, and February; repairing fences around fields in March and April; "brambling" or cutting back hedgerows in July and August; making hay in June; and harvesting the small plantings of tomatoes and sweet corn in July and August.

These tasks all took a substantial amount of time. A three-horse or mule team plowed two acres a day when fields were prepared for wheat; three plows could plow the two fields for wheat in sixteen days. When wheat was planted, eighteen acres a day of sowing with a drill behind a team was considered a big day. This October planting was much quicker than plowing had been—100 acres could be planted in six days. When wheat was threshed in July, farmers cooperated in groups of ten: each farmer contributed two wagons with men and a team of horses or mules. A gas-powered threshing rig and crew were hired and the rig made a "run" to all ten farms, two days at each. Wet weather delayed the process, and threshing continued into August—even September—some years. The wheat was bagged in sacks, carried on scows to schooners, and shipped to market.

Corn demanded a lot of work. Fields were manured in March, plowed in April, planted by cross-checking in May, and cultivated in June. In September, corn was cut with a one-row cutter and mule or by men with corn knives and in October and November it was husked, thrown on the ground, then picked up and hauled to a crib. The fodder-caps and blades (or roughage) were fed to stock in winter. Then in March or April, after the corn had dried, a sheller came and shelled the corn, which was packed in 1 1/2–bushel bags. Until the late 1930s, corn was packed in these bags, slid along chutes at the river edge at Tunis Mills and Miles River Bridge into scows, then transported to schooners which went to Baltimore.

Woodcutting was a constant chore in the winter months, and in the months of December through February wood was cut for the following year. A typical house used from ten to twenty cords per year.

The stock required continual attention, particularly in winter. Cows were milked morning and evening. Loose straw for bedding and fodder had to be hauled in for them. When the animals were in pounds, in winter, more work was required to bring them bedding, hay, and silage. And fields were fenced against stock, and barley and corn were grown for them.

Work days were long, largely because of the stock. In October, for example, the day began at 5:00 A.M. when cows were hand milked and all stock fed; then, after a half-hour breakfast, wheat was sowed all day with a drill behind a team. The men broke for one hour at lunch. At 4:30 P.M., planting stopped and cows were milked again. The men tried to quit at 6:00 P.M., just before supper.

Tenants hired men by the month or by the day to work for them. Tenants were white in Miles River Neck, with a single exception. Men hired by the tenants were usually black, but sometimes white. Most were hired for the year, but paid by the month. When extra men were needed, at corn-cutting or wheat-shocking time, for instance, they were hired by the day (at $1 for a 10-hour day in 1931) and paid by the week. Men hired by the month in the 1930s were paid $25 a month, provided with a house, firewood, and a "lay-in": in one case, each house was allocated twenty-five pounds of cured hog meat, two bushels of wheat (which made seventy pounds of flour) and two bushels of corn (for chickens and hogs) each month.

By the early 1930s, a number of changes were beginning to affect the amount of labor needed on farms: trucks replaced two-horse farm wagons, and trucks and tractors began to replace horse and mule teams. Seldom were fields plowed by moonlight after the early 1930s; horse-drawn spreaders spread manure in one-third the time it took using pitchforks; wheat combines that cut and threshed wheat replaced horse-drawn binders and hand-cut and -bound wheat. The number of black tenants needed to work the farms declined, and many blacks were leaving for Baltimore and other cities in the North. Some farmers forecast the end of this aspect of the tenant system.

In addition, by the early 1930s, the tenant-landowner relationship was subject to stress. For one thing tenants began to devote more time and acreage to tomatoes and sweet corn for the canning industry and less to wheat and field corn. Tomatoes and sweet corn brought ready income to the tenant, although owners demanded a portion of the revenue. Tenant dairy herds further reduced the wheat acreage. But health regulations demanded improved dairy facilities, and many owners were reluctant to comply and then be taxed on the improvements, when revenues from the milk were going to the tenant.

In the following decade, the amount of livestock on farms dwindled, and a greater emphasis was placed on corn. Hybrid corn was developed in 1940, and not only could more corn be grown but more remained upright to be picked by one-row machines by 1942 and shelled by harvesters by the end of the decade. Machine picking, the use of tractors, and fewer livestock all lowered labor demands.

All these changes altered the ratio of the number of men needed to work the land. In the antebellum nineteenth century, there were from fifteen to twenty-five slaves resident on Lloyd's farm, "400 Acres." One-half dozen were adult males. In 1829, seven of twenty were adult males.[74] One hundred years later, three men worked that farm's 260 tilled acres.

There was a substantial canning industry during this period. In 1900, peaches were an important crop, though susceptible to March frosts and August storms. There were peach orchards in Miles River Neck and in other sections of the county. Both peaches and tomatoes were canned. In 1902, a cannery was built at Tunis Mills in Miles River Neck to peel, process, can, cap, and send out tomatoes and fruit. By 1916, corn, peas, and potatoes were added. The Talbot County canning industry employed 2,500 men, women, and children around this time, in a short August-September season. The price for tomatoes varied wildly, and some years it didn't pay to pick and tomatoes were left to rot in the fields. Price problems deepened in the early 1930s. There was a dependence on migrant labor for picking, and migrant whites and blacks, called "Bohemians" by some, came to Talbot County each summer to pick. Talbot County blacks apparently were reluctant pickers.

Complaints about labor surfaced during the 1920s and 1930s. In 1920, the Talbot County Agriculture Advisory Committee compiled a wage list said to be fair to both farmers and laborers: laborers should receive 25 cents/hour or $2.50 for a ten-hour day of ordinary day work (without board), $3.50/day for harvesting hay, wheat, or for threshing wheat, and $4.00/day for cutting corn.

There were complaints of labor scarcity, even though it was said that laborers received more than clerks in town. In 1920, several farmers estimated that men hired by the month earned the equivalent of $1,300/year. Only $300 of this was in actual wages ($25/month), with the rest being the replacement value of keeping a horse fed with corn and hay ($365/year), one gallon of milk each day ($146/year), ten cords of wood ($100), raising two hogs out of the corn house ($100), seventy-five pounds of flour each month ($72), twenty-five pounds of meat per month ($60), and some other expenses.

By 1926, some complained that Talbot County blacks wouldn't work for more than three days at a time: one farmer said he had to pay $6/day for labor; others brought in laborers from outside the county at $3/day.

There were occasional difficulties with migrant laborers. One black who had come from Virginia to work in canning houses, then worked at odd jobs when the houses closed, robbed the Longwoods store of $75 in 1926. In 1933, the same store was robbed twice in a month and the owner was said to

> blame the present losses to some strange colored people who were
> brought here from Virginia to work in the neighborhood of Long-
> woods. He says they come here to work for low wages, being paid
> all they are worth, and then when they are paid off they have to
> steal to get back home. The idea of bringing in the county a lot of
> strange colored people does not do the county any good, still it is
> hard for the farmers to get the local help to work. Judge Slaughter
> of the Orphans' Court stated on Monday that he had to go to
> Caroline County for help to cut his corn after local colored men
> were offered $2 a day but refused to work after promising to do
> so. They said they could get food from the county and did not have
> to work. Mr. Slaughter stated that some farmers near Longwoods
> got corn cutters from Queen Anne County.[75]

Oystering was an extremely important economic activity in Talbot County. The oyster season lasted from September through April. In 1900, 900 tongers, 100 scrape boats, and twelve dredging boats were operating in Talbot County. In 1898, there were almost 300 boats in St. Michaels, many of them canoes equipped with rakes for tonging. The tongers started in September, the dredgers in November, and the dredgers were not allowed on tonging ground in many rivers, including the Wye and Miles. Bad weather, ice and early winter especially, restricted the time spent on the oyster grounds, and tongers averaged only 100 working days in a 240-day season.

The independence of Talbot County watermen is legendary, and there were numerous infractions of culling laws (in 1891, the law to replace oysters less than 2.5 inches in length was broken often), invasions of privately owned oysterbeds in the Miles River, the infringing by scrapers on tonging grounds, and oystering beyond the April closing of the season. Some fines were steep: scrapers caught working at night illegally on Miles River tonging bars were fined $100; a dredger caught 2.5 miles inside the dredging limit in 1902 defaulted $600 bail, and his boat was tied to the St. Michaels wharf. Those who violated the April end-of-season law were sent to the House of Corrections for four months. And in 1898, there was a boundary dispute between Queen Annes and Talbot counties in the Wye River; "local law" established one line as the boundary, while the police schooner reinforced another law.

Although oystering was independent work, it was also rough and often not economically rewarding. Oysters were sometimes scarce: in 1902, it was difficult to get five bushels/day, and the top price was $1.10/bushel. In the 1932-1933 winter, the price was only 25 cents/bushel, and neither tongers nor dredgers made expenses. Oysters were scarce that year, tongers getting only five bushels a day. The following December, tongers were getting six bushels/day and dredgers 75 to 100 bushels, and the price had improved, though not dramatically, to a range of 30 to 65 cents/bushel. In September 1936, the price was still 35 to 50 cents/bushel.

Working in icy conditions was something that everyone had to endure. The work was sometimes dangerous: in 1898, one man was stuck on Herring Island at the mouth of the Miles River for forty-eight hours, and finally rescued.

Many blacks participated in the oyster industry, some as tongers or in dredging, others shucking in the packing houses. Shuckers were paid by the piece, 20 cents/gallon in 1890, when a fast shucker cut out 100 oysters in 4-5 minutes and produced twenty-seven gallons a day.

In other seasons, oystermen worked by the day in agriculture, cutting corn, thrashing wheat, or hauling grain to market in their boats, or fished for herring in spring, rock and perch in summer with pound nets, haul seines or fykes, and crabbed during summer.

From time to time, violence erupted in this traditionally independent industry. In 1926, dredgers were encroaching illegally on tongers' grounds at night, and although the police patrolled the waters and fired on the dredgers, fining those they caught $200, many got away.

The oyster industry was substantial. In Talbot County in 1938, there were 132 oyster bars producing an estimated 2 million bushels worth $1 million. Forty thousand acres on 1,200 farms were producing roughly 800,000 bushels of wheat, in 1938 worth approximately $600,000. Miles River Neck oysterers worked thirty bars in the Miles and Wye rivers, a combined acreage of over 3,500 acres producing almost 275,000 bushels of oysters.

There were very few manufacturers in Talbot County. At the turn of the century, there were two machine shops, two flour and several grist mills, two fertilizer factories, a brick and tile factory, broom factory, and several shipyards. A shirt factory employed 100 women. There was a lumber and planing mill at Tunis Mills, which was important for Miles River Neck people.

Talbot County was linked to the Maryland Western Shore and to points north by railroad and steamer. The Queen Annes RR went to Baltimore; the Delaware Branch of the Pennsylvania RR went to Baltimore, Washington, Wilmington, Philadelphia, and points north twice a day. Many people went to Baltimore by taking a train which ran from Easton to Claiborne, then a steamer to Baltimore. The trip took four hours. Steamboats also came into the Miles and Wye rivers.

In sum, the general economic picture of Talbot County during this period, especially in the 1920s and 1930s, is of a poor, rural county with many people working in agriculture at all seasons and some oystering in winter. Austerity peaked in the early 1930s, at the height of the Depression, when prices for crops and oysters were extremely low, when wheat acreage was set aside, and when men worked on ditching and drainage projects created by funds from the Civil Works Administration. Rural, agricultural Talbot County in the 1920s and 1930s was like much of rural America: agriculture slumped in the early 1920s after relative prosperity in the late 'teens, and it never really recovered during the next two decades; the 1929 crash and the early 1930s depression was not significantly alleviated by the Agricultural Adjustment Act and other New Deal policies. Farmers were not prosperous, and laborers on farms were even less so.

The adverse economic climate and the complaints about the difficulty of hiring blacks seem to have been reflected in other developments in Talbot County, notably in voting patterns and court cases.

The attitudes of Talbot County whites toward blacks that had resulted in the antebellum resistance of whites to emancipation and the post-emancipation apprenticeships did not alter dramatically in the 1885-1940 period. Talbot County was segregated, Jim Crow customs prevailed, blacks were portrayed as less than human, superstitious, unintelligent, and prone to violence, and in the early 1930s the most severe sort of mob rule erupted just south of Talbot County.

This 1885-1940 period was difficult for blacks throughout the United States, and particularly so in the South. The North did not escape: in 1919, for example, race riots were most severe in Chicago. In Mississippi, South Carolina, Tennessee, and other southern states, lynch mobs sanctioned implicitly by public opinion terrorized blacks in the 1870s, in reaction to blacks behaving as if they were not a subordinate race.[76] The entire Jim Crow system of racial proscription emerged and flourished during this period, and the segregation codes were sanctioned by law or firmly enforced by custom. Blacks were first excluded by law from railroad cars, then in other forms of public transportation; the black codes then affected virtually every aspect of life—housing, eating and drinking, restrooms, schools, hospitals, churches, recreation, and cemeteries. Disfranchisement, on the basis of property or literacy clauses and with the benefit of so-called understanding or grandfather clauses and of Supreme Court decisions, spread throughout southern states from Mississippi in the late 1890s. It probably was not coincidental that Jim Crow customs and laws and mob violence and lynchings intensified at a time when there was substantial economic deprivation and political frustration.[77]

Maryland was affected less than were other states by Jim Crow legislation and mob violence. Still, there was a concerted move on the part of Democrats in the period from 1904 to 1911 to disfranchise blacks. Three amendments, one with a harsh "understanding" of the constitution clause, another with an impossible test, and the third with a property clause, were drafted, presented to the voters, and, although supported in general on the Eastern Shore when not in conflict with unwanted changes in oyster laws, rejected by 54 to 65 percent of the state. Although Maryland Democrats failed to disfranchise black voters, they did succeed in enacting some Jim Crow legislation: in 1904, railroads and steamships were segregated by law; in 1908, steamship toilets and sleeping areas were segregated; voting rights were restricted in local elections in some Eastern Shore towns in 1904; in Baltimore in 1911, a law was passed prohibiting the sale to blacks of property in all-white sections of the city; and informal codes all over the state resulted in de facto segregation in many aspects of life.[78]

Talbot County facilities and all recreations were segregated through this period. In education, the salaries of black schoolteachers and the maintenance of schoolhouses were paid in the early 1890s from state funds and from black tonging licenses. Approximately $6,000 was spent on Talbot's 1,300 black pupils, compared to over $26,000 spent on 2,700 white students. There were salary differences between white and black teachers: in Miles River Neck in 1908, the white principal at Tunis Mills, received $320, the white teachers at Miles River Neck school received $300, and the black principal at Unionville was paid $164. There was a stress on vocational education in the black schools, in part because a "domestic sciences" department in the Easton School received from the state almost as much money as it cost the entire school to run, thus saving county taxpayers money. The vocational education of blacks was regarded as a panacea for racial trouble. In 1898, the *Easton Gazette* editorialized:

> The more intelligent the negro becomes, the more he sees his dependence upon the republic that made his advancement possible, and

the more he respects and treats with deference the dominant race, and the less boisterous, clamorous and abusive he becomes. . . . Education is therefore the necessity . . . education that educates along broad lines of usefulness. . . . The first essential for the colored people is to be taught labor, taught to feel the blessings of properly employed time in the shop, mills, fields, and house.[79]

In 1902, the *Easton Ledger* apparently editorialized that blacks shouldn't be educated to the point that they would compete with whites for jobs. The *Easton Gazette* commented:

The Ledger, ever and anon, breaks out in a wail of fear lest the negro be taught something, and so prove himself smart enough to compete with the white race in the struggle for existence. We have a higher opinion of the white people than that and believe they can easily keep the lead if they want to. While it is true the negro needs to be taught more work and less books for his own good, yet it will not hurt him to be taught along with it all a greater respect for toil— manual toil. His brain need not burden itself with the affairs of the County too much, and it should be more burdened with the responsibility of teaching his offspring the value of diversified and abundant labor. Let the negro enjoy life somewhere else besides "in the woodpile" as the Ledger would fain keep him. Let him learn to build houses, pave streets, make clothes, paint and plaster as well as do better on the farm what he now poorly does, and then, perhaps, there will not be seen so many worthless idlers on our street corners while the industries are calling for help. What the negro needs is to be taught and shown that labor is his salvation— not books. The state appropriation is intended to encourage that teaching.[80]

There was a tendency to portray blacks in newspapers as slightly less than human, lacking in intelligence, superstitious, drunk, and violent. The Volstead Act was defied by blacks and whites alike in Talbot County, although the illegal activities of blacks at camp meetings, especially, drew more attention. Camp meetings were popular (and segregated) annual events during this period, and crowds of blacks gathered in August at Concord Camp, Wye Camp, or, in the case of many Miles River Neck blacks, the camp at Dixontown between Miles River Neck and Easton. Initially, the camps were occasions for preaching and sermons and for socializing. By the 1890s, though, there began to be arrests for shooting craps, and fighting and whiskey drinking took place. In 1916, some black Methodist ministers from Easton and Saint Michaels joined others in a trip to Annapolis to try either to have the camps taxed heavily so that fewer occurred or to put a stop to the increased gambling, violence, and drinking which took place. A law was in fact passed, and camp meetings had to be licensed; permits were not granted unless signed by twenty-five taxpayers who lived in a three-mile radius. Fines were levied when the permit regulations were not followed.

In 1920, nearly every Monday morning there were cases in court of intoxication. Point Road and Grahams Alley, both black sections of Easton, were regarded by whites as dens of iniquity. Sentences and fines for drunk and disorderly conduct varied, mostly it seems depending on whether a person had been in trouble before. However, more blacks than whites appeared in court, which is probably a reflection of black drinking being more open and of the police acting more readily on complaints of noise and violence. Many assaults in the late 1930s near the black "beer gardens" led to a move to close them down. Throughout this period the sheriff had no salary. In 1938, he was paid for every prisoner who went in or out of jail (25 cents), for each summons (75 cents), and for every warrant issued ($1.75). He was also paid for transporting prisoners each day court was in session.

Blacks were regarded as superstitious. In March 1920, northern lights lit the sky and "Negroes got down on their knees and prayed, believing that some supernatural event was about to take place, it is said."[81] In January 1938, the eastern horizon was streaked red and blacks were said to have "showed more or less fear,"[82] interpreting the streaks as a sign of war, famine, or indicative of local troubles.

It is quite clear that the ideal black, from the standpoint of whites in Talbot County, modeled himself after passive slaves. In 1926, one white commented:

> I knew many Uncle Toms and Black nannys who were slaves, and I never knew one who was maltreated or who did not receive the greatest consideration from those of the master's household. . . . One of the very last to go of these good old negroes of my recollection died here in Talbot not so long ago. His name was Harrison. He occasionally came to see me, for he at one time was a slave of a branch of my family. He was a most interesting old man. He lived to be over 95, and his mind was clear to the last. He was a slave of the Lloyd's at Wye House and no working man had it better than Harrison. He always said he never had it easier after he became free. He was a teamster and market man on the Lloyd's plantation. He took all the produce from the farm and the output of the grist mill to Easton once a week in one of the old-time covered wagons. He had four of the best horses in the whole county, and they each were held as part of their equipment as was the custom in those days. The wagons contained potatoes, butter, eggs, poultry, wheat and corn flour, buckwheat, hominy and every-

thing the farm or mill could produce. Harrison could not read or write, but yet he would come back from market and give an accurate account of his sales and his cash account was always right. . . . The colored people today, with all their advantages, can do no better than to study the characters of those loyal, grateful, and faithful servants of more than half century ago, for education alone is not sufficient for success in life. The qualities I have referred to must be cultured also.[83]

Talbot County was neither overwhelmingly Republican nor Democratic during this period (though the Democrats tended to have a majority after 1920). There was some interest in capturing the black vote. For example, in 1891 the *Eastern Star* (a Democratic paper) editorialized:

Were elections a year off [the Republicans] would not have time to think of the colored man . . . not so with Democrats. The Democrats have the care and charge of a great many of the colored people in this county on their hands from year to year. . . . It is unnatural for the colored man to vote against the man upon whom he relies for money and help when in need of a friend. The Republicans have in the past by threats and intimidations driven the colored man to vote against his best interest and inclination of his mind and heart.[84]

The white Republicans were accused of organizing "military companies of colored men for service on election day"[85] in order to bring out the black Republican vote. Blacks in Talbot County, as elsewhere, voted for the Republicans, the party of Abraham Lincoln. In 1916, the registration of voters fell, which was said to be due to the northward emigration of black men to work in New Jersey potteries and other industries.

In 1920, Talbot County women voted for the first time (following the passage of the Nineteenth Amendment), and the Democratic *Star-Democrat* urged "women of good class" to register. If they didn't:

We shall have all public affairs dominated by a class that is not fitted for the role of masters. . . . Negro men and negro women are going to register and vote, and so are ignorant and vicious men and women of the white race. It is necessary for the best men and women to also register and vote in order to keep the government out of the hands of an undesirable class.[86]

In October 1920, 702 black women registered, 701 of them Republican.

In 1926, the *Star-Democrat* played on the fears of the population in order to bring out the Democratic (white) vote. In the county, there were over

8,200 registered voters: 4,800 were Democrats, all white; 3,100 were Republicans, white and black; and there were several hundred Independents. In Tilghman precinct, there had never been a black voter.

In 1926, it was reported that blacks were learning how to read and vote ballots at night, working with sample ballots, according to the *Star-Democrat,*

> so that the negro voter can be taught to memorize the ticket and vote the dication [*sic*] of the Republican leaders, not by sizing up the qualifications of the candidate, not by the study of a single issue of the campaign, but by measuring down the column in the ballot and voting by inches and numbers, not even able to read the names of the men who are before the people as candidates for office. . . .
>
> Is it any wonder that white voters . . . at the last minute lay aside their bitterness and unite in the honorable determination to overthrow a system which is a thorn in the side of Talbot's best citizenship?
>
> No wonder that the white voter steps into the voting booth and marks with an extra heavy cross, when in the booth next to him stands a negro who is racking his brain to make a mark in the exact spot, 16 inches from the top of the ballot and 23 lines of type from the first line at the head? If Talbot Republicans had the votes without the negro, they would not need to spend so many weary hours teaching Rastus how to use the rule and tape; and just so long as this is the condition that confronts the white voter of Talbot County the Republican bosses will have greater and greater need to buy more tapes and burn more oil in the midnight schools of the black settlement.[87]

In late October 1926, the fears of voters were played upon more explicitly, when Democratic voters were reminded that few blacks paid land taxes, and that a "double responsibility rests upon all Democratic voters," that it was "not only necessary but wisest" to vote Democratic.[88] The county did vote Democratic in local elections that year.

By the mid-1930s, these tactics were disappearing, and some blacks were said to be considering a Democratic vote. Still there were complaints that some registering black women in 1936

> were unable to read, and how they can vote intelligently is more than can be intelligently answered. They probably are buoyed up with the age old tradition that the Republicans liberated them and therefore they owe the party their support.[89]

Court cases reflected the increasing tensions between the races and the uneven treatment in major cases, although this latter point does not appear to have obtained in minor cases heard at Talbot County Circuit Court.

Throughout the 1890s, both blacks and whites were fined in circuit court for selling whiskey, infractions of oyster laws, and theft. The fines and punishments varied greatly, as much it seems because of prior record as because of any other factors. Some sentences seemed steep: in 1916, a black man pleaded not guilty to stealing three turkeys but was sentenced to one year in the House of Corrections; in 1898, a black woman from Trappe was fined $25 for rioting and a black man sentenced to six months in jail for assaulting a police officer on Nace Hopkins Day—a perennial march in Trappe started by Nathaniel Hopkins to celebrate the emancipation. It seems that at the turn of the century, however, most if not all prisoners in jail were black and no blacks were considered as jurors for the circuit court.

Blacks seem always to have been implicated in the more serious crimes. In 1898, one man was accused of manslaughter in the death of his son, who froze to death during a snowstorm during which the father was said to have been intoxicated. In 1902, one black man was sentenced to death (a sentence commuted to life in prison) for the murder of a woman (also black); another black man was accused of killing a white man and was found guilty of second-degree murder. Lynching was threatened in this case.

Other incidents involved blacks and whites: in 1890, a sixty-five-year-old "infirm" black man was accused in Kent County of assaulting and attempting to rape two white girls and sentenced to ten years in jail. The most notorious cases occurred after the turn of the twentieth century. In 1919, a black man named Isaiah Fountain, who owned fourteen acres and a two-story house in Trappe, was accused of raping a thirteen-year-old white girl. Fountain said that he "was in town when they claim the crime was committed,"[90] but after his Easton trial for criminal assault he was sentenced to death. A new trial was requested and granted on the Western Shore, where the verdict was upheld in spite of Fountain's statement, "I do not know anything about the crime they got me charged with at all."[91] Fountain was taken back to Easton. He escaped from jail but was recaptured by a 100-man posse, and state police were called up to prevent lynching. Fountain was hanged shortly after 3:00 A.M. on July 24, 1920, not without controversy: the sheriff was charged in Western Shore newspapers with brutality to Fountain, but a November 1920 grand-jury hearing exonerated him.

In the 1920s, the Prohibition amendment was violated frequently, and most openly and violently it seems in two black sections of Easton, Graham's Alley and Point Road. In 1926, for example, one dancing, drinking, and crap-shooting party on Point Road was broken up by the police, but not before shots were fired. In another incident, a black was arrested in Graham's Alley, three other blacks threatened to riot at the Easton jail, and one white was shot and wounded in what seems to have been an unprovoked attack. The reaction to this was mild, compared to other southern states; apparently, no violence against the blacks was threatened (but this might not have been reported in county papers: see below), and the *Star-Democrat* editorialized that the blacks should "feel the arm of the law to the fullest extent possible."[92]

This reaction was mild compared with the savagery that erupted in Wicomico, Somerset, and Worcester counties, just south of Talbot, in the early 1930s. In 1931, a thirty-five-year-old black man named Matthew Williams was charged with the murder of his white employer, and a mob estimated at 2,000 took him from the Salisbury jail, lynched him at the courthouse, and dragged his body to the black section of town where, doused with gasoline, it was burned while the mob applauded. No one was indicted in a grand-jury investigation the following spring.[93]

Some blamed this lynching on what many whites regarded as stalled "justice" in the concurrent case of Ewell Lee. Lee was accused just before the Williams case of killing his white employer and the latter's wife and two children. A lawyer employed in Baltimore by the International Labor Defense managed through the court of appeals to get the case removed from Snow Hill in Worcester County to the Western Shore, where Lee was convicted in two trials by all-white juries.[94]

In 1933, an Eastern Shore mob estimated at between 1,000 and 3,000 lynched George Armstrong, a twenty-eight-year-old black man accused of raping a seventy-one-year-old white woman. Armstrong signed a confession in Baltimore, was returned to Princess Anne in Somerset County, where he was taken from jail, then lynched, dragged through the streets, and an attempt was made to burn his body while the crowd was said to have chanted, "Here's what we do on the Eastern Shore!" Although four whites were suspected of being ringleaders in this violence and, with the help of 300 National Guardsmen holding off a crowd of 2,000 in Salisbury, were taken to Baltimore, they were soon freed, and a hearing in 1934 failed to identify any single individual responsible.[95]

The 1933 lynching drew little immediate comment in Talbot County newspapers, although letters to the editor suggested that the slow court system, with only two jury terms each year, be changed to allow the immediate judging of crimes in continual court session. The Lee case was singled out as illustrative of slow justice. In November 1933, one month after the lynching of Armstrong, the *Star-Democrat* editorialized:

> There is a right way and a wrong way to do everything—the mob
> that lynched a negro in Princess Anne selected the wrong way, and
> as a consequence brought shame upon Somerset County and the
> State of Maryland as well. The crime for which the negro paid the
> penalty at the hands of the Princess Anne mob was shocking. Lynch
> law has prevailed. The brutality and barbarism of pre-historic times
> has been re-enacted. All rules of religion have been violated. Little

or no effort on the part of the Sheriff or the State Police was made to stop the mob, and it wreaked its vengeance. Upon the altar of cruelty it immolated not merely a negro fiend, but justice and decency which form the foundation of a civilized community. The deed is done—another blot has been placed upon the map of Maryland.[96]

One of the results of the Lee case was establishing a precedent for moving the location of a trial to a more neutral court; a second result was the significant legal decision that the exclusion of blacks from juries was unconstitutional.[97] In 1933, a black sat on the circuit-court grand jury in Easton. There still were only two jury trials a year in the mid-1930s. And there remained conspicuous differences in the treatment of criminal cases.

In 1936, a black man was killed by a car in St. Michaels in Talbot County. The accident was judged unavoidable, the black said to have been drunk. That same year a white man was sent to the House of Corrections to serve a three-year sentence, "accused of obtaining carnal knowledge of two little girls who live at Easton Point."[98] The man was said to have undressed one eight-year-old girl and partly undressed a nine-year-old. He was found guilty only of the first act. Easton Point residents insisted that the (black) parents take the case to court. Was this really any different from 1865, when a white in Miles River Neck shot and killed a black man whom he said threatened him with a pitchfork, and upon deliberation a jury returned a verdict of "self-defense"?[99]

Notes

1. Jeffrey R. Brackett, 1969. *The Negro in Maryland* (New York: Negro University Press, 1969), p. 26; Homer Bast, "Talbot County, Maryland: A History," in C. B. Clark. *The Eastern Shore of Maryland and Virginia*. Vol. II. New York: Lewis Historical Publishing Company, Inc., p. 961.
2. Bast 1950:944; Giddens, Paul H. 1933. Land Policies and Administration in Colonial Maryland, 1753–1769. *Maryland Historical Magazine* 28(2):142–171, p. 144.
3. Earle, Swepson. 1923. *The Chesapeake Bay Country*. New York: Weathervane Books, p. 351; Howard, McHenry. 1923. Wye House, Talbot County, Maryland. *Maryland Historical Magazine* 18(4): 293–299; Skirven, Percy. 1923. The Eastern Shore of Maryland, in Swepson Earle, *The Chesapeake Bay Country*. New York: Weathervane Books, p. 280.
4. Giddens 1933:142; Land, Aubrey C. 1972. The Planters of Colonial Maryland. *Maryland Historical Magazine* 67(1):109–128; Land, Aubrey

C. 1965. Economic Base and Social Structure: The Northern Chesapeake in the Eighteenth Century. *Journal of Economic History*
25(4):639–655.

5. Land 1965:644–648; Tilghman, Oswald. 1967. *History of Talbot
County, Maryland 1661–1861.* 2 Volumes. Baltimore: Regional Publishing Co., p. 142–143.

6. Tilghman, J. Donnell. 1953. Wye House. *Maryland Historical Magazine*
48(2):89–108; Bast 1950:944.

7. Bast 1950:949ff.; Clemens, Paul G. E. 1975. From Tobacco to Grain:
Economic Development on Maryland's Eastern Shore 1660–1750.
Journal of Economic History 35(1):256–259.

8. Giddens 1933:158; Clemens 1975; Clark 1950. Slavery and the Free
Negro, in *The Eastern Shore of Maryland and Virginia.* Vol. I. New
York: Lewis Historical Publishing Co., Inc., pp. 511–537.

9. Clemens 1975; Giddens 1933:156.

10. Clark 1950:514; Best 1950:951, 957.

11. Papenfuse, Edward C., Jr. 1973. Economic Analysis and Loyalist
Strategy During the American Revolution: Robert Alexander's
Remarks on the Economy of the Peninsula or Eastern Shore of Mary-
land. *Maryland Historical Magazine* 68(2):173–195, pp. 189–193;
Clark 1950:513–514; Giddens 1933: 142; Bast 1950:965.

12. Bast 1950:963, 966.

13. Clark 1950:513–514; Slave Census 1850: Slave Inhabitants Maryland.
Vol. 3. Talbot County.

14. Wright, James M. 1921. *The Free Negro in Maryland 1634–1860.*
Columbia University Studies in History, Economics and Public Law.
Vol. XCVII(3). New York: Columbia University Press, pp. 86–91;
Clark 1950:513; Brackett 1969:37, 52.

15. Kimmel, Ross M. 1976. Free Blacks in Seventeenth Century Maryland.
Maryland Historical Magazine 71(1):19–25.

16. Clark 1950:524–525.

17. Wills Records Talbot County 4 April 1829.

18. Bridner, Elwood L., Jr. 1971. The Fugitive Slaves of Maryland. *Maryland
Historical Magazine* 66(1):33–50; Clark 1950:529ff.

19. Clark 1950:521–523; Brackett 1969:97–99; Bast 1950:961.

20. Douglass, Frederick, 1969. *My Bondage and My Freedom.* New York:
Dover Publications (originally 1855), pp. 37–38.

21. Douglass 1969:48–60 passim.

22. Douglass 1969:68–78 passim.

23. 1856 Talbot County W. R. Lieber 10/412.

24. Douglass 1969:68–78 passim.

25. Douglass 1969:69–74, 108, 124.

26. Douglass 1969:105–110; see Tilghman 1967:203.

27. Douglass 1969:111–112.

28. Tilghman 1967:198–293.

29. Douglass 1969:54, 69, 90–91, 109–110.

30. Douglass 1969:118.

31. Douglass 1969:92–117 passim.
32. Douglass 1969:89; 76–114 passim.
33. Douglass 1969:74–75, 132.
34. Douglass 1969:92.
35. Douglass 1969:85–122 passim.
36. Douglass 1969:72; 83–123 passim.
37. Douglass 1969:120–121.
38. Douglass 1969:86, 95
39. Douglass 1969:122–124.
40. Douglass 1969:127.
41. Douglass 1969:69, 115–117.
42. Douglass 1969:134.
43. *Easton Gazette.* 3 December 1859.
44. *Easton Gazette.* 13 November 1858.
45. *Easton Gazette.* 30 October 1858.
46. *Easton Gazette.* 11 December 1858.
47. *Easton Gazette.* 15 May 1858.
48. *Easton Gazette.* 18 December 1858.
49. *Easton Gazette.* 1859.
50. There were exceptions to this oversimplification: for example, riots
    broke out in Baltimore over whether Northern troops should be
    allowed to pass through the city to fight for the North and, in 1862,
    the Maryland Senate adopted an antiwar position and many resented
    the pro-Union measures of federal and military officials, which were
    reported as repressive. Bast 1950; C. B. Clark 1952 *Politics in Maryland
    during the Civil War.* Chestertown, Md. R. R. Duncan 1977 The Era
    of the Civil War, in *Maryland: A History, 1632–1974.* Eds. Richard
    Walsh and William W. Fox. Baltimore: Maryland Historical Society.
51. Duncan 1977:355. Again it would be a mistake to assume that Eastern
    shore whites, even those in Talbot County, were uniformly opposed to
    the Union; there were some pockets of pro-Union sentiment (see, e.g.,
    Preston, D. 1976. *Trappe: The Story of an Old Fashioned Town.*
    Easton, Md.: Economy Printing Co.)
52. Clark 1952:2.
53. Clark 1952:78–142 passim; Duncan 1977:361–375.
54. Mulliken, J. C. 1959. Talbot County's Company H in the Civil War.
    Easton Star-Democrat, April 8–May 22, 1959.
55. *Easton Gazette.* 7 November 1863.
56. Blassingame, John W., 1967. The Recruitment of Colored Troops
    in Kentucky, Maryland and Missouri, 1863–1865. *The Historian*
    29(4):533–545.
57. Duncan 1977:366–370. By January 1869, a board of claims was solici-
    ting applications for compensation from loyal slaveowners who "offer
    their slaves for enlistment, or whose slaves have enlisted without their
    consent" (*Easton Gazette.* 9 January 1864).
58. *Easton Gazette.* 29 August 1863. This apparently was the final sale of
    slaves in Talbot County.

59. Wagandt, Charles L., ed. 1967. The Civil War Journal of Dr. Samuel
    A. Harrison. *Civil War History* 13:131–146, pp. 134–135.
60. Wagandt 1967:135.
61. Wagandt 1967:135–136. (material in quotation marks). *Easton Gazette*.
    12 September 1863, 19 September 1863.
62. *Easton Gazette*. 5 March 1864, 19 March 1864, 26 March 1864.
63. Koger, A. B. 1942. The Maryland Negro in Our Wars.
64. Duncan 1977:377; Clark, C. B. 1950. Slavery and the Free Negro, in
    The Eastern Shore of Maryland and Virginia, Vol. I. Ed. C. B. Clark.
    New York: Lewis Historical Publishing Company, Inc., p. 512.
65. Wagandt 1967:138–139.
66. *Easton Gazette*. 5 November 1864.
67. Wagandt 1967:137.
68. *Easton Gazette*. 5 November 1864. This policy of binding or appren-
    ticing children was not reflected in the *Gazette*, in which there were
    only three notes on apprenticing between 5 November 1864 and
    November 1865: a note offering a reward for the return of an appren-
    tice who ran away; a second note on the "semi-slavery" of apprentice-
    ship; and a third on the court decision remanding to their parents
    several apprenticed black children (*Easton Gazette*. 18 February 1865,
    25 February 1865, 3 June 1865).
69. Gutman, Herbert G. 1976. *The Black Family in Slavery and Freedom,
    1750–1925*. New York: Pantheon, pp. 402–403.
70. Fuke, Richard Paul. 1976. A Reform Mentality: Federal Policy toward
    Black Marylanders, 1864–1868. *Civil War History* 22:214–235,
    pp. 222–226.
71. Low, W. A. 1952. The Freedmen's Bureau and Civil Rights in Maryland.
    Journal of Negro History 37:221–247, pp. 238–243.
72. Unless noted otherwise, all information in this final section of the
    appendix has been drawn from Talbot County newspapers located in
    the Talbot County Free Library and the *Easton Star-Democrat*.
    Particularly helpful were the *Easton Star* (1890, 1891), *Easton
    Gazette* (1886, 1887, 1894, 1898, 1901, 1905), and the *Easton Star-
    Democrat* (1908, 1914, 1916, 1920, 1926, 1933, 1936, 1938). The
    particular locations of direct quotations have been referenced.
73. The following information on farming practices, labor needs, and tenant-
    landowner relationships was provided by Sidney Mielke, Percy
    Shortall, and Hazel Clark, Miles River Neck farmers.
74. Lloyd Papers. Ms. 2001. Roll 14. Maryland Historical Society.
75. *Star-Democrat*. 13 October 1933.
76. Nolen, Claude H. 1968. *The Negro's Image in the South*. Lexington:
    University of Kentucky Press, pp. 40–50.
77. Woodward, C. Vann 1974. *The Strange Career of Jim Crow*. New York:
    Oxford University Press, pp. 4–7, 68–116 passim. Scruggs, Otley M.
    1971. The Economic and Racial Components of Jim Crow, in *Key*

Issues in the Afro-American Experience. Ed. Nathan I. Huggins, Martin Kilson, Daniel M. Fox. New York: Harcourt Brace Jovanovich, pp. 70–87.

78. Callcott, Margaret Law. 1969. *The Negro in Maryland Politics 1870–1912*. Baltimore: The Johns Hopkins Press, pp. 101–138; Fox, William Lloyd. 1974. Social-Cultural Developments from the Civil War to 1920, in *Maryland: A History*. Ed. Walsh and Fox. Baltimore: Maryland Historical Society, pp. 499–589; Crooks, James B. 1974. Maryland Progressivism, in *Maryland: A History*.
79. *Easton Gazette*. 19 November 1898.
80. *Easton Gazette*. 26 July 1902.
81. *Star-Democrat*. 27 March 1920.
82. *Star-Democrat*. 28 January 1938.
83. *Star-Democrat*. 14 August 1926.
84. *Easton Star*. 20 October 1891.
85. *Easton Star*. 3 November 1891.
86. *Star-Democrat*. 11 September 1920.
87. *Star-Democrat*. 23 October 1926.
88. *Star-Democrat*. 30 October 1926.
89. *Star-Democrat*. 16 October 1936.
90. *Easton Star*. 17 July 1920.
91. *Easton Star*. 22 May 1920.
92. *Star-Democrat*. 10 April 1926.
93. I am indebted to Arthur F. Raper, whose files of newspaper clippings on this lynching and on the Armstrong lynching two years later were made available to me. *Washington Post*. 5 December 1931; *Sun* (Baltimore). 14 March 1932, 15 March 1932. See also H. Alan Wycherly. H. L. Mencken vs The Eastern Shore: December 1931. New York Public Library Bulletin, pp. 381–390.
94. McQuinn, Henry J. 1939. Equal Protection of the Law and Fair Trials in Maryland. *Journal of Negro History* 24:143–166.
95. *Washington Daily News*. 19 October 1933, 30 November 1933; *Time*. 30 October 1933.
96. *Star-Democrat*. 10 November 1933.
97. McQuinn. 1939:162–163.
98. *Star-Democrat*. 11 September 1936.
99. *Easton Gazette*. 8 July 1865.

Appendix B

On Methods, Reliability, and Dialect

Several decades ago, Gordon Allport remarked in a report on life histories and other personal documents that a most serious criticism of such documents is that they may take their meaning from a framework of conceptions that is "arbitrary and predetermined by the writer or by the commenter."[1] Other criticisms include not specifying the setting and the manner in which material was obtained, the types of questions asked, and both the motivations of the informant and the aims of the interviewer.[2] In this appendix, the methods used in this study are set out in some detail, in hopes that this will allow a fuller evaluation of Joseph Sutton's narrative. Additional comments are made on the reliability of some aspects of Mr. Sutton's testimony and on dialect.

Methods

As noted in the Introduction, this life history began unintentionally—though by deliberate interviewing—in 1976, when I and an anthropology colleague spoke with several people in Talbot County, Maryland. We entertained thoughts of a joint field project, but the collaboration never resulted, due more to the competing pulls of other research interests than to any other factor. One of the people we spoke with was Joseph Sutton. A comparison of information he provided on genealogies, household composition, and land transfers with nineteenth-century federal census manuscript schedules and land records data revealed substantial correspondences and strong indications of reliability, albeit limited to this data (see below). This, together with his advanced age (ninety in 1976) and the fact that he was a willing informant who responded to my interest in his past and who agreed to taping, made life-history work attractive. Most important was his apparent knowledge of the postemancipation growth of all-black settlements and his memories of the diversions and meaning of kinship networks in the Miles River Neck section of Talbot County, as these topics interested me as an anthropologist.

As mentioned in the Introduction, I began taping well aware of two potential drawbacks: first, Joseph Sutton and I were not total strangers, and second, I had not preceded the interviews with anthropological fieldwork.

That Mr. Sutton and I were not total strangers may have affected the selection of information he presented to me and the meanings he assigned to it. I had grown up in Miles River Neck; specifically, vacations from school in the period 1955-1967 were spent at my parent's home there. Before he retired, my father was a doctor—a general practitioner—and Joseph Sutton was one of his patients. My father is also a farm owner, having bought in the early 1950s White House Farm, part of the nineteenth-century estate of Edward Lloyd, who had been the largest landowner and slaveowner in Miles River Neck and the owner of some of Joseph Sutton's ancestors. Thus Mr. Sutton could place me firmly in the race and class structure of Talbot County, which may have conditioned both his responses to my questions as well as information he offered spontaneously. It is possible that a researcher who could be assigned by him to another ethnic group and to a different socioeconomic category and who also was a stranger to Talbot County would elicit information with substantially different meaning attached to it; it is also possible that this might not be the case.

The second drawback was not preceding the interviews with intensive participant-observation and other standard techniques of anthropological fieldwork. The criticism may be made that in the absence of prior anthropological work, one can assume only with extreme caution that relevant questions are being asked of an informant.[3]

Offsetting these admitted drawbacks were previous anthropological fieldwork experience, the selection of an informant with certain problems in mind; and concurrent secondary data collection. First, previous fieldwork among Athapaskan Indians in the Canadian Northwest Territories in the early 1970s, preceded by graduate training in anthropology in the late 1960s, in theory provided some awareness of informant work, interviewing techniques, and the sorts of problems I might encounter given my childhood residence and lack of anthropological immersion in Talbot County. Second, Joseph Sutton seemed to be an excellent informant for the sort of information I was interested in: the reconstruction of the late-nineteenth-century growth of all-black settlements in Miles River Neck, the dimensions of kinship groups—families especially—in these settlements, the degree to which emigrants retained ties to their relations, and the late-nineteenth-century adaptations of blacks in Talbot County. The aim was to recover a former way of life through the documentation of a single life, and an old informant who had a good memory, who at first glance seemed reliable, who was lucid and articulate, and with whom rapport was good seemed an excellent place to begin.[4]

Finally, a substantial amount of secondary data was gathered: formal interviews were conducted with thirteen other Miles River Neck residents;

both primary sources—including the Lloyd Papers (MS 2001, Maryland Historical Society), Talbot County Land Records, United States Census schedules for 1870, 1880, and 1900, and Talbot County newspapers—and secondary sources were consulted (see Appendix A) in order to provide additional ethnohistorical data for this oral history.

Interviews were conducted with Mr. Sutton over a period of approximately forty-five days in 1976-1978. Most of these days—thirty-three, to be exact—were in August 1976, January 1977, and June 1977. Most interviews were taped; some of the earliest conversations in 1976 were not, and some of the most recent meetings in 1978 (and 1979) were not taped. Each taping session lasted from one to three hours, depending mainly on how strong and alert Mr. Sutton seemed.

All interviews were conducted in Joseph Sutton's home in Unionville, Talbot County. On no occasion was anyone else present during the interviews, although brief interruptions—the delivery of oil, Mr. Sutton's daughter coming from the adjoining house to see if she could get something for him in town, his granddaughter's husband coming from the adjacent house to see whether he needed a Saturday ride to Easton—did occur. Although Mr. Sutton was paid (at a rate of $2.50 per hour), the money, while welcome, seemed incidental to his genuine interest in talking about his life in the context of Talbot County.

The interview questions varied greatly (although they were of course directed at the general interests just mentioned). Every attempt was made to conform to fairly standard guidelines in interviewing procedure: impossibly long and obtuse questions were avoided; questions on Mr. Sutton's own direct experiences as well as on the experiences of others were asked; and areas of sensitivity were dealt with lightly at first. Some questions were open, designed to elicit nondirected, free-association types of responses; other questions were closed, directed often at the clarification or expansion of points made in open responses.[5] The following excerpts illustrate the use of both types of questions:

SK: Did you go to church very often those days?
JS: Oh yea. Yea.
SK: Every Sunday?
JS: No, no. I didn't go every Sunday. I used to go to church. As
      a child comin up I used to go to Sunday School every
      Sunday. But when growed up and some distance from the
      church had no way to go but walk. I didn't go as often. But
      when we lived there in Copperville I went to Sunday School
      every Sunday. And if I hadn't I wouldn't been able to spell
      my name. That's where I got my start. I learnt what I had.
      And I never went to day school until after I was ten years

old. And I went to work nine years old. So it wasn't a convenience, it was neglect. I went to Sunday School every
Sunday. And then first job I had was on a schooner, Bay
schooner, nine years old. Some people laugh when I say that
but what I did. We had two men on the schooner and times
he went to sailin he need two men on deck or when they was
loadin stuff like wheat, corn, anythin like that. And my job
was to keep the fire up under the food after the cook, one of
em was cook, after he put it on the stove I was to keep the
fire up under it. So it wasn't no heavy work but anyhow it
kept me out of school. And then when I went culling oysters,
I think I was there three or four months on the boat. Man
never sent my mother a cent. So she took me off and I went
cullin oysters and I'd culled oysters until it'd get too cold for
me. And the other children goin to school. School open they
goin to school. And then when it'd get too cold for me, why
lots of times very bad roads and when it got too cold for me to
cull oysters wouldn't be long before the river would freeze up
and then I didn't get my breakfast in time then to go to
school. And that went all the winter. The next spring I'd go
back cullin oysters. If it was warm the last part of March I
would but every year it wouldn't be any later than April. And
got nothin for cullin oysters. Twenty-five cents a day. Cause
the reason I didn't get the education as much as was goin then
for a colored person was neglect.

SK: Who neglected you?

JS: The ones that was above me.

SK: And who was above you?

JS: Well, lot of people was above me. I went but be late some
     mornings I'd have to stop in Millerstown and wait until eleven
     o'clock recess and all sorts of stuff like that. . . . [Tape 21A
     3-4 January 6, 1977]

SK: You never wanted to oyster yourself?

JS: I did oyster awhile by myself, yea. I oystered awhile by
     myself.

SK: When was that, Joe?

JS: When was it?

SK: Before you got married?

JS: Yea, that was before I got married; I was a boy. And then
     years after that I oystered again by myself. Cause I rent the
     boat from Saint Michaels. One season I oystered by myself
     and then I cut it out—that was years after I was married.

SK: You just did that one season?

JS: I think that was all, was after I was married.

SK: Why did you quit?

JS: Well, it was inconvenient and a long walk. That was clear down here to Wye House and next to Bruffs Island. And if I had something better when the season opened, I wouldn't oyster. Cause all of it was walkin. Them were hard days, though. I remember one evenin I come in from oysterin, land in a cove they called Ice Pond, that was right next to Bruffs Island. I had a sail boat and didn't have enough wind up enough to go to St. Michaels sellin oysters and wasn't no buy boats in the mouth of Wye River and this was on a Saturday. And I only had very little bit of money in my pocket. And on my way home, walkin along, I was thinkin about it. Of the family and got to get some food and I looked down on the side of the road and there was a paper dollar had blowed up layin against the grass that was standin there. And then it was dusk but it come plain to me that it was money and I reached down and got it. It was a paper dollar. And with what I had in my pocket was enough to buy food enough. That was lucky, though. Now it was dusk and I saw it, I'd never noticed it layin flat but it was layin up against the grass on that angle. And it come to me soon as I saw it, it was money and I reached down and picked it up. And there was a dollar. Well, if you try to do the Lord will always make a way for you to get along. Don't you believe that?

SK: It sounds all right.

JS: Yea, but that ain't answerin my question. I asked you did you believe it?

SK: I think so.

JS: Well you ain't answering neither way—I answer your questions. You won't answer mine. I don't believe you believe in it.

SK: I think I do sometimes. Joe, that's as honest an answer I can give you.

JS: Yea. Well that's the kind of answer I'm goin to give you from now on.

SK: Do you believe it?

JS: Certainly do! Yea.

SK: At that time you didn't have enough money to get any food before you found that dollar?

JS: No I wouldn't had enough. Course I could've got it without it.

SK: How could you?

JS: But I didn't want to go in debt for it.

SK: And you could borrow money?

JS: No, I didn't have to borrow money.

SK: But could have if you needed to?

JS: Well, I don't know, never did borrow any money. But I was a
friend of the man who had that store there in Tunis Mills. Him
and I was play boys together but I didn't like to get things
what they called "on trust." Never did. It has been times I had
to get somethin there from him and then when I'd go to pay
him I'd say, "Well, there's the last of the money." [unintelli-
gible brief phrase] "You don't have to pay for all of it, just
pay for part." Told him, "No I'd rather pay every cent I owe
you even if I have to come back tomorrow." Now we was
boys together.

SK: Did many people get things on trust from him?

JS: I don't know. I know people that did—white and colored. But
I don't know how many it was.

SK: Did he charge interest?

JS: No, no.

SK: Not like Ennals Tull?

JS: You know about Ennals Tull?

SK: I read a little bit about him in the newspaper. Around 1900,
1910.

JS: Yea, he'd charge you. Oh, he couldn't have bad, I mean good
luck the things that man done. He saved his money, bought
one of the largest houses in Easton. And on the big street.
That's where the money people, the most of em, was on that
street, Royal Street. And then wasn't there long before he
got so he couldn't walk. Lot of them things will come home
to you. [Tape 21A 11-14, January 6, 1977]

More than sixty tapes were transcribed, and the approximately 1,800
pages of transcript were checked against the tapes for the accuracy both of
content and of the orthographical representation of Mr. Sutton's speech
patterns (see below), first by a student assistant and lastly by myself.

The final step was the editing process, in which decisions were made
(1) to arrange the material in chronological order; (2) to interweave data
elicited by direct questions with indirect, more free-association passages,
in appropriate contexts, in order to construct the fullest accounts of events;
and (3) to preserve as totally as possible Joseph Sutton's phonological and
syntactical patterns. The selection of material was made easier by the large
amount of genealogical, demographic, and land-transfer data elicited from
Mr. Sutton, most of which could not be used in the life history, by a fairly

large amount of information told two or more times, and by other material that is not of direct utility.

On Reliability and Validity

How reliable is Joseph Sutton as an informant? Is his record of past events, his version of history, "valid"? These are questions of some importance, and they will be examined here.

The validity of any single version of historical events cannot be taken for granted. Biases are inevitable in *all* historiography. The writing of history demands choosing some "facts" and neglecting others, on the basis of some criteria considered significant by the historiographer.[6] The notion that oral testimony is less valid than documentary evidence (if it is useful at all) is no longer tenable. Although the belief that in the absence of documents there can be no history reached its zenith in the late nineteenth and early twentieth centuries,[7] the idea that oral testimony is inferior to documents as historical evidence unfortunately persists today,[8] in spite of impressive correspondences between oral history and geological,[9] archaeological, and genealogical and other forms of documentary evidence.[10] There are also cases where written records are scanty and oral testimony is the sole major basis of historiography,[11] or where primary sources do not accurately record events. A good example of the latter was the reported death in an East Texas newspaper in 1900 of a black Populist leader who actually died in 1923.[12]

To argue that any single collection of historical data represents a true or objective history is difficult, if not impossible, in many cases. It has been recognized for some time that different societies have different notions of time and of what constitutes historical truth, and that the preservation of historical accounts is directly related to the structure of a society.[13] The more important task may be to show just how particular historical accounts and beliefs reveal basic cultural attitudes, values, and sentiments held by members of a society. Any set of historical beliefs held by members of a society (or folk history),[14] whether preserved and transmitted in oral or written form, reveals much of the culture of a society. When one folk history can be compared to another, the congruities and discrepancies throw cultural values into relief, revealing the differential importance and significance of events. In many cases, the discrepancies between different accounts defy reconciliation, leaving one no closer to the "truth" but rather with a healthy awareness of the existence of diametric accounts and of the relativity of historical validity.[15]

The most important way to measure Joseph Sutton's reliability as an anthropological informant is to compare his version of historical events with the versions of other informants, with documentary data, by observation, or by repeated interviews on the same topic and checks on the internal consistency of his oral history.[16]

Of these, the comparison with documentary data has yielded the most information on reliability. Some examples follow.

(1) Comparison of genealogies and household composition data provided by Mr. Sutton compares very favorably with federal census manuscript schedules (United States Census Archives) for Miles River Neck, Talbot County, for 1870, 1880, and 1900.

a. Sutton said that Solomon Deshields, his mother's mother's mother's brother, married Sarah (or Sally) and that their children (males named first) were John, Charles, William, Isaac, Sarah, and Hester. John married Mary Elizabeth (surname unknown) and moved to Millerstown; Sarah married Charles Kinslow and moved to Baltimore; Charles married Mary (surname unknown) and moved to Germantown; William first married Minnie, and second, a woman in the "canning-factory bunch" and stayed in Copperville; Hester married Phil Moaney and went to Baltimore. Isaac died before 1885.

The 1870 federal census manuscript shows Solomon Deshields and Sallie, and children John, Sallie, Isaac, and Charles. William and Hester do not appear. The 1880 federal census manuscript shows Solomon Deshields married to Sallie, with children Isaac, Charles, Hester, and William (the latter two born since 1870); also resident in the household is John Deshields, married to Elizabeth, with a daughter, Nannie.

b. Sutton said his stepfather's father, Ezekiel Emory, married Millie, with children Robert, Ezekiel, Prissy, Hanna, Rosetta, Lizzie, and Sally.

The 1870 federal census manuscript shows Ezekiel Emory and Milly, children Priscilla, Elizabeth, Sallie, and Robert. The 1880 manuscript shows Ezekiel Emory married to Milly, with children Robert, Rosetta, and Ezekiel. Hanna is missing from the schedules; she may have been born after 1880, or she may have returned to her father's house in Queen Annes County, north of Talbot County, where, according to Sutton, many of the Emory children returned.

c. Sutton said that a Copperville resident, Eliza Kellum, had four children: Charlie, William, Nettie, and Solomon. The 1880 federal census manuscript shows Eliza Kellum with children Charles, Willie, Letty, and Solomon.

Extensive genealogical information on Miles River Neck blacks was collected from Mr. Sutton. Much of this information, the above examples included, shows a good "fit" with 1870, 1880, and 1900 federal census manuscript date.

(2) Information on the leasing and sale to blacks of land in Miles River Neck and on the growth of all-black communities was compared to the Talbot County Land Records, on file in the Talbot County Courthouse, Easton, Maryland. Information was collected on the transfer of land to blacks in Miles River Neck in the nineteenth and twentieth centuries. The growth of the all-black settlements of Copperville, Unionville, Millerstown, and Germantown was reconstructed in part. Impressive correspondences between this and Mr. Sutton's data were revealed; there are also differences in the data.

a. Sutton maintained that John Copper, Solomon Deshields, and Phil Moaney were the first to buy land in what became Copperville, that they bought it from a Captain Horney right after the Civil War, and that Colonel Lloyd never sold to blacks any land in Copperville. The Talbot County Land Records confirm an 1867 transaction between Horney on the one hand, and Copper and Deshields on the other. Lloyd never did sell blacks any land in Copperville, nor it appears in any other area in Miles River Neck. The Land Records do not show, however, a transaction between Horney and Phil Moaney. In fact, the lot where Joe Sutton said Phil Moaney built and lived was sold to Moaney's widow, Morena Moaney, in 1898 by Captain Horney's widow. An 1877 map of Talbot County, on the other hand, shows Phil Moaney resident precisely where Sutton maintained he was, and on the same land that Morena Moaney later bought. Was the 1898 transaction the first? Was the lot purchased twice? Was Moaney leasing the land? The answers to these questions are unknown, but the available information supports Sutton's view that Moaney was an early resident of Copperville.

b. Sutton said that Unionville was started soon after the Civil War, and that a Quaker named Cowgill leased much of the land to blacks for thirty years, and that the land was subsequently purchased. Sutton said further that he thought that Matthew Roberts was the first purchaser of land in Unionville. Talbot County Land Records confirm that Cowgill owned the land, that thirty- (and fifty-) year leases were made by him to blacks and that Matthew Roberts became in 1867 the first purchaser of land. (And Cowgill was a Quaker.)

c. Sutton reconstructed the settlement pattern in Copperville when he lived there in 1895. The comparison of this data to Talbot County Land Records reveals some interesting departures. The Land Records did show that twelve of nineteen household heads named by Sutton owned lots where Sutton said they did. Of the seven others named by Sutton, two rented houses from the owners, one lived in a double house on property registered in the name of the man living in the other part of the double house, one is not listed as owning property in 1895 (see section (a) above), and the deed search in three cases has not been successful (due to incomplete information on the deeds). The Land Records list five owners, but according to Sutton, although they had purchased land, they had not yet built houses. Thus a very different (and, I believe, inaccurate) reconstruction of Copperville would result from the Land Records as the sole source: according to Sutton, of the nineteen people listed as property owners, five had not yet built houses, two were not living in them, and an additional five names were missed.

Leasing is a dimension of land use that does not appear at all in the Miles River Neck Land Records data (except in the leasing of land by a white, Ezekiel Cowgill, to blacks in Unionville in the nineteenth century). When Sutton lived in Copperville in 1895, his stepfather was renting the house from the owner, who was living in another part of Miles River Neck. Renting land occurred frequently, for a number of demographic, economic, and social reasons. Sutton moved his residence over twenty times in his life, almost always to houses in Miles River Neck, and often renting from other blacks. The leasing of land and this type of frequent movement is not revealed by the Land Records data.

(3)   The comparison of information provided by Mr. Sutton on slavery is more difficult to check. There is one major source of documentary data, the Lloyd Papers (MS. 2001) in the Maryland Historical Society. Many Miles River Neck blacks were slaves for the Lloyds, and there are occasional slave lists in the Lloyd Papers. Although the information is fragmentary and difficult to check, Sutton's data does seem to correspond to documentary evidence.

For example, Sutton's belief that John Copper was a houseboy at Wye House is borne out by an 1862 list of slaves; Sutton's belief that Harrison Roberts lived on 400 Farm seems to be correct: a Harrison (no surname, but the only Harrison of approximately 275 slaves), age nine, appears in 1853 on 400 Farm (Roberts' birthdate is given variously in the 1870, 1880, and 1900 census as 1843, 1835, and 1858). (Lloyd Papers MS. 2001, Ross 40 and 41)

(4)   Mr. Sutton provided a considerable amount of information on the Civil War period: on the recruitment in Miles River Neck of blacks, the

bravery in battle of black recruits, the attitude of Edward Lloyd to the enlistment of blacks, Talbot County whites who fought for the Confederacy, the role of Quakers in the emancipation process, and a number of quite specific incidents about Miles River Neck blacks who fought for the Union. A comparison of this information to a range of primary and secondary sources has revealed three things:[17] first, a considerable amount of oral data just isn't going to appear in any document; second, the general statements on Lloyd's attitude, the enlistment process, Southern sympathizers in Talbot County, and the bravery of black recruits correspond to documentary information; and third, information on Lloyd, the bravery of blacks, the role of the Quakers, the accomplishments in battle of specific blacks, and the adaptations of blacks—especially their creativity—in avoiding recruitment, escaping from slavery just prior to recruitment, failing a sharp-shooting test because of a sudden realization of sharp-shooter mortality, and shooting off a forefinger to avoid the front lines reveal criteria meaningful to Mr. Sutton's interpretation of this historical period. These include deep pride in black strength, accomplishments, and adaptations, a caustic view of a slaveowner who never sold blacks any land in Miles River Neck, and an appreciation of Quakers who sold land to blacks in Miles River Neck.

(5) A number of other checks demonstrated the reliability of Mr. Sutton's information.

> Sutton maintained that John Copper worked very little for Colonel Lloyd after he came back from the Civil War, but that Ike Johnson and Perry Blake, two other Copperville residents, worked a great deal for Lloyd. Johnson was apparently one of the "ditchers," a man who prepared the ditches so that fields would drain and in order that the stock would stay in specific fields. Farm account ledgers for 1882 (Lloyd Papers MS. 2001, Roll 14) show that twelve men, most from Copperville, worked that year. Perry Blake worked 16½ days, Isaac Johnson, 22½ days, and John Copper 1½ days. Ike Johnson and Phil Moaney (another Copperville resident) were ditchers. Perry Blake and Ike Johnson did work longer than anyone else, and John Copper worked less than two days.
>
> Sutton said that he lived for a while with his father's brother, William Sutton, at one of Lloyd's farms named Wye Town, where William Sutton had been "for years." In 1882, at least (three years before Joseph Sutton was born), William Sutton was employed by the month (at $10/month) at Wye Town. (Lloyd Papers MS. 2001, Roll 14)
>
> Sutton named two Unionville men who died in late February 1908, crossing the ice on the Wye River from Wye Island to Miles River Neck. There is an account of this drowning in the *Easton Gazette* on February 15, 1908, which corresponds to Sutton's recall on the time, the exact

place on the river, the names and ages of the men, and the fact that
they had been woodcutting for a mill.

Sutton named a white man who charged blacks high interest on
loans to them of money. There is an article titled "A Talbot County
Shylock" in the *Easton Gazette* on July 28, 1894, corroborating
Sutton's testimony.

The impression from a comparison of Mr. Sutton's testimony to documentary data is that he is a reliable informant. Although there were a number of discrepancies between documentary information and Mr. Sutton's data which have been pointed to above, these can be explained.

Another way to evaluate the reliability of Mr. Sutton's testimony is to examine the document from the standpoint of internal consistency. Does the document "hang together"? Are events consistent with one another? Do questions asked at two separate times elicit similar responses? Responses to these questions should give some indication of the reliability of the testimony.[18]

On a number of occasions during the interviews, either I asked the same question at different times or Joseph Sutton mentioned an incident that he had commented on previously. The purpose of my asking redundant questions was two-fold: to see whether the responses differed and to elicit a second account of an incident, one hopefully fuller and requiring less intrusion in editing. On almost all occasions, redundant accounts are highly consistent. Three transcript examples follow. First, on the death of Joseph Sutton's great-great-grandmother:

a. She was, the men cut wheat with a cradle and the women used to
   bind it. And she had a baby just a little over a month old. And I
   wish you could see that tree left in the field there, dead now. That
   tree limb spread was far as from here to that house, pretty near. It
   may not've been quite that far but it wasn't far from it. And the
   body, I guess, was eight to ten feet across—one whole tree. It had
   great big limbs, the limbs was big and long and when it was de-
   stroyed, it broke down and why, why it growed like that, sombody
   cut the top out of the top of it when it was a sapling comin up and
   that's why it growed that way. Then it start decayin in the middle
   where that top was cut out of it and it kept decaying until it got,
   the weight got so that, the weight from them big long limbs until
   it just broke down like, broke right down there. And my great-
   grandmother's mother died under that tree. Charl [? slurred] was,
   she was nursin this baby, the baby wasn't much over a month old
   and she was nursin it. And she would nurse it fore she would go to
   work in the morning and then they'd bring the baby out in the field

to her at nine o'clock. And course, they'd go home twelve o'clock. And it was awful hot and she went under that tree and that sudden change, that's where she died. [Tape 4B12. 5 August 1976]

b. [Q: Did [your great-grandmother] ever tell you the name of her mother?] Yea. But I couldn't—I've heard. Didn't tell me in particular but I've heard her mother's name called but I don't remember it now. That's been a long time. Her mother died over here on Hopewell. Died cuttin wheat. She was bindin wheat. Every man with a cradle had a woman to bind after him. And she died under that big tree I was tellin that used to be there. She had a young baby and they always had an old woman was too old to be in the field to work or a young girl wasn't old enough to take care of the children. And this baby I don't think was but two months old. And the girl used to bring it out. She'd nurse it before she left home and then bring it out again bout nine o'clock to nurse, next they'd go in for their dinner. And this was either the morning session or evenin session cause they used to bring em out again at three o'clock in the evenin. But anyhow it was hot. And she went under the tree to nurse the baby and that's where she died. She died right under that tree. [Tape 26A12. 12 January 1977]

On Harrison Roberts and recruitment:

a. Well, [my mother and stepfather] lived down there after they got married and when they left there they come back to Copperville and rented Harrison Roberts' house. That was a slave that stayed with the Lloyds until he was disabled and died. Never worked for nobody else. The men went to war and he didn't go. The man that was recruitin soldiers went to different farms that was down on Colonel Lloyd's, all of them that owned farms here, and picked up the men cause there was no law to stop em. And they went to Wye and went to Colonel Lloyd's old farm. He had, I guess, pretty near a dozen farms besides Wye, and old man Harrison, I think he was born and raised up to that time on "400." Well, anyhow that's where he lived, his mother and him lived, on "400." Well, he didn't want to go and the man, Ben Blackwell, told him he had to go. "You don't," say, "you're gonna be put in jail." So, anyhow, he went with em and he got out to the meetin house—you've heard talk of the meeting house, well, he got put there and he stopped and told Ben Blackwell he had to go in the woods to do a job. Old man Ben stopped the men and they waited, waited for Harrison to come back. And old man Ben say he thought there was somethin wrong. He commenced callin Harrison. No Harrison answered. So old man Ben told

the men, "Well, come on, we'll go," say, "and I'll report it and
they'll get him." In the meantime, before he stopped the men for
goin in the woods, one of em said, "Harrison," say, "you gonna
leave them two big fat hogs you got there at "400"? That's the time
he say he had to go in the woods. And they went on and old man
Harrison from that day went back down to Wye to be close to
Colonel Lloyd for protection and he stayed there until he was
disable to work, a young man then, stayed right there on Wye, but
he owned a piece of land, a house in Copperville, but he never lived
in it until he got disable to work. [Tape 2A1-2. 3 August 1976]

b. [Q: And [Ben Blackwell] was born here?] Oh yea. Yea. He was
relations to John Blackwell. He was one time, maybe the onliest,
he was over here recruitin down at Colonel Lloyd's farms and old
man Harrison Roberts was livin on 400. Him and his mother. Was
living together on 400 and he went over to them farms and got men,
men that looked like they was able to make able soldiers. And he
got old man Harrison. That was on his way down to Wye. And he
went down there and he went up, come out the front way from
Wye, come from the front door and I don't know he told Colonel
Lloyd somethin. But anyhow, old man Harrison was in the bunch.
And he got out here. Do you know where the meetin house used to
be out chere? Down that way. [Q: Meeting House Corner?] Yea.
Well, they got there, old man Harrison say he had to go aside. So
old man Ben he stopped the men. "All right." Say, "Go ahead."
Say, "We'll wait for you." So old man Harrison kept turnin around.
Say thought he was lookin for somethin—figurin on getting away.
But he looked all around. So he went in the woods. Old man Ben
said they waited and waited a long time. Then they commenced to
callin him, didn't think he went out of hearin distance. And they
called and called. And they never saw old man Harrison until the
war was over and they come back here again. Old man Harrison had
pulled that woods over em. And that was the day he went down to
Wye to Colonel Lloyd's. And never left there until he got an old
man. Years after the war. That was the first day he went down to
Wye. Went down there and course the Colonel kept him. And was
glad to get him because all his able man was gone. Old man Harrison
Roberts stayed here. [Tape 27B22-23. 12 January 1977]

On going to work at age nine:

a. I went to work nine years old. Always did go to Copperville, I mean
Tunis Mills, it was then Copperville. [?] And this man picked me
out. I used to go over there and play with the white boys and this

man, I heard he told a man there in the store, say, "That seems to be a bright intelligent boy, I'd like to have him." Say, "I've got two men on this schooner but when I have to load or unload and one of them men is a cook and I have to load or unload," say, "I've got nobody to cook. And he have to try to cook and load and unload" and he say, "I'd like to have that boy just to keep the fire up under it, the food and watch it and put water into it when it need." So he asked me one day would I like to go with him? So I told him yes and I was only nine years old. I say, "But you have to see my mother." And he saw my mother. Told my mother he give me four dollars a month. Four dollars, that was big money them days. And she let me go, and I think maybe I was gone bout three months. And never got thirty cents, never got nothin. Never got a cent. In them months I should've been goin to school. [Tape 1A3–4. 30 July 1976]

b. As a child comin up I used to go to Sunday School every Sunday. But when growed up and some distance from the church, had no way to go but walk I didn't go as often. But when we lived there in Copperville I went to Sunday School every Sunday. And if I hadn't I wouldn't been able to spell my name. That's where I got my start. I learnt what I had. And I never went to day school until after I was ten years old. So it wasn't a convenience, it was a neglect. I went to Sunday School every Sunday. And then first job I had was on a schooner, bay schooner, nine years old. Some people laugh when I say that but what I did. We had two men on the schooner and times he went to sailin he need two men on deck or when they was loadin stuff like wheat, corn, anythin like that. And my job was to keep the fire up under the food after the cook, one of em was cook, after he put it on the stove I was to keep the fire up under it. So it wasn't no heavy work but anyhow it kept me out of school. And then when I went cullin oysters, I think I was there three or four months on the boat. Man never paid my mother a cent. So [she] took me off and I went cullin oysters and I'd culled oysters until it'd get too cold for me. And the other children goin to school. School open they goin to school. And then when it'd get too cold for me why, lots of times very bad roads and when it got too cold for me to cull oysters wouldn't be long before the river would freeze up and then I didn't get my breakfast in time then to go to school. And that went all the winter. The next spring I'd go back cullin oysters. If it was warm the last part of March I would but every year it wouldn't be any later than April. And got nothin for cullin oysters. Twenty-five cents a day. Cause the reason I didn't get the education as much as was going then for a colored person was neglect. [Tape 21A3–4. 6 January 1977]

The least satisfactory check on Joseph Sutton's data was its comparison to the testimony of other informants. Although interviews were conducted with other residents of Miles River Neck and other sections of Talbot County, none was able to corroborate or contradict Sutton's versions of nineteenth-century events. Other informants said simply that they didn't know a great deal about what went on. It is unfortunate that there are no longer many Miles River Neck residents who were born in the 1880s and 1890s and that many who are this old do not have the degree of precision for the recall of events that Mr. Sutton has.

Also unsatisfactory is the degree to which Joseph Sutton's emotions, attitudes, sentiments, and motivations can be checked, although this is a criticism that can be applied to any personal document. It is almost impossible to judge whether motivations ascribed by Mr. Sutton to his actions at age fourteen actually obtained, or whether they were developed later in life. The subjectivity of any account, the difficulty of reporting motives, the tendency to oversimplify, the relationship of mood changes, memory losses, and the sheer selection of data, unintentional self-justification, and deception are problems in the collection of any life-history materials.[19] Still, the liberal use of close-ended, aggressive questions interspersed with free-flowing responses to open-ended questions and the stress by Mr. Sutton on honest responses (and his local reputation for honesty) do support the opinion that Sutton is truthful. On a number of occasions, Mr. Sutton railed against men and women who had the reputation for lying; he insisted that honesty was one of the most important things that the "old people" advocated; and, rather than be put in a compromising position, he often said he'd rather not answer specific questions.

This leads to a final point: if Joseph Sutton has selected even some data to withhold (or to present), then how "valid" is his history? A judgment on this is difficult, if it is possible at all; my only tentative conclusion is that this most decidedly is one black man's history, a chronicle of events selected as meaningful to a black informant, and that it reveals a considerable amount of the adaptations of blacks in late nineteenth- and early twentieth-century Talbot County.

Speech Patterns and Orthographical Representation

One of the priorities in the preparation of edited versions of the taped conversations was to ensure that the transcription of the taped conversations and the orthographical representations reflected Joseph Sutton's speech patterns. Prior to the preparation of a manuscript, the transcript of each tape was checked against the tape by a student assistant and by myself. Subsequent manuscript versions were proofed for orthographical accuracy.

One aim was to avoid so-called eye dialect—the use of nonstandard spellings to represent speech peculiarities. There are risks in the use of eye dialect, the most innocuous of which is readability (assuming that the orthography has been faithful), and the more serious ones the exaggeration of speech peculiarities or a signal of low literacy and lack of education. One example of the misuse of eye dialect—and of the sort of orthography avoided in this book—is the short, 700-word "Story of Uncle George Scruggs, a Colored Slave," collected in Kentucky by workers of the Federal Writers' Project.[20] The following nonstandard spellings (with the standard spellings in brackets) are clearly eye-dialect spellings: rite [right], frum [from], uv [of], staid [stayed], no [know], nives [knives], liv [live], ofis [office], cuntry [country], midel [middle], telin' [tellin'], sole [sol(d)], caus [cause], wood [would], caut [caught], ant [aunt], muther [mother], strate [straight], sez [says]. These spellings indicate more of the writer's impression of the literacy of the storyteller than they do the storyteller's speech patterns. B. A. Botkin has said of the Federal Writers' Project that "many interviewers were betrayed by their zeal for accurate recording into stressing truth to pronunciation, which led them into new and worse inaccuracies."[21] Equally to the point is that many interviewers were betrayed by their own (cultural) assumptions of the speech and literacy of their subjects. Eye dialect such as this is avoided here, in favor of "qualities of style, of word choice and word order";[22] these latter, however, did not take precedence over the primary responsibility of preserving Joseph Sutton's speech style.

CHARACTERISTICS OF JOSEPH SUTTON'S SPEECH PATTERNS

Joseph Sutton's speech patterns are consistent and highly predictable and are a reflection of his birth and residence on the Eastern Shore of Maryland, his race, age, and socioeconomic status. His pronunciation of some words reflects also the fact that he has no teeth (and does not use false teeth); understandably, there was some variation in the pronunciation of the same word, depending on such factors as whether it was the beginning or the end of a taping session, whether Mr. Sutton was particularly tired, and so forth. The following patterns are characteristic:

(1) In most present participles, /n/ is substituted for the velar nasal /ing/, as in whippin, runnin, gettin, standin, blowin. This phonological substitution occurs far less, however, in nouns ending in /ing/, such as thing, anything, everything. But this is variable, especially somethin/something.

(2) Voiced and voiceless /th/ are always heard, in they, then, that, think, three, and so forth. However, the initial /th/ in /them/ is rarely pronounced.

(3) Final consonants and consonant clusters are sometimes simplified. The final /d/ in /and/ is omitted roughly one-half the time. /And/ is the only

word, however, in which the final stop is dropped; it is retained in other words ending in /d/ or /t/.

There is some tendency to simplify consonant clusters and to reduce final clusters to a single consonant, as /kep/ for /kept/ or /Mack/ for /Max/. The absence of terminal /s/ or /z/ is not common, although we do find /post/ where pluralization /posts/ is standard, and rarely, the zero (absence of) possessive, as in 'my dog['s] nose.'

(4) /Here/ is sometimes pronounced /chere/, a shift that does not seem to depend on the preceding word: e.g., /here/ occurs after out, left, down, up, over; /chere/ following out, right, it.

(5) The transposition of 'to' for 'at' or 'in,' as in 'he was to Wye' or 'we were livin to Copperville,' is common.

(6) Initial elements in 'because' /cause/, 'of course' /course/, 'about' /bout/, and 'before' /fore/ are almost always omitted. 'Across' /cross/ is variable.

(7) Articles, prepositions, and pronouns are commonly deleted, as in 'owned [a] good size piece'; 'there was people [who] could tell you'; 'he was [the] oldest'; 'he got married [in] Philadelphia'; 'he worked [at] the saw mill.'

(8) Hyperconnections occur frequently, as in 'onliest,' or occasionally, as in 'mostest.'

(9) Many pronouns are undifferentiated, as in 'it [there] was one man'; 'care of them [those] children'; 'them [those] that [who] didn't wear clothes'; 'wife and him [he] separted'; 'theirself [themselves] ; 'them [those] days.' The exotic form 'whosomever' occurs.

(10) The present participle sometimes is in an a-prefix form, as in 'sons a-working.'

(11) Double negatives are very common, as in 'wasn't in no pail'; 'never smelled no musk oil on no cooked muskrat'; 'didn't cut no wood'; 'didn't no colored people live there'; 'nobody never told them'; 'I never used sugar on neither one'; 'wasn't nothing'.

(12) The absence of copula (zero copula) is rare, though it does occur, as in 'stumps that [are] gone now'; 'they [were] going to.'

(13) 'Ain't' ('it ain't like it is today') is common.

(14) In the formation of past tenses:

   a. Noncommittal time is rare in the be-been-was forms, though it does occur: 'after I'd be [I was] gone everyday.'
   b. 'A' is often used, as in 'it a [would have] worried them to death'; 'they couldn't a [have] stand [stood] it up here.'
   c. Singular is used for plural (especially with was/were): 'they wasn't [weren't] living.'

d. The present is used often for the past: 'after what they call [called]';
   'he come [came] to a'; 'when winter come [came]'; 'never know
   [knew] him to'; 'I never takin [took] it seriously.'

e. The past is otherwise "incorrectly" formed: 'I knowed [knew] I'd got
   [I would have been] locked up'; 'I'd left [I left] and come [came]
   back home again'; 'growed [grew]'; 'it was tore [torn] down'; 'you
   better had [have had] clothes on.'

RACE, GEOGRAPHY, AND SUTTON'S SPEECH

Among the distinctive sounds of black English are the replacement of voiceless /th/ by /t/ and /f/, of voiced /th/ by /d/ and /v/, and of the valar nasal
/ing/ by /n/; the simplification of final consonants, for example, /-ks/ becomes /-k/, of voiced and voiceless /z/, and the dropping of final stops; and
the loss of postvocalic /r/.[23] Many of these phonological shifts are *not* unique
to black English. In Sutton's speech, /ing/ is frequently replaced by /n/ and
voiced and voiceless /z/ are sometimes, though certainly not consistently,
simplified. The final stop /d/ in /and/ is dropped 50 percent of the time in
Sutton's speech, but other stops are rarely dropped, and the reduction of
final consonant clusters is variable.

Some other phonological shifts characteristic of black dialect[24] do not
occur in Sutton's speech. For example, the substitution of /t/ or /f/ for
voiceless /th/, in which 'thick,' 'tooth,' and 'south' become 'tick,' 'toof,'
and 'souf,' respectively, does not occur. Nor is voiced /th/ replaced by /d/
or /v/, as when 'them' becomes 'dem' or 'brother' becomes 'bruvver.'

The simplification of final consonants in the treatment of /s/ and /z/
is a phonological shift with syntactical implications.[25] For example, the
absence of /z/ in the third-person singular alters 'he walks' to 'he walk.' It
produces the so-called zero possessive: without /z/, there is no possessive
form. And this phonological shift results in the absence of (zero) copula,
as in 'he['s] ugly.' As noted, the simplification of consonant clusters is
highly variable in Sutton's speech.

Undifferentiated pronouns, particularly the treatment of possessive
pronouns[27] and the substitution of 'they' for 'their,'[28] are characteristics
of black speech. Of these, the first is most common in Sutton's speech.

The signal of noncommittal time in the use of be/been/was and the absence
of copula[29] and the substitution of 'ain't' for 'don't'[30] also are characteristic
of black speech verb forms. There are important grammatical differences
between black and white speech in the use of 'be' as a marker of time orientation and in the use of an unmarked form of a verb that is noncommittal in
time.[31] While the use of 'ain't' is common in Sutton's speech, it is not sub-

stituted for 'don't; zero copula, and noncommittal time in verb forms, while occurring, are not spoken with frequency.

Zero copula, zero possessive, undifferentiated pronouns and other aspects of the sounds and grammar of black English are also found in regional (southern) speech and are characteristic of black speech more perhaps in terms of frequency than anything else.[32]

Many aspects of Sutton's speech are of regional distribution and are characteristic of older people who received little education and who tend to be "old-fashioned." Some patterns are shared by other members of a low-educated "rustic" group, though not by so-called "cultured" people (with extensive education) in the Southern states, including the Eastern Shore of Maryland.[33]

Examples of the regional distribution of speech forms are the overwhelming prevalence among "rustic" Southern states residents of the following tense forms [with the "cultured" form in brackets]: begin [began], bit [bitten], blowed [blew], broke [broken], come [came], drownded [drowned], give [gave], growed [grew], knowed [knew], run [ran], spoilt [spoiled], tore [torn], throwed [threw]. 'Chunked' is a Chesapeake Bay variation on 'throwed.' 'He do' [he does] and 'he don't' [he doesn't], 'you was' [you were], 'here's' [here are], 'there's' [there are], 'I ain't [I am not], 'I ain't done' [I haven't done] are all commonly used by "rustic" southerners, regardless of race. And 'It's (many people)' is a Chesapeake Bay variation; 'There's (many people)' ['There are many people'] is the "cultured" form. Also, 'a-singin' [singing], an a-prefix participle form, is a common Chesapeake Bay variation. And the common "rustic" present participle is 'singin' [singing]. So also is 'goin' [going] common among the rustic group.[34]

Many terms in Sutton's lexicon are of regional distribution, including 'grass-sack,' 'shock,' 'rick,' 'rail fence,' 'singletree,' 'clabber,' and 'right smart.'[35]

In sum, Sutton's speech reflects his position in the "rustic" Tidewater class as much if not more than it does his race. There certainly is a wide difference between Sutton's speech and inner-city black English vernacular,[36] and even, in the use of *be*, there is a gap between Sutton and blacks in Mississippi.[37]

The transcription of the narrative tries to reflect these considerations of phonology and syntax. There is only one exception to the straightforward transcription of morphological patterns: the simplification of the consonant /d/ in /and/, which occurs half the time in Sutton's speech, is largely ignored, solely for the sake of readability. Otherwise, an attempt has been made for the narrative to reflect faithfully what was said. Two final notes are these: first, I have not had any formal training in linguistics, and have without doubt missed some phonological shifts; and second, all speakers are able to switch codes from one dialect to another, something that occurred in stories told by Sutton of the slavery period in which he indicates different phonological patterns and that may also occur if Sutton is conversing not with a white anthropologist, but rather with another black in the Tidewater "rustic" class.[38]

Notes

1. Allport, Gordon. 1942. *The Use of Personal Documents in Psychological Science.* Bulletin 49. New York: Social Science Research Council, p. 142.
2. Kluckhohn, Clyde. 1945. The Personal Document in Anthropological Science, in *The Use of Personal Documents in History, Anthropology and Sociology.* Ed. L. Gottschalk, C. Kluckhohn and R. Angell. Bulletin 52. New York: Social Science Research Council, p. 94; Langness, L. L. 1965. *The Life History in Anthropological Science.* New York: Holt, Rinehart and Winston, p. 9.
3. Langness 1965:35.
4. This point should perhaps be emphasized. Life-history work in anthropology is decades old, and the collection of data ranges from studies whose intent is to focus on psychological dimensions to those which reconstruct, through the rich description of a single life, a particular culture. The interests which led to the collection of this life history, and the material that was elicited, place this study with the latter type—those which are descriptive, cultural, and, to some degree, humanistic. This life history has clear affinities to the life of Nate Shaw (Rosengarten, Theodore. 1975. *All God's Dangers: The Life of Nate Shaw.* New York: Knopf), among recent black American documents. It is rooted firmly in an anthropological heritage, the literature for which is summarized in Kluckhohn (1945) and Langness (1965).
5. See Maccoby, N. and E. E. 1954. The Interview: A Tool of Social Science, p. 449–487 in G. Lindzay, ed. Handbook for *Social Handbook of Psychology,* v I. Cambridge: Addison-Wesley; C. F. Cannell and R. L. Kahn. 1968. Interviewing, p. 526–595 in G. Lindzay and E. Aronson, eds. *The Handbook of Social Psychology,* v. II. Second edition, Reading, Mass.: Addison-Wesley; also Kluckhohn 1945:125; Langness 1965:38ff.
6. Sturtevant, William C. 1968. Anthropology, History and Ethnohistory, in *Introduction to Cultural Anthropology.* Ed. J. A. Clifton. Boston: Houghton Mifflin, p. 466–467. Kessel, William B. 1974. The Battle of Cibecue and Its Aftermath: A White Mountain Apache's Account. *Ethnohistory* 21(2):123–134.
7. Thompson, Paul. 1978. *The Voice of the Past: Oral History.* Oxford: Oxford University Press, p. 47; Dorson, Richard M. 1968. The Debate Over the Trustworthiness of Oral Traditional History, in *Volksuber-*

lieferung: Festschrift fur Kurt Ranke. Eds. F. Harkort, K. C. Peeters, R. Wildhaber. Gottingen: Verlag Otto Schwartz & Co., pp. 19–35.

8. Dorson 1968; Montell, William L. 1970. *The Saga of Coe Ridge: A Study in Oral History.* Knoxville: The University of Tennessee Press, p. viii.

9. de Laguna, Frederica. 1958. Geological Confirmation of Native Traditions. *American Antiquity* 23:434.

10. Sturtevant 1968:466–467.

11. Montell 1970:viii.

12. Goodwyn, Lawrence D. 1971. Populist Dreams and Negro Rights: East Texas as a Case Study. *American Historical Review* 16:1435–1456.

13. Vasina, Jan. 1973. *Oral Tradition: A Study in Historical Methodology.* Chicago: Aldine, pp. 100–103, 170–171.

14. Hudson, Charles. 1966. Folk History and Ethnohistory. *Ethnohistory* 13(1–2):52–70.

15. Day, Gordon M. 1972. Oral Tradition as Complement. *Ethnohistory* 19:99–108; Hudson 1966: 54–60; Kessel 1974; Sturtevant 1968; Goodwyn 1971; Gould, Richard A. 1966. Indian and White Versions of "The Burnt Ranch Massacre." *Journal of the Folklore Institute* 3:30–42. Gould details disagreements mainly in emphasis between white and Indian accounts and concludes that whereas the accounts "provide valuable guides to the different cultural attitudes involved, . . . it would be hard to claim that there is to be found in the narratives . . . very much in the way of 'objective' history which is more accurately represented by one side than the other" (1966:42). Goodwyn's analysis of "Populist Dreams and Negro Rights" points to "the dangers inherent in relying on such "primary sources [as local newspapers] for details of interracial tension in the post-Reconstruction South but also the value of received oral traditions in correcting contemporary accounts. Nevertheless, the problem of evaluating such source material remains; white and black versions of the details of racial conflicts are wildly contradictory" (1971:1456).

16. Dorson 1968:35; Kluckhohn 1945:129–131; Langness 1965:39–43. Langness (1965:38) has said of the value of redundant elicitation that "it is difficult to sustain a web of falsehoods over a long period of time."

17. Krech, Shepard, III. 1980. Maryland Blacks in the Civil War: Some Perspectives from Oral History. *Ethnohistory.* forthcoming.

18. Klukhohn 1945:131; Langness 1965:42–43; see also Allport 1942: 128ff.

19. Allport 1942:125–142; Langness 1965:39.

20. Rawick, George P., ed. 1972. *The American Slave: A Composite Autobiography.* Volume 16: Kansas, Kentucky, Maryland, Ohio, Virginia, and Tennessee Narratives. Westport, Conn.: Greenwood Press, pp. 29–30.

21. Botkin, E. A., ed. 1945. *Lay My Burden Down.* Chicago: University of Chicago Press, p. viiff.

22. Botkin 1945:viiff.

23. Moulton, William G. 1976. The Sounds of Black English, in *Black English: A Seminar*. Deborah S. Harrison and Tom Travasso, eds. New York: John Wiley and Sons, pp. 149–197.
24. Moulton, 1976:149–197.
25. Labov, William. 1972. *Language in the Inner City*. Philadelphia: University of Pennsylvania Press; Wolfram, Walt. 1971. Black-White Speech Differences Revisited, in *Black-White Speech Relations*. Walt Wolfram and Nora H. Clarke, eds. Washington, D.C.: Center for Applied Linguistics, pp. 139–161; Stewart, William A. 1971. Continuity and Change in American Negro Dialects, in *Black-White Speech Relations*. Walt Wolfram and Nora H. Clarke, eds. Washington, D.C.: Center for Applied Linguistics, pp. 51–73 (originally 1968).
26. Stewart 1971.
27. Wolfram 1971.
28. Bailey, Beryl Loftman. 1965. Towards a New Perspective in Negro English Dialectology. *American Speech* 40:171–177.
29. Bailey 1965; Wolfram 1971; Stewart 1961.
30. Bailey 1965.
31. Bailey 1965; Wolfram 1971.
32. Labov 1972; Wolfram 1971.
33. Atwood, E. Bagby. 1951. *A Survey of Verb Forms in the Eastern United States*. Studies in American English 2. University of Michigan Press.
34. Atwood 1951.
35. Kurath, Hans. 1949. *A Word Geography of the Eastern United States*. Studies in American English. University of Michigan Press.
36. Labov 1972.
37. Wolfram 1971.
38. See Bailey 1965 on this point.